PATTERNS OF URBAN GROWTH IN THE RUSSIAN EMPIRE DURING THE NINETEENTH CENTURY

by

Thomas Stanley Fedor

Richmond College of the
City University of New York

THE UNIVERSITY OF CHICAGO
DEPARTMENT OF GEOGRAPHY
RESEARCH PAPER NO. 163

1975

Library of Congress Cataloging in Publication Data

Fedor, Thomas Stanley, 1943–
    Patterns of urban growth in the Russian Empire during the nineteenth cen-
tury. (Research paper—University of Chicago Dept. of Geography; no. 163)
    Bibliography: p. 225
    1. Urbanization—Russia. 2. Russia—Statistics, vital. I. Title. II. Series: Chi-
cago. University. Department of Geography. Research paper; no. 163.
H31.C514 no. 163 [HT145.R9] 301.36′1′0947
74-84783
ISBN 0-89065-070-5

Research Papers are available from:
The University of Chicago
Department of Geography
5828 S. University Avenue
Chicago, Illinois 60637
Price: $6.00 list; $5.00 series subscription

To my father, Stanley

and

To the memory of my mother, Anna

Thank you

ACKNOWLEDGEMENTS

I wish to express my sincere gratitude to Professor Chauncy D. Harris for his intellectual stimulation and guidance and for his most valuable contributions and enthusiastic support of this study. I am also greatly indebted to Professors Arcadius Kahan and Peter G. Goheen for sharing with me their knowledge of Russian economic history and urban geography, respectively, and for their constructive criticism which they so generously offered during the course of this work. I am especially grateful to my colleague in graduate school, Marshall A. Worden, who contributed through many long discussions to the clarification and refinement of the themes developed in this study.

I wish to express my appreciation to Mr. Vaclav Laska and to Miss Helen M. Smith of the Joseph Regenstein Library of the University of Chicago for their assistance in procuring materials from other libraries, especially in the Soviet Union, without which this study would have been impossible.

I also wish to thank the Department of Geography and the Committee on Slavic Area Studies for their generous financial support which made possible my graduate study at the University of Chicago.

Finally, words alone are insufficient to express my gratitude to my wife, Lucia, and to my children, Liza and Stefan. Their contributions, assistance, encouragement and sacrifices are reflected throughout this entire work.

INTRODUCTION

Writing at the end of the 19th century, Adna Ferrin Weber observed in the introduction to his classic study that "the most remarkable social phenomenon of the present century is the concentration of population in cities," and he considered the tendency towards population concentration to be "all but universal in the Western world."[1] Forty years later, Hope Tisdale defined the tendency towards population concentration and the increase in the number and size of the points of concentration as the process of urbanization. She saw urbanization as a "process of becoming," which implied a movement, "not necessarily direct or steady or continuous. . . , from a state of less concentration toward a state of more concentration."[2] The definition of urbanization in these terms provided a relatively unambiguous framework for the study of the growth of cities. Urbanization was conceived as a societal process resulting in the formation of cities.[3]

Within each phase of societal development, however, there exists an enormous diversity in the environmental, demographic, technological, and institutional conditions which give rise to urbanization. As a result of this diversity, various types of urbanization in respect to origin, process, and consequence have emerged.[4] In turn, "distinctive types of cities with markedly

---

[1] Adna Ferrin Weber, The Growth of Cities in the Nineteenth Century: A Study in Statistics (Originally published in 1899 for Columbia University by the Macmillan Company, New York, as Volume XI of Studies in History, Economics and Public Law; reprinted, Ithaca, N.Y.: Cornell University Press, 1967), p. 1.

[2] Hope Tisdale, "The Process of Urbanization," Social Forces, XX (March, 1942), p. 312.

[3] Eric E. Lampard, "American Historians and the Study of Urbanization," American Urban History: An Interpretive Reader with Commentaries, ed., Alexander B. Callow, Jr. (New York: Oxford University Press, 1969), p. 635.

[4] Philip M. Hauser and Leo F. Schnore, eds., The Study of Urbanization (New York: John Wiley and Sons, Inc., 1965), p. 210.

different outlooks" have developed in different regions of the world, "creatures of their varying growth histories and resource orientations."[1] The variety of urbanizing experiences and urban forms serves to underscore that "population concentration is everywhere an _adaptive_ process," and as such, every urban tradition, like every city, "represents a continuing accommodation of general societal tendencies to particular sets of demographic and environmental exigencies."[2]

In addition to achieving an understanding of the dynamics of urbanization, one must also search for an explanation of how this process has changed through time and how it has expressed itself spatially on the earth's surface. As focal points in the occupation and utilization of the earth by man, cities "develop in definite patterns in response to economic and social needs."[3] At various points in time these economic and social conditions attain certain quantitative and qualitative thresholds which not only permit and encourage urban growth to take place, but also integrate cities into coherent, functioning systems. As urbanization proceeds through time such conditions undergo change and the consequent distribution and role of cities within a system as well as the system itself is affected not uniformly, but differentially, both in time and space.[4] Consequently, in studying urbanization one must seek to explain not only the dynamics of the process by which cities have grown, but also the distribution of that growth and the changing nature of the urban system.

Although the study of urbanization has attracted increasing attention from social scientists in the last several decades, we still know little beyond a bare outline of what factors and

---

[1] Brian J. L. Berry and Frank E. Horton, eds., _Geographic Perspectives on Urban Systems_ (Englewood Cliffs, N. J.: Prentice-Hall, Inc., 1970), p. 106.

[2] Eric E. Lampard, "Historical Aspects of Urbanization," _The Study of Urbanization_, ed. Philip M. Hauser and Leo F. Schnore, p. 539.

[3] Chauncy D. Harris and Edward L. Ullman, "The Nature of Cities," _Annals of the American Academy of Political and Social Sciences_, CCXLII (November, 1945), p. 277.

[4] Norton S. Ginsburg, "Urban Geography and Non-Western Areas," _The Study of Urbanization_, eds. Philip M. Hauser and Leo F. Schnore, p. 314.

combinations of factors have prevailed at different times and in diverse geographic settings in affecting the pattern of urban growth and the nature of cities. Before we can expect to achieve a general theory of urbanization, we need to know more not only about how urban growth was and is possible, but how such growth has and is taking place relative to the diversity of conditions found in the world.[1] It is with this intention that the study of urban growth in pre-Revolutionary Russia is undertaken.

This study examines urban growth in the Russian Empire from the beginning of the 19th century until the commencement of the First World War. More specifically, this study seeks to describe and analyze the structural, spatial, and temporal patterns of urban growth in the Russian Empire during the 19th century and to explore the more important forces and factors accounting for these patterns. Since the growth of cities is intimately associated with economic development, this study will focus on the relationships between urban and economic growth in general and between urban and industrial growth in particular.

Nineteenth-century Russia provides a particularly interesting background for the historical study of urban growth. The 19th century was for Russia, as it was for most of the Western world, an era of very rapid changes in all aspects of life.[2] In Russia it was a century marked by intense intellectual activity and remarkable cultural achievements, the enlargement of the Empire and the incorporation of numerous, diverse ethnic groups, the rapid expansion of Russian settlement and the opening of new lands to production, and the restructuring of many old economic, social, and political institutions and emergence of new ones. Perhaps the outstanding feature of the 19th century, however, was the dissolution of a long-established economic system and the formation of a new one. Under the impact of modernization, Russia found herself in the midst of a transition from an agrarian to an industrial-based economy. This transition involved, among other things, a rapid increase in industrial output through the application of new technology, advances in

---

[1]Frederick Gutheim and Atlee E. Shidler, "The Building Blocks of Urban History," The Historian and the City, eds., Oscar Handlin and John Burchard (Cambridge, Mass.: The M.I.T. Press and Harvard University Press, 1963), p. 250.

[2]Cyril E. Black, ed., The Transformation of Russian Society: Aspects of Social Change Since 1861 (Cambridge, Mass.: Harvard University Press, 1960), p. 6.

in the division of labor, a growth in capital investments, the expansion of trade and commerce, and the growth of cities.

The process of modernization in Russia, however, took place within a socio-physical milieu which stood in sharp contrast to that of the West[1]. The role of the state was omnipresent in all phases of Russian life. With a virtual monopoly on political power, the state not only provided for the organization and regulation of social groups, but out of its own interests, it also provided the primary stimuli to economic growth and development. Although the economic role of the nobility was sharply curtailed with the emancipation of the serfs in 1861, they still continued to possess enormous social and political privileges. Throughout the century the nobility, together with the Orthodox Church, provided the principal pillars around which Russian society was organized and rendered reliable social and political support to the autocracy.

In contrast, the middle class in Russia was weakly developed and was viewed generally with suspicion by the autocracy as well as by the other classes. Entrepreneurs were held in disesteem and there existed in Russian society a general aversion to entrepreneurial activities that extended to all new forms of economic activity.[2] At the bottom of Russian society stood the peasantry. Treated with contempt, burdened by heavy taxation, exploited and abused, the huge majority of peasants found themselves in a pitiful state of misery and deprivation. Various institutional structures, moreover, not only deprived the peasants of many civil rights and bound them to the land, but also fostered among them a tradition of fatalism, servility, and acquiescence to authority. Finally, the enormous expanse of the country, the relatively low level of population density, the shortcomings of the transportation and communication networks, and the inadequacies and poor distribution of

---

[1] Ibid., p. 669.

[2] Alexander Gerschenkron, "Social Attitudes, Entrepreneurship, and Economic Development," Economic Backwardness in Historical Perspective: A Book of Essays, Alexander Gerschenkron, (Cambridge, Mass.: The Belknap Press of Harvard University Press, 1966), pp. 60-62.

natural resources presented major obstacles to the integration of the diverse parts of the Empire and to economic growth.[1]

While focusing solely on the urbanizing experience of Russia in the 19th century, this study, in its broader conceptual outline, seeks to explore the proposition that the pattern urbanization assumes in a country is to a large degree dependent on the nature of its historical traditions and institutions. More specifically, it is suggested that the process of urbanization, the growth in the number and size of cities, which occurred in Russia during the 19th century, while similar in many regards, varied from the urbanization process in the West in several respects, most notably in the nature of the relationship between urban and industrial growth, and that these variations can be explained by the distinctive institutional arrangements of Russian society.

Although improved means of transportation and communication, the formation of national and international markets, the growth of trade and commerce, and the rise of a middle class were essential factors in the growth of cities, the unprecedented increase in the number and size of cities in the Western world during the 19th century was largely the product of industrialization. The relationship between the simultaneous expansion of industry and the growth of cities in the West has been well documented and need not be recapitulated here.[2] In nineteenth-century Russia, however, the relationship between urban and industrial growth has not been clearly established. In fact, the few investigations made into this subject have resulted in conflicting opinions.

On the basis of urbanization-industrialization rank correlations made by Robert A. Lewis and Richard H. Rowland, it was found that industrialization was not a significant factor in urbanization in Tsarist Russia, and, in fact, "by 1897 its effect on urbanization as a whole was negligible . . ."[3] In contrast, A. G. Rashin

---

[1]Alexander Baykov, "The Economic Development of Russia," The Economic History Review, 2nd Series, VII (1954), pp. 140-142.

[2]See for example, Weber, pp. 185-209 and Eric E. Lampard, "The History of Cities in the Economically Advanced Areas," Economic Development and Cultural Change, III (January, 1955), pp. 81-136.

[3]Robert A. Lewis and Richard H. Rowland, "Urbanization in Russia and the USSR: 1897-1966," Annals of the Association of American Geographers, LIX (December, 1969), p. 791.

concluded on the basis of an analysis of the growth in the urban
population in Tsarist Russia that "in the course of the entire
period studied (1800-1913) the essential factor accounting for
the large increase in the urban population was the significant
development of industry."[1] This conclusion has received support
in a recent study by Roger L. Thiede. On the basis of his analysis of data pertaining to the growth in the urban population and
employment in factory industry in European Russia between 1854
and 1908, Thiede found a positive correlation between urbanization and industrialization and concluded that there was "a significant relationship between industrialization and urbanization
in Tsarist Russia . . . ."[2]

Perhaps part of the difficulty in ascertaining the relationship between urban and industrial growth in Russia during the 19th
century may be related to, among other things, the nature of the
spatial dimension of these two processes. Urban and industrial
growth in the West were not only interrelated temporal processes,
but they were interacting spatial processes as well.[3] The economic rationale for the spatial convergence of urban and industrial
growth was efficiency. The fact that "contiguity of related
economic units whenever permitted by the productive process is
economical, and the cost of dispensing with it is high," made
these two processes natural accompaniments to each other.[4]

The spatial relationship between urban and industrial growth
in the West can be interpreted as one of alternating causes and
effects. On one hand, cities possessed a number of advantages
which made them locationally attractive to industry. The presence
of a concentrated and affluent body of consumers offered a ready

---

[1] A. G. Rashin, "Dinamika Chislennosti i protsessy formirovaniia
gorodskogo naseleniia Rossii v XIX- nachale XX vv.," Istoricheskie
Zapiski, XXXIV (1950), p. 35.

[2] Roger L. Thiede, "Urbanization and Industrialization in Pre-
Revolutionary Russia," The Professional Geographer, XXV (February,
1973), p. 17.

[3] Allan R. Pred, The Spatial Dynamics of U.S. Urban-Industrial
Growth, 1800-1914: Interpretive and Theoretical Essays (Cambridge,
Mass.: The M.I.T. Press, 1966), p. 3.

[4] Simon Kuznets, Economic Growth and Structure. Selected
Essays (New York: W. W. Norton and Co., 1965), p. 97.

market for many types of manufacturing.[1] Cities provided a favorable infrastructure in which the broad array of scale-type economies made possible by new productive techniques and modes of industrial organization could most fully be exploited.[2] Finally, the new scale of industrial production, represented by the factory system, required access to relatively large and permanent supplies of labor.[3] Such supplies were most readily available in the cities.

On the other hand, as large-scale industry became established in cities further growth in the concentration of both population and industry was generated through a "circular and cumulative process" in which the primary and secondary multiplier effects created by the new demands thrust upon the local economy brought into being a whole host of additional economic, social, and political activities.[4] At the same time the establishment of new industries created additional demands for labor that in turn attracted an ever increasing stream of migrants to the city. While reinforced through time by the growing importance of the city as a market, the accumulation of economies of agglomeration, the centralizing tendencies of advances in transportation and industrial technology, this "circular and cumulative process" of urban-industrial growth was contingent largely on the ability of cities to amass increasingly larger reserves of labor.

Although natural increases in the urban population added to the supply of labor, the enormous build-up of the labor force in the cities which occurred during the 19th century was primarily the result of a massive influx of population from the countryside.[5] The impetus to this migratory movement was twofold. On one hand, people were drawn to the city by the opportunities it afforded for

---

[1] Weber, p. 198.

[2] Lampard, "The History of Cities in the Economically Advanced Areas," p. 95.

[3] Leonard Reissman, The Urban Process: Cities in Industrial Societies (New York: The Free Press, 1970), p. 172.

[4] Pred, pp. 15, 25-26.

[5] Weber, pp. 230-284.

a better life. The higher standard of living, the material comforts, the variety of images, and the excitement of life found in the city were powerful attractions to many people dissatisfied with the poverty, isolation, and boredom of rural life.

On the other hand, there were many who were not pulled to the city, but rather were pushed out of their rural environment. Structural changes in agriculture, which sharply reduced the relative proportion of labor required to produce food, and in industry, which destroyed village handicraft and cottage industries, effectively displaced great numbers of people from the countryside for whom the city was their only refuge. Whether people were pushed from the countryside or pulled by the city is actually of secondary interest. Of primary importance, however, is the fact that in the Western world the population was more or less free to move.[1]

In Russia, however, the overwhelming majority of the population was not entirely free to move. The most formidable barrier to the movement of population, until its abolition in 1861, was, of course, serfdom, but other institutional arrangements, such as the communal organization of agriculture, the structure of village government, and the rigidity of social classes, also acted to curtail the mobility of population in Russia. How did cities develop within an institutional framework that impeded the movement of population and what effects did the institutional constraints on the mobility of population have on the spatial interaction of urban and industrial growth? These are questions which form central themes in this study. The answer to these questions should provide a clearer insight into how urbanization occurred under conditions very different from those in the West.

This study does not introduce any new techniques or methodology to the study of urban growth. What this study does do, however, is to bring together in a systematic manner statistical information and other pertinent source materials relating to the population and changes in the population of cities in the Russian Empire during the 19th century.

Some of the characteristics of the data presented in this study, which were compiled largely from 19th and early 20th century publications of the Tsarist government, are discussed together with the problem of delimiting urban settlements in Chapter I.

---

[1] Ibid., pp. 214-215.

Chapter II examines the patterns of growth in the total population of the Russian Empire and its major geographic units during the 19th century.

Chapters III through VII are devoted to an analysis of the data on the growth of urban population in the Russian Empire at various intervals during the 19th century. The patterns and changes in the patterns of urban growth are described and analyzed against the general background of economic development and social change.

Chapter VIII is concerned with the growth in the population of cities by natural increase in in-migration.

Chapter IX examines the urbanization process occurring in Russia during the 19th century in terms of an increase in the number and size of cities and as a structural change in the distribution of population and their economic activities.

Chapter X focuses on the evolution of the spatial relationship between urban and industrial growth. Primary attention is devoted to describing the nature of this relationship and the factors which shaped it.

Chapter XI presents the summary and conclusions of this study.

The scope of this study is admittedly rather broad and, as a consequence, many important aspects of urbanization are either omitted entirely or treated only superficially. It is hoped, nevertheless, that the broad context will not only provide a useful developmental framework and historical perspective for other studies dealing with more specific subjects or phases of urban development, but will also aid in the explanation of other facets of economic development and social change in the Russian Empire during the 19th century.

Figures 1 and 2 are provided to aid the reader unfamiliar with the geography of nineteenth-century Russia. Figure 1 lists and locates on a map the guberniias, or provinces, and their names as of the beginning of 1910. Because the number and configuration of guberniias underwent frequent changes during the 19th century, it was decided in the interests of clarity and uniformity to use the arrangement of guberniias as of 1910 for the entire period of study.

Figure 2 depicts the regions utilized for the presentation and analysis of much of the data in this study. The grouping of guberniias into the regions shown in Figure 2 was based on a consideration of historical traditions, ethnic patterns, and basic economic characteristics. Because of the unique historical and economic significance of Moscow and St. Petersburg guberniias, it was decided to group them together as one region rather than merge them with surrounding guberniias.

NAMES OF GUBERNIIAS

1. St. Petersburg	30. Chernigov	60. Viatka
2. Moscow	31. Poltava	61. Perm
3. Vladimir	32. Khar'kov	62. Tobol'sk
4. Iaroslavl'	33. Bessarabia	63. Tomsk
5. Kostroma	34. Kherson	64. Enisei
6. Nizhnii Novgorod	35. Tavrida	65. Irkutsk
	36. Ekaterinoslav	66. Zabaikal
7. Kaluga	37. Voiska Don	67. Iakutsk
8. Tula	38. Astrakhan'	68. Amur
9. Riazan'	39. Kazan'	69. Primorsk
10. Orel	40. Simbirsk	70. Ural'sk
11. Kursk	41. Penza	71. Turgai
12. Voronezh	42. Saratov	72. Akmolinsk
13. Tambov	43. Samara	73. Semipalatinsk
14. Pskov	44. Ufa	74. Semirech'e
15. Novgorod	45. Orenburg	75. Fergana
16. Tver'	46. Chernomorsk	76. Samarkand
17. Estliand	47. Kuban'	77. Syr Dar'ia
18. Lifliand	48. Stavropol'	78. Zakaspisk
19. Kurliand	49. Terek	79. Suwałki
20. Vitebsk	50. Tiflis	80. Płock
21. Smolensk	51. Kutais	81. Łomża
22. Mogilev	52. Kars	82. Siedlce
23. Minsk	53. Erivan	83. Lublin
24. Grodno	54. Elisavetpol'	84. Warszawa
25. Vil'na	55. Dagestan	85. Radom
26. Kovno	56. Baku	86. Kielce
27. Volyniia	57. Olonets	87. Piotrków
28. Podoliia	58. Arkhangel'sk	88. Kalisz
29. Kiev	59. Vologda	

Note: Finland, Bukhara, Khiva, and Sakhalin Island are not included in this study.

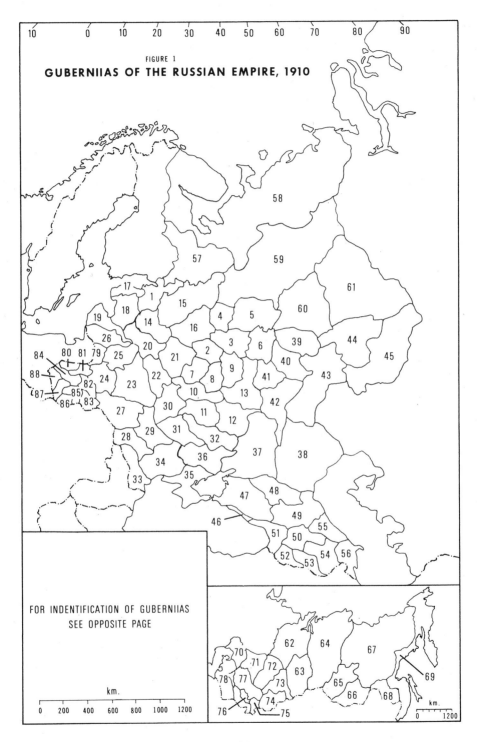

FIGURE 1

GUBERNIIAS OF THE RUSSIAN EMPIRE, 1910

FOR INDENTIFICATION OF GUBERNIIAS
SEE OPPOSITE PAGE

km.

0   200   400   600   800   1000   1200

km.

0   1200

FIGURE 2
REGIONS IN THE RUSSIAN EMPIRE

FOR THE GROUPINGS OF GUBERNIIAS
INTO REGIONS SEE OPPOSITE PAGE

—·—·—·— INTERNATIONAL BOUNDARY
━━━━━ REGIONAL BOUNDARY
───── GUBERNIYA BOUNDARY

km.

0   200   400   600   800   1000   1200

REGIONS OF THE RUSSIAN EMPIRE
AND THEIR GUBERNIIAS

Region	Guberniias
Capitals	1. St. Petersburg 2. Moscow
Central Industrial	3. Vladimir 4. Iaroslavl' 5. Kostroma 6. Nizhnii Novgorod
Southern Industrial	7. Kaluga 8. Tula 9. Riazan'
Black Earth	10. Orel 11. Kursk 12. Voronesh 13. Tambov
Northwest	14. Pskov 15. Novgorod 16. Tver'
Baltic	17. Estliand 18. Lifliand 19. Kurliand
West-Central	20. Vitebsk 21. Smolensk 22. Mogilev
Western	23. Minsk 24. Grodno 25. Vil'na 26. Kovno
Right Bank Dnepr	27. Volyniia 28. Podoliia 29. Kiev
Left Bank Dnepr	30. Chernigov 31. Poltava 32. Khar'kov
Southwest Steppe	33. Bessarabia 34. Kherson 35. Tavrida
Southeast Steppe	36. Ekaterinoslav 37. Voiska Don 38. Astrakhan'
Middle Volga	39. Kazan' 40. Simbirsk 41. Penza
Lower Volga	42. Saratov 43. Samara
Trans Volga	44. Ufa 45. Orenburg
Pre Caucasus	46. Chernomorsk 47. Kuban' 48. Stavropol' 49. Terek
Caucasus	50. Tiflis 51. Kutais 52. Kars 53. Erivan
Caspian Sea	54. Elisavetpol' 55. Dagestan 56. Baku
North	57. Olonets 58. Arkhangel'sk 59. Vologda
Northeast	60. Viatka 61. Perm
Western Siberia	62. Tobol'sk 63. Tomsk
Eastern Siberia	64. Enisei 65. Irkutsk 66. Zabaikal 67. Iakutsk 68. Amur 69. Primorsk
Central Asiatic Steppe	70. Ural'sk 71. Turgai 72. Akmolinsk 73. Semipalatinsk
Central Asia	74. Semirech'e 75. Fergana 76. Samarkand 77. Syr Dar'ia 78. Zakaspisk
Eastern Tsarist Poland	79. Suwałki 80. Płock 81. Łomża 82. Siedlce 83. Lublin
Western Tsarist Poland	84. Warszawa 85. Radom 86. Kielce 87. Piotrków 88. Kalisz

TABLE OF CONTENTS

Page

ACKNOWLEDGEMENTS   v

INTRODUCTION   vii

LIST OF TABLES   xxii

LIST OF ILLUSTRATIONS   xxiv

Chapter
 I.   THE CONCEPT OF THE CITY AND THE PROBLEM OF DELIM-
       ITING URBAN SETTLEMENTS IN TSARIST RUSSIA   1

 II.   PATTERNS OF POPULATION GROWTH IN THE RUSSIAN EM-
        PIRE DURING THE NINETEENTH CENTURY   18

 III.   URBAN DEVELOPMENT IN THE PRE-REFORM PERIOD, 1811-
         1856   39

 IV.   FACTORS OF URBAN GROWTH IN THE PRE-REFORM PERIOD,
        1811-1856   54

 V.   URBAN GROWTH DURING THE REFORM PERIOD, 1856-1870   71

 VI.   ECONOMIC DEVELOPMENT IN THE POST-REFORM PERIOD,
        1870-1910   80

 VII.   PATTERNS OF URBAN GROWTH IN THE POST-REFORM PERI-
         OD, 1870-1910   99

 VIII.   URBAN GROWTH: NATURAL INCREASE AND MIGRATION . .   116

 IX.   URBANIZATION AND THE GROWTH OF CITIES   122

 X.   INDUSTRIAL DEVELOPMENT AND THE RUSSIAN CITY: AN
       INTERPRETATION   138

 XI.   SUMMARY AND CONCLUSIONS   173

APPENDICES

 I.   Population of Cities in the Russian Empire, 1811-
       1910   179

 II.   Occupational Categories of the Gainfully Employed
        Population in the Russian Empire, 1897   217

 III.   Sources of the Figures   223

SELECTED BIBLIOGRAPHY   227

        РЕЗЮМЕ   239

LIST OF TABLES

Table   Page

1. Natural Movement of the Population in the Fifty Guberniias of European Russia, 1861-1913   29

2. Per Cent of the Total Growth in Urban Population in the Russian Empire Between 1811-1910 Attributable to New Entries   41

3. Growth in the Population 1811-1910 of the Original 570 Cities in the Russian Empire as of 1811 . . .   42

4. Absolute Growth and Per Cent of Total Growth in Urban Population by Region in Russian Empire, 1811-1856   45

5. Growth in the Number of Factories and Workers in European Russia, 1811-1860   60

6. Absolute Growth and Per Cent of Total Growth in Urban Population by Region in Russian Empire with and without Tsarist Poland and Central Asia, 1856-1870   75-76

7. Growth in the Value of Foreign Trade, 1860-1910   88

8. Growth in the Output of the Main Branches of Heavy Industry, 1870-1900   90

9. Growth of the Cotton Textile Industry, 1870-1897   92

10. Growth of Large Factory Industry in European Russia and the Concentration of Employment in Large Industry, 1897-1902   96

11. Distribution of Factories and Employment According to Size of Factory in the Russian Empire for 1902   96

12. Distribution of Employment in Manufacturing in 1897 and Employment in Factory Industry in 1902 by Region   97

13. Absolute Growth and Per Cent of Total Growth in Urban Population by Region in the Russian Empire, 1870-1910   101-102

14. Growth in Factory Employment by Major Branch of Industry, 1870-1897   104

15. Comparative Growth of the Urban Population in Selected Industrial and Agricultural Regions in the Russian Empire by Major Periods, 1870-1910   107

16. Growth in the Number of Factories and Workers Subordinated to the Factory Inspectorate, 1901-1910   110

17. Births, Deaths, and Natural Increase of Urban and Rural Population in European Russia, 1859-1863 and 1909-1913   117

18. Distribution of the Urban Population in the Russian Empire in 1897 According to Place of Birth by Major Region   119

Table   Page

19. Growth in the Number and Size of Cities and the
     Distribution of the Urban Population According to
     City Size, 1811-1910   124

20. Total Population, Urban Population, and Per Cent
     Urban for Russian Empire and Its Major Regions,
     1811-1910   126

21. Comparative Growth of the Urban and Rural Popula-
     tion in the Russian Empire, 1811-1856, 1870-1910,
     and 1811-1910   132

22. Growth Rates of the Urban and Rural Population Dur-
     ing the Post-Reform Period, 1870-1910   132

23. Persons Occupied in Manufacturing in the Russian
     Empire in 1897 by Guberniia and Per Cent of Employ-
     ment Located in Cities in Each Guberniia   140-
                                                                 142

24. Persons Occupied in Manufacturing in the Russian
     Empire in 1897 by Type of Manufacturing and Loca-
     tion in Cities   144

25. Occupational Structure of the Urban Population in
     the Russian Empire in 1897   146

26. Occupational Structure in Manufacturing of the Ur-
     ban Population in 1897   147

27. Distribution of Cities with $\geq$10,000 Inhabitants by
     Size of Population and Per Cent of Gainfully Occu-
     pied Population Employed in Manufacturing in 1897   148

28. Cities in the Russian Empire with More Than 20,000
     Persons Occupied in Manufacturing in 1897   149

29. Distribution of Factory Industry by Size Category
     and Location, 1902   151

30. Cities in the Russian Empire with More Than 5,000
     Persons Employed in Factory Industry in 1902 . . .   152

LIST OF ILLUSTRATIONS

Figure		Page
1.	Guberniias of the Russian Empire, 1910	xvii
2.	Regions in the Russian Empire	xviii
3.	Growth of Population in the Russian Empire, 1810-1910	23
4.	Growth of Population in European Russia, 1811-1910	25
5.	Population Growth in European Russia, 1811-1910, by Guberniias	27
6.	Population Growth in European Russia, 1863-1914, by Guberniias	31
7.	Natural Increase in the Population of European Russia, 1861-1913, by Guberniias	32
8.	In-Migration, as Percentage of Population, 1897, by Guberniias	33
9.	Out-Migration, as Percentage of Population, 1897, by Guberniias	34
10.	Growth of Population in Tsarist Poland, 1820-1910	36
11.	Annual Volume of Gross Migration into Asiatic Russia, 1885-1913	38
12.	Urban Growth in the Russian Empire, 1811-1910, by Major Periods	43
13.	Percentage Increase in Urban Population of European Russia, 1811-1856, by Guberniias	51
14.	Absolute Growth in Urban Population of European Russia, 1811-1856, by Guberniias	53
15.	Growth in Urban Population, 1856-1870, as Percentage of the Growth in Urban Population, 1811-1856, by Guberniias	74
16.	Expansion of the Railroad Network in the Russian Empire, 1860-1910	81
17.	Growth in Total Employment in Railroad Transportation, 1860-1910	83
18.	Employment in Factory Industry, 1902, by Guberniias	84
19.	Percentage Growth in the Urban Population of the Russian Empire, 1870-1910, by Guberniias	98
20.	Absolute Growth in Urban Population of the Russian Empire, 1870-1910, by Guberniias	115

Figure   Page

21. Absolute Change in the Percentage of Urban Popula-
     tion, 1870-1910, by Guberniias   129

22. Percentage of Population Residing in Urban Areas,
     1910, by Guberniias   131

CHAPTER 1

THE CONCEPT OF THE CITY AND THE PROBLEM OF DELIMITING
URBAN SETTLEMENTS IN TSARIST RUSSIA

A serious difficulty encountered in undertaking an analysis
of urban growth in Tsarist Russia is the uncertainty over what
constituted an urban settlement. For various historical reasons,
a clear distinction between urban and rural settlements was never
firmly established in Tsarist Russia.

By the end of the Tsarist period under the name gorod (plural,
goroda) or city, was officially understood, "those populated points
which were self-governed on the basis of city charters by elected
city councils and possessed the right of taxation for the needs of
its public welfare by means of a valuation tax on all persons, . . .
who have electoral rights within the recognized forms of self-government."[1] On the surface the meaning of a city appeared rather unambiguous and concise. The problem, however, lay not so much in the
legal distinction made between urban and rural settlements, although
even that was not entirely clear, but according to what criteria and
in what sort of manner populated settlements were conferred with
these privileges. In Tsarist Russia, unfortunately, the bestowing
of urban rights and privileges upon settlements never, "found a
satisfactory application either in the very legislation or in
reality."[2]

In Tsarist Russia, three basic types of urban settlements were
recognized: gorod, posad, and mestechko. Of these three the most
important and also the oldest was the gorod, or city.

---

[1]E.Z. Volkov, Dinamika narodonaseleniia SSSR za vosem'desiat
let (Moskva: Gosudarstvennoe Izdatel'stvo, 1930), p. 238.

[2]Russia. Tsentral'nyi statisticheskii komitet. Statisticheskiia tablitsy Rossiiskoi Imperii. Vypusk vtoroi. Nalichnoe
naselenie Imperii za 1858 (S.-Peterburg, 1863), p. 85.

The City as a Fortified Center

According to various sources, the word gorod probably originated from the verb gorodit' (to protect, secure; to enclose), and it
came to be used in ancient Rus to designate an enclosed and fortified locality, ogorozhennoe mesto, or a citadel, ograda.[1] Thus the
Russian gorod was initially none other than a fortified settlement
which offered temporary shelter and protection from the ravages of
enemy forays to the inhabitants of the surrounding region. On the
basis of fortifications, the gorod gradually secured pre-eminence
over other, unfortified settlements and the latter eventually fell
into relative dependency to it.

In time, however, the inclinations of the surrounding population to look to the gorod for protection and leadership imparted to
it a significance over the other settlements beyond the presence of
fortifications. Although the gorod continued as the seat of military power and was entrusted with the protection of the region, it
also emerged as the center of community life in the region. It was
in the gorod where the native councils or veche gathered for consideration of local affairs and where the contacts between the people
and the ruling powers took place. The collection of taxes and duties and the implementation of justice and punishment also became
centralized in the gorod. Consequently, as the means of power and
control over the surrounding region were gradually concentrated in
the gorod, the very word began to assume additional significance,
that of a ruling place, a capital over a given territory.

This meaning of the city was consolidated with the arrival of
the Varangian princes. In this sense, the goroda, subordinated to
Rurik and his descendants, became the fortified abodes of the prince
and the men chosen by him, namestniki and voevody, to represent him
and his authority in the localities.[2] At the same time a distinction
among cities based variously on their relative strength, age, and
position in the hierarchy of power emerged. Thus goroda became known
as sil'neishie (stronger) and slabeishie (weaker), starshie (older)

---

[1]P. Mullov, Istoricheskoe obozrenie pravitel'stvennykh mer po
ustroistvu gorodskago obshchestvennago upravleniia (S.-Peterburg,
1864), p. 4 and Veniamin Semenov-Tian-Shanskii, Gorod i derevnia v
Evropeiskoi Rossii. Ocherki po ekonomicheskoi geografii s 16
kartami i kartogrammami ("Imperatorskoe Russkoe Geograficheskoe
Obshchestvo, Zapiski, Tom X, vypusk 2," S. -Peterburg, 1910), p. 39.

[2]Tsentral'nyi statisticheskii komitet. Statisticheskiia
tablitsy Rossiiskoi Imperii. Vypusk vtoroi. Nalichnoe naselenie
Imperii za 1858, p. 76.

and mladshie (younger), bol'shie (greater) and men'shie (lesser), or simply into goroda and prigorody. The latter type of city in each instance was subordinated to the former. The basic distinction between cities and rural settlements, however, remained until the 17th century in the presence of fortifications. As soon as this external distinction disappeared, "the gorod either ceased to be called by this name altogether, or without any distinction was called at times an urban settlement, and at other times a rural settlement."[1]

The City as Constituting a Special Social Order

The security and protection provided by the fortifications of the gorod attracted in time increasingly larger numbers of people to settle permanently within it. But very soon the goroda, as fortified localities, were no longer able to contain all the persons who desired to settle in them, and eventually around the gorod proper settlements grew up which received various names according to their population structure and position in relation to the gorod. Thus closest to the gorod were founded posady (singular, posad), the name of which most likely originated from the form of their settling: ". . . the inhabitants of the neighboring localities, which were near to the already existing or newly built gorod, came and settled, sadilis', around the gorod, so that the posady encircled the gorod."[2] These posady became the foci of commercial and industrial activity. Still later another ring of settlements appeared around the gorod, called slobody, which, in many instances, resembled the posady by the acquisition of commercial and industrial activities, but on the other hand, were often purely agricultural communities settled by free persons.

As the gorod became encircled by other forms of settlement, the meaning of the word gorod was gradually broadened to embrace the entire settled community, and not just the citadel. As this transition occurred, what was formerly referred to as the gorod, that is, the citadel, became known as the kreml' or kremlin.[3] In

---

[1]Russia. Ministerstvo vnutrennikh del. Gorodskiia poseleniia v Rossiiskoi Imperii, Tom I (S.-Peterburg, 1860), p. vi.

[2]Mullov, p. 5.

[3]Ibid.

a sense, this transition in the meaning of the word for city represented a consolidation of the fortress and the market.

As the city became more complex, both in regard to its internal physical arrangement and to the number and kinds of functions carried on, its inhabitants also became distinguished from the rest of Russian society. Beginning in the 17th century the population of the newly conceived gorod was bestowed with various rights and privileges as well as duties and obligations which served to set them apart from rural society.

At first only one segment of the population of the gorod, the commercial, and only one part of the gorod, the posad, were given special recognition. Under the Ulozhenie of 1649, the state, in an effort to protect an important source of its revenues, attempted to make trade and industry a monopoly solely of the inhabitants of the posady. It ordered that such activities could henceforth be carried on only in the posady and in order to effectuate this order, it attached permanently all merchants and craftsmen not only to the posady, but also to their occupations.

The provisions of the Ulozhenie also bound the peasants permanently to their place of residence and occupation, and in the process for the first time, "a distinction between cities and villages was made by estate, and at the same time the administration of urban settlements received a special character."[1] Thus posady were viewed under the law as settlements inhabited by tradesmen and craftsmen, while villages were inhabited by peasants engaged in agriculture.

In the 18th century the special recognition accorded to the inhabitants of the posady was extended to include other segments of the population of the gorod. Under the provisions of the Reglament Glavnogo Magistrata, introduced by Peter the Great in 1721, all the residents of the gorod, with the exception of the nobility, government officials, clergy, foreigners, and those who belonged to one of the already established estates, were organized into an urban estate.[2] At the same time the cities were given a governmental structure distinct from all other settlements and the citizens of the city, that is, members of the urban estate, were

---

[1] "Goroda," Entsiklopedicheskii slovar', ed. I. E. Andreevskii (S.-Peterburg: Izdateli: F.A. Brokgauz and I. A. Efron), Tom IX, p. 323.

[2] Tsentral'nyi statisticheskii komitet. Statisticheskiia tablitsy Rossiiskoi Imperii. Vypusk vtoroi. Nalichnoe naselenie Imperii za 1858, p. 260.

invested with certain limited electoral rights that enabled them to have a voice in the administration of municipal affairs.

The urban estate as established by Peter the Great was divided into two categories, the regular and non-regular citizens, with the former category being divided again into two guilds largely on the basis of property qualifications. To the first guild belonged bankers, "prominent" merchants, physicians, master artisans, and other similar types, while the second guild consisted largely of petty traders and handicraftsmen. To the non-regular category belonged wage earners, unskilled laborers, and other such "base" people. Although recognized as citizens of the city, the non-regulars remained largely excluded from participation in city affairs.

With the establishment of an urban estate the city, or gorod, "came to mean the society of the people of this estate, which belonged to a recognized locality and . . . to which they are considered affiliated."[1] For the formation of a city it no longer was required that a settlement be fortified, but "only that a law be declared to the people, living in the particular locality, who are able and willing to be counted in among the urban estate, to belong to the 'urban society,' with all the rights which are granted to a society of this type."[2]

The concept of the city was further refined during the reign of Catherine II. Of the rather large amount of urban legislation promulgated during her reign, the most important was the Gorodovoe Polozhenie, or the Charter to the Cities, published in 1785. The Gorodovoe Polozhenie, which was an attempt to summarize all existing legislation dealing with cities, outlined in a general way the meaning of the city and further delimited the privileges and obligations of its residents.

On the basis of the Charter, all cities were instituted by the state. In order for a settlement to be a city, it had to possess "a charter, a coat of arms, and a plan signed by the hand of the Imperial majesty."[3] More importantly, however, the concept of the

---

[1]K. A. Nevolin, "Izsledovaniia o gorodakh Russkikh," Ministerstvo vnutrennikh del, Zhurnal, Chast' VIII (1844), p. 187.

[2]Ibid.

[3]Ministerstvo vnutrennikh del. Gorodskiia poseleniia v Rossiiskoi Imperii, Tom I, p. ii.

city as constituting a special social order was confirmed in the
Charter: "The inhabitants of the city form a separate society and
are enrolled in the city's registry of citizens. Land, industries,
and other articles of the urban citizenry are taxed for the benefit
of the city's coffers, which are then spent on the needs of the
city. The inhabitants of the city are united in a recognized estate and are granted the right to choose from among themselves
persons for the management of their social, economic, and legal
affairs."[1]

At the same time the urban estate was enlarged to include "all
of those, who in the given city were long-term residents, were born
there, or settled there, (and) who have houses or other structures,
or places, or land, or are enrolled in the guilds or shops, or in
the service of the city administration, or in the employ of the
given city, and bear services, or are taxed."[2] Even the nobility,
who had a permanent residence in the city, were for the first time
included into the ranks of the urban estate, although by virtue of
their "noble dignity", they were exempt from personal services and
taxes. The urban estate, moreover, was divided into six categories,
largely on the basis of property qualifications and occupation. The
sphere of urban self-government was also expanded under the Gorodovoe Polozhenie.

On the basis of the legislation of the 18th century, therefore,
"one should look at urban settlements as specially privileged
communities which, it is true, for the most part present several
signs of industrial life, but most of all are distinguished from
other settlements by their special social organization and by the
citizen's rights of the native residents."[3] The determination of
which settlements became cities, moreover, from the time of Peter
the Great was reserved solely as a prerogative of the state: "From
this time, the declaration by the government of a known place as a
city, made it a city, equally as the exclusion of it by the government from the list of cities stripped it of its status as a city."[4]

---

[1] Ibid.

[2] "Goroda," Entsiklopedicheskii slovar', Tom IX, p. 324.

[3] N. A. Miliutin, "Chislo gorodskikh i zemledel'cheskikh
poselenii v Rossii," ("Imperatorskoe Russkoe Geograficheskoe
Obshchestvo. Statisticheskii otdel. Trudy: Sbornik statisticheskikh svedenii o Rossii," Knizhka I, S.-Peterburg, 1851),
p. 236.

[4] Nevolin, p. 190.

Absence of Clearly Defined Criteria and Procedures for Advancement of Settlements to Urban Rank

While the legislation of the 18th century, particularly the Gorodovoe Polozhenie, delineated in a general way the legal distinctions between urban and rural settlements, it did not clearly set forth any criteria by which a settlement qualified for status as a city. The failure to do so resulted in the condition whereby the legal definition of the city, which was, in part, a recognition of the social and economic development which had taken place in the city, was subverted by what became de facto the concept of the city as perceived by the criteria actually utilized by the state in bestowing urban status on settlements. Beginning with Peter the Great, urban status came to be determined largely by the needs of the state in regards to the civil administration of its territory. In many respects the performance of an administrative function became almost as important a distinguishing characteristic of cities in the 18th and 19th centuries as the presence of fortifications were for cities in ancient Rus. The state, in essence, while recognizing in principle the concept of a city as a relatively complex and multifunctional social and economic entity on one hand, continued to view the city, as in former times, primarily as "a ruling place."

With the first territorial-administrative division of Russia into guberniias, or provinces, introduced by Peter the Great in 1708, in each guberniia were established, solely for administrative purposes, settlements which were designated as goroda, or cities, and under them administratively were instituted other, smaller cities called prigorody.[1] As the territorial-administrative map of Russia underwent frequent changes during the 18th and 19th centuries, however, the distinction made between types of cities became at the same time both more refined and confused.

The repeated division of Russia into guberniias and guberniias into uezds, or districts, formed the notion of gubernskie goroda, uezdnye goroda, zashtatnye goroda, and bezuezdnye goroda. The difference among these goroda, or cities, was based largely on the relation to the administration of territorial units which they were

---

[1]Ministerstvo vnutrennikh del. Gorodskiia poseleniia v Rossiiskoi Imperii, Tom I, p. vi.

designated by the state.[1] Thus <u>gubernskie</u> and <u>uezdnye goroda</u> were
simply cities in which the administration of either a guberniia or
as uezd was entrusted. <u>Zashtatnye goroda</u> were those cities which,
with one or another division of Russia into guberniias and uezds,
played an administrative role, but then, according to changing
circumstances, had the administrative function taken away from them.
This category of cities began to pose problems for the legal distinction between urban and rural settlements, for when many such
cities lost their administrative function they were termed at first
in the general usage and then, in the official acts, as <u>posady</u> or
even <u>sela</u>, that is, villages.[2] As an example of the confusion that
developed pertaining to the status of such cities, the Senate in
1797 ordered that all <u>zashtatnye goroda</u>, or those cities which found
themselves outside the established administrative order, have their
status changed to <u>posady</u>, while later on in the same year an <u>ukaz</u>
was issued directing that the cities which were not placed into the
administrative structure retain their status as <u>goroda</u>.[3]

Adding to the confusion over the delimitation of cities was the
problem of those settlements which had never been included in the
administrative structure, but for some reason, often historical,
preserved the name <u>gorod</u>. These cities became known as <u>bezuezdnye</u>
<u>goroda</u>, or cities without the administration of an uezd. This term
was also utilized at times to include without any distinction
<u>zashtatnye goroda</u>. This problem became particularly acute when it
came to the designation of new settlements, which for reasons of
their commercial, industrial, or even military significance acquired
urban status but were never given any administrative function.

These settlements never did acquire an exact nomenclature and
were sometimes referred to in official publications as <u>bezuezdnye</u>
<u>goroda</u> and at other times as <u>mestechka</u>.[4]

Although the grant of an administrative role to a settlement
was normally accompanied by its elevation to the rank of city, a
practice which fostered the concept of a city solely as an administrative center, the bestowing of urban status on a settlement did

---

[1]<u>Ibid</u>., p. viii.

[2]Tsentral'nyi statisticheskii komitet. <u>Statisticheskiia</u>
<u>tablitsy Rossiiskoi Imperii</u>. Vypusk vtoroi. <u>Nalichnoe naselenie</u>
<u>Imperii za 1858</u>, p. 77.

[3]<u>Ibid</u>., p. 79.

[4]Miliutin, p. 232.

not necessarily mean that it was given an administrative function.
This was apparent from the category of bezuezdnye goroda. Consequently, there were other criteria which ostensibly entered into
the decision not only to elevate a settlement to urban status, but
also to designate it as a center of administration. Although not
clearly defined in the legislation, it was possible to ascertain
from the general meaning of the statutes pertaining to cities,
"that the basis for the division of settlements into urban and
rural serves the occupation and industries of the inhabitants.
Residents who are engaged in agriculture form hamlets and those
engaged in industry, trade, and handicrafts are attached to goroda
and posady . . ."[1] Moreover, in regard to the distinctions made
among the various types of cities, they were apparently conditioned
not only by the importance of the city in relation to the hierarchi-
cal structure of administration, but also, "by its geographic position, the development of industries in it, the amount of population,
and the particular way of life of its inhabitants."[2] Consequently,
on the basis of the foregoing observations together with the practice of designating the "main city" of a region, in terms of its
relative size and economic importance, also as the administrative
center, it would appear that the two concepts of the city, the city
as an administrative center and the city as a relatively complex and
multifunctional social and economic entity, did in fact often coincide.

It was true, however, that the two concepts of the city often
did not coincide. Many settlements became cities for no other
reason than being designated an administrative center, while on the
other hand, a number of settlements which had developed into industrial and/or commercial centers were denied urban status.[3] The
former condition was particularly evident during the period of the
territorial-administrative reforms of Catherine II when approximately 216 new cities were created primarily on the basis of administrative needs.[4] When Catherine II introduced her reforms in the

---

[1] Tsentral'nyi statisticheskii komitet. Statisticheskiia
tablitsy Rossiiskoi Imperii. Vypusk vtoroi. Nalichnoe naselenie
Imperii za 1858, pp. 82-83.

[2] Ministerstvo vnutrennikh del. Gorodskiia poseleniia v
Rossiiskoi Imperii, Tom I, p. iii.

[3] Semenov-Tian-Shanskii, p. 46.

[4] Iu. R. Klokman, "Gorod v zakonodatel'stve Russkogo absoliutiz-
ma vo vtoroi polovine XVII-XVIII vv.," in Akademiia Nauk SSSR,
Absoliutizm v Rossii(XVII-XVIII vv.). Sbornik statei, ed. B. B.
Kafengauz (Moskva: Izdatel'stvo "Nauka", 1964), p. 339.

latter part of the 18th century, she found it necessary for the administration of the new uezds to raise to the rank of city a total number of settlements equal to the number of newly created uezds. Most of the settlements selected by Catherine for city status were in reality nothing more than agricultural villages. The fact that, "a whole hundred of such villages transferred into the ranks of cities were eventually stricken from the list of cities," was sufficient testimony to the often arbitrary and superficial manner in which cities were instituted in Russia.[1] While it was true, however, that many such settlements which received urban status in such a fashion were not removed from the ranks of cities and remained until the very end of tsardom little more than villages, many such settlements, on the other hand, benefited from their newly bestowed status and attracted other activities which served as the basis for further growth and development.[2]

The opposite condition, that of settlements which in the course of time became commercial and industrial centers in their own right but never received legal recognition as cities, did not become a serious problem until the second half of the 19th century when the industrialization of Russia gathered momentum. Although the actual procedures and criteria for the elevation of a settlement to urban status, aside from administrative significance, were never clearly defined in the legislation, it was commonly assumed that, "if in some kind of hamlet industry would be strengthened to such a degree that the means of livelihood of the inhabitants will depend more on industry than on agriculture, then a degree is made concerning the transformation of such a hamlet into a posad or a gorod."[3]

In reality, however, the number of cities created solely on the basis of occupation was comparatively small. The state was, in general, reluctant to act on petitions for urban status from such settlements because, "it considered the expansion of such a type of self-governing units as a great evil for political considerations."[4]

---

[1]P. Miliukov, Ocherki po istorii Russkoi kul'tury. Chast' pervaia. Naselenie, ekonomicheskii, gosudarstvennyi i soslovnyi stroi (S.-Peterburg, 1904), p. 228.

[2]Klokman, pp. 341-344.

[3]Tsentral'nyi statisticheskii komitet. Statisticheskiia tablitsy Rossiiskoi Imperii. Vypusk vtoroi. Nalichnoe naselenie Imperii za 1858, p. 83.

[4]Volkov, p. 238.

There were other factors, however, that impeded the transfer of
"qualified" industrial and commercial settlements to the rank of
city. Since the elevation to the rank of city carried with it
additional tax burdens for the population of the settlement, "fear-
ing these taxes, the rural commune, as a rule, did not submit petitions on such a transformation of their settlements."[1] In the absence of any initiative from the settlement involved, only the district rural council, in the interests of the economy of the region,
could submit a petition for the transformation of its status. In
regard to factory settlements, which were often dominated, if not
owned outright, by one or more powerful industrialists, even the
district rural council proved to be impotent in altering their
status. In these settlements, "the interests of the factory owners,
who also did not wish the extra taxes on their revenues and property, appeared as the greatest obstacle to the introduction of city
statutes."[2] As a consequence of these factors, many settlements
which apparently merited urban status on the basis of their industrial or commercial character, remained until the end of tsardom
officially listed as rural settlements.

Other Urban Settlements: Posady and Mestechka

In addition to cities, there were two other basic types of
settlements which, although they did not officially carry the name
goroda, nonetheless, were considered as urban settlements. These
were posady and mestechka. As in the case of the various types of
goroda, a clear distinction between posady and mestechka, and between them and cities, was never firmly established. In many respects they were viewed as transitional forms of settlement between
villages and cities and, in reality, they possessed characteristics
of both: "The composition of their populations is mixed, and their
social organization is sometimes very similar yet at other times,
on the contrary, sharply different from cities."[3] Under the laws
they were considered, "sometimes on the level with cities and at
other times with villages."[4] Since these settlements were generally inhabited in part by merchants and meshchany, that is, members
of the urban estate, it was largely on this basis that they were
considered as urban settlements.

---

[1] Ibid.
[2] Ibid., p. 239.
[3] Miliutin, p. 232.
[4] Ibid.

Of the two, the posady approached nearest to the concept of a
city in Russia. As was pointed out previously, posady generally
appeared after a gorod, or, in its initial meaning, a fortress was
established. In time the posady became, in essence, the commercial
and industrial "suburbs" of the gorod, but as the gorod expanded,
both physically and conceptually, most of them lost their independence and were incorporated within the enlarged city. There were
many posady, however, which, although located near the city, remained independent from it, and in places where the need to be located near the city for security was no longer important, other
posady were established as separate and distinct settlements and
remained as such until the end of tsardom.[1]

While the posady, in various regards, possessed many characteristics of cities, in the case of the mestechka this was less
true. The mestechka were of Polish rather than Russian origin, the
word coming from the Polish miasteczko, connoting a smaller or
lesser city, and came to Russia largely with the annexations of
Polish territories. The institution of many mestechka dated back
to the time of the Polish Kingdom when the crown gave to the nobility special commercial rights which allowed them to establish markets
and fairs in their villages on the same level as in the cities.[2]
Although populated initially largely by the owner's peasants, many
of the mestechka, by virtue of their special privileges, were able
to attract merchants and handicraftsmen to settle permanently in
them. When the Kingdom of Poland was dismantled and large parts
of it were absorbed into Russia during the 18th century, these
rights, the right of the nobility to establish mestechka on their
land, which was extended in 1785 to the nobility in the other parts
of Russia, and the right, reserved normally only for urban settlements, to conduct trade and establish industries, were transferred
unaltered into Russia.[3]

---

[1]Ministerstvo vnutrennikh del. Gorodskiia poseleniia v
Rossiiskoi Imperii, Tom I, p. vi.

[2]Ibid., p. ix.

[3]Tsentral'nyi statisticheskii komitet. Statisticheskiia
tablitsy Rossiiskoi Imperii, Vypusk vtoroi. Nalichnoe naselenie
Imperii za 1858, p. 84.

The legal basis for the claim to urban status in Russia, however, was very tenuous for many mestechka. Not only had the documents given by the Polish crown to the owners of these settlements at the time of their institution been lost in many instances, but as internal order waned in Poland during the latter days of her existence, many owners took it upon themselves, "to rename their villages as mestechka, establish markets and bazaars, and attracted to them people of the free estate, szlachty, merchants, handicraftsmen, and especially Jews."[1] Consequently, not only did the number of mestechka greatly increase, in many instances they formed over two-thirds of the total number of urban settlements in the former Polish territories, but at the time of their inclusion into Russia it was all but impossible to distinguish those mestechka which existed de facto from those which did have a legal basis. Aside from their tenuous legal foundations, most mestechka were virtually indistinguishable from other rural settlements. Perhaps the most characteristic feature of mestechka which set them apart from villages, according to one observer of urban development in Russia, was the presence of a Jewish community. "It is known, that it is possible to find them (Jews) everywhere where there is the slightest embryo of urban life, and as their settlement in villages is prohibited by law, then it is possible with a full basis to consider as a city or a mestechko all those settlements (in the Western region) in which exists a separate Jewish community."[2]

Problems in the Enumeration of Urban Settlements and Their Population in the Statistical Publications of the Russian Empire

From what has been said about the precarious nature of the foundations upon which the concept of a city rested, the lack of clearly formulated criteria which might have determined the basis for the promotion of a settlement to urban status, and the often arbitrary manner in which urban status was bestowed upon settlements, the difficulty in making a calculation of the urban population of Russia becomes apparent. The uncertainty over the status of many settlements in the 19th century resulted in this condition, that for a long time, "there was no possibility of determining exactly the number not only of urban settlements in general, but even of

---

[1]Miliutin, p. 232.

[2]Ibid., p. 233.

cities in the proper sense."[1] This was nowhere more apparent than in the official statistical publications pertaining to urban settlements, the aim of which consisted not so much, "in the enumeration of all existing settlements of this type, but in presenting the main statistical data about some of them, which for some reason deserve special attention."[2]

Among the numerous deficiencies present in the statistical publications on the cities of the Russian Empire, perhaps the most obvious was the inconsistency in the listing of urban settlements from one publication to another. Although this problem pertained most of all to the settlements designated other than goroda, primarily posady and mestechka, there were many cities which were omitted in some years but included in others. The number of settlements other than goroda, for example, varied from 21 in the list of urban settlements for 1840 to 418 in the list for 1885.[3] As a consequence of such inconsistency in the official publications, which served as the basis for the official calculation of the urban population, the use of such figures, without the necessary adjustments, resulted in a distorted picture of urban growth in the Russian Empire.

This was particularly true for the second half of the 19th century. In the list of cities for 1870, in addition to 809 goroda, 24 other settlements were listed with a total population of 106,083.[4] In 1885, however, besides the enumeration of 856 goroda, 418 other settlements were listed with a total population of 994, 066.[5] Then in 1897, the number of settlements listed other than the 869 goroda, declined to 64 with a total population of

---

[1] Tsentral'nyi statisticheskii komitet. Statisticheskiia tablitsy Rossiiskoi Imperii. Vypusk vtoroi. Nalichnoe naselenie Imperii za 1858, p. 82.

[2] Ministerstvo vnutrennikh del. Gorodskiia poseleniia v Rossiiskoi Imperii, Tom I, p. iii.

[3] Russia. Ministerstvo vnutrennikh del. Statisticheskoe otdelnie. Statisticheskiia tablitsy o sostoianii gorodov Rossiiskoi Imperii, Velikogo Kniazhestva Finliandskogo i Tsarstva Pol'skogo (Sanktpeterburg, 1842). and

Russia. Tsentral'nyi statisticheskii komitet. Statistika Rossiiskoi Imperii. Sbornik svedenii po Rossii za 1884-1885 gg. Gorodskiia poseleniia Imperii (S.-Peterburg, 1887).

[4] Russia. Tsentral'nyi statisticheskii komitet. Statisticheskii vremennik Rossiiskoi Imperii. Seriia II. Vypusk desiatyi. Ekonomicheskoe sostoianie gorodov (Sanktpeterburg, 1875).

[5] Tsentral'nyi statisticheskii komitet. Statistika Rossiiskoi Imperii. Sbornik svedenii po Rossii za 1884-1885 gg. Gorodskiia poseleniia Imperii (S.-Peterburg, 1887).

308,384.[1] It might be pointed out, moreover, that for the publications of 1870 and 1885, under "other settlements" were included primarily posady and mestechka, while in the 1897 publication posady and mestechka accounted for less than a third of the "other settlements." The remaining ones, most of which appeared for the first time, were largely agricultural or military settlements which were included in the list on the basis of their performing some kind of administrative function. Consequently, an examination of the pattern of growth in the urban population based solely on the official figures would result in a rate of growth greater than what actually took place in the urban population between 1870 and 1885, and a lesser rate for the period 1885-1897. Nevertheless, despite such an obvious defect in the statistical publications, the official figures given for the urban population have been consistently cited in studies dealing in one way or another with urban growth in Tsarist Russia.[2]

The official statistics on the populations of the cities in the Russian Empire are suspect in many other respects, but in most instances the defects are not readily detectable, and when they are, little can be done to correct them. One case in point was the distinction made between the postoiannie and nalichnoe population of the city. The postoiannie naselenie were the permanent citizens of the city. They usually owned a house or other property in the city and were inscribed in the city's register of inhabitants. The nalichnoe naselenie included the permanent residents of the city in addition to most of the others who for one reason or another found themselves living in the city. The total of the nalichnoe naselenie was the figure normally used in the statistical publications. Depending on the time of the year the enumeration of the population present in the city was taken and the diligence of the local officials in carrying out the enumeration, however, the final figure forwarded to the central statistical office seldom reflected the actual population of the city.

---

[1]Russia. Tsentral'nyi statisticheskii komitet. Pervaia vseobshchaia perepis' naseleniia Rossiiskoi Imperii 1897 g. Vypusk 5. Okonchatel'no ustanovlennoe pri razrabotke perepisi. Nalichnoe naselenie gorodov (S.-Peterburg, 1905).

[2]The main Soviet work dealing in part with the growth of urban population in Tsarist Russia during the 19th century is: A.G. Rashin, Naselenie Rossii za 100 let, 1811-1913. Statisticheskie ocherki (Moskva: Gosudarstvennoe Statisticheskoe Izdatel'stvo, 1956). The figures he presents, taken from the official statistical publications, have normally been cited in subsequent Soviet and non-Soviet works.

Then too, one is seldom certain whether the population figures given for cities represented only the population found within the city's official boundaries, or whether adjacent settlements were included. In the 1897 census, for example, when all the settlements were enumerated, "the Central Statistical Committee, already in the process of working out the data from this census, decided in the apportioning of the population into urban and rural not to adhere to the strict limits of the city boundaries, and included in the number of the population of the formal city also the population of suburban slobody and other settlements which were connected with the territory of the city's boundaries by a contiguity of buildings."[1]

In the data on the population of cities for 1910, aside from the problem of whether their populations were determined on the same territorial basis as in 1897, another problem emerged in regard to military personnel. In Russia military forces stationed in cities were normally counted in among their total populations for statistical purposes, and the shifting of garrison forces often was a factor, if not the only factor, in the seemingly inexplicable abrupt growth or decline in the population of many cities. In the publication on cities for 1910, however, the figures on military personnel were presented separately for the first time, and in over sixty cities, including many of the larger ones like Moscow, St. Petersburg, and Warsaw, an indication was given that military personnel were present in the city, but the actual figures were omitted.[2]

Although these are but a few of the deficiencies to be found in the official statistics on cities for the 19th century, they do serve to point up the difficulties inherent in their utilization. Nevertheless, although the official statistics on population, particularly on the urban population, are far from being as satisfactory as one would desire, they do provide, in lieu of anything better, a sufficiently close approximation to actuality upon which general analyses can be based.

Definition of Urban Settlements Used in this Study

For the purposes of this study, therefore, in determining the urban population of the Russian Empire at various intervals during

---

[1]Volkov, p. 240.

[2]Russia. Tsentral'nyi statisticheskii komitet. Goroda Rossii v 1910 godu (S.-Peterburg, 1914).

the 19th century, it was decided to select all those settlements
which were designated as goroda by 1910, and those posady and
mestechka which had a population of 2,000 or more inhabitants as of
1910 and, moreover, had been listed in the official statistical publications for three or more consecutive dates.

It is recognized that such a definition of the urban population
is far from being entirely satisfactory. The major shortcoming in
adopting what was essentially the legal delimitation of urban settlements used in Tsarist Russia, even with the modifications indicated,
is that a number of settlements which had little, if any, economic
significance are included in the number of cities, while on the
other hand, a number of settlements which were largely industrial
in character, but legally considered as non-urban, are excluded.[1]
In view of the fact that little statistical information is available,
concerning occupation as well as population, particularly for non-
urban settlements, this situation is regretfully unavoidable.

Nevertheless, despite the inherent weakness of the definition,
it is felt that it does introduce a certain degree of uniformity
and consistency in the determination of the urban population which
not only provides a more accurate basis for the analysis of urban
growth in the Russian Empire than has hitherto been possible, but
can serve as the basis for further refinements in the calculation
of the urban population.

---

[1]For example, in the 1897 census, "thirty-five predominantly
mining and manufacturing centers with populations between 15,000
and 41,000 were not included in the urban population." On the
other hand, "very small uezd centers, which were little more than
agricultural villages were considered urban." Citation taken from
footnote in: Robert A. Lewis and Richard Rowland, "Urbanization
in Russia and the USSR: 1897-1966," Annals of the Association of
American Geographers, LIX (December, 1969), p. 778. The authors,
however, failed to show on what basis such determinations were made.

CHAPTER II

PATTERNS OF POPULATION GROWTH IN THE RUSSIAN EMPIRE
DURING THE NINETEENTH CENTURY

The absolute growth and territorial redistribution of the
population in the Russian Empire provided the basis from which
the growth in the number and size of cities during the 19th century was possible. The rise in the rate of natural increase,
brought about by the sharp reduction in death rates, affected the
growth of the population in the cities as well as in the countryside, while the spread of population into the formerly uncultivated
and largely unpopulated regions of the Empire were accompanied, and
often even preceded, by the rise of cities. This expansion of
settlement, by bringing into use previously inaccessible natural
resources, together with the absolute growth in the population
provided a broader resourse base which permitted an extension of
the territorial division of labor and gave further impetus to
economic development. The importance of cities in this process
as nodal points in the assembly and distribution of goods was
thus greatly enhanced.

Some Observations on Nineteenth Century Russian Population Statistics

The population data utilized in this study were obtained
primarily from statistical information published by the Tsarist
government during the 19th and 20th centuries. In view of
possible unfamiliarity of the reader with the statistical sources
available for Tsarist Russia and with the general deficiencies inherent in the materials themselves, a brief review of the nature
of the data utilized in this study and the means by which they were

compiled is in order.[1] It might be noted at the onset that for the
entire period of this study, 1811-1910, there was only one general
census taken of the entire population of the Russian Empire. This
was the 1897 census.[2] For the remainder of the period under study
the calculation of the population and its composition was effected
through other methods and means.

A convenient demarcation date for a review of the statistical
data on population is 1858. This was the year in which the Central
Statistical Committee (Tsentral'nyi Statisticheskii Komitet) was
officially established under the auspices of the Ministry of Internal Affairs (Ministerstvo Vnutrennikh Del). With the establishment
of the Central Statistical Committee, the compilation and publication of statistical information on population acquired a certain
measure of accuracy, uniformity, comparability, and regularity
which was not entirely true for the first half of the century.

Until the middle of the 19th century the determination of the
population and its composition was based primarily on the periodic
registrations of the population undertaken by the government called
revizii (reviziia, singular) or revisions. Initiated by Peter the
Great in 1718 for the purpose of registering the male population
of the empire subject to the poll tax, or more precisely, the
"soul tax," ten revizii were carried out: five in the 18th century
(1719, 1744, 1762, 1782, and 1794) and five in the 19th century
(1811, 1815, 1833, 1850, and 1856).

Since the principal objective of the revizii was fiscal,
they did not enumerate the entire population. Only those classes
liable to the poll tax, mainly peasants and common citizens, were
registered while only part of the non-taxed categories were included.
Because of the fiscal nature of the revizii, moreover, the peasants
strove by all means to avoid registration, and, "although comparatively few were successful, all of the revizii, undoubtedly, give

---

[1]For a more detailed discussion and analysis of statistical
materials from the 19th century see: V. M. Kabuzan, Narodo-
naselenie Rossii v XVIII-pervoi polovine XIX v. Po materialam
revezii (Moskva: Izdatel'stvo Akademii Nauk SSSR, 1963), A. Kaufmann,
"The History and Development of the Official Russian Statistics,"
The History of Statistics. Their Development and Progress in Many
Countries, ed. John Koren (New York: The MacMillan Company, 1918),
pp. 469-534, A. G. Rashin, Naselenie Rossii za 100 let, 1811-1913
(Moskva: Gosudarstvennoe Statisticheskoe Izdatel'stvo, 1956), and
E. Z. Volkov, Dinamika narodonaseleniia SSSR za vosem'desiat let
(Moskva: Gosudarstvennoe Izdatelstvo, 1930).

[2]Tsentral'nyi statisticheskii komitet. Pervaia vseobshchaia
perepis' naseleniia Rossiiskoi Imperii 1897 g. 89 vols. (S.-
Peterburg, 1899-1904).

somewhat underestimated figures for the number of the tax-paying population."[1] The registration of the population in the revizii, moreover, took considerable time, often extending over one or two years, and was carried out at different times for different parts of the country. Tsarist Poland, the Caucasus, and Finland were never included in the revizii.

The data obtained from the revizii were supplemented with information on population secured through the civil administrative authorities. The provincial governors were entrusted with the duty of collecting information about the composition of the population, particularly the categories not included in the revizii, the population of cities, natural movement, and migration. This information, obtained primarily from the district police and the Orthodox Church, was then forwarded to the statistical division of the Ministry of Internal Affairs where it was collated, ostensibly verified, and occasionally published. Estimates of the population between revizii were made on the basis of the data from the preceding reviziia with adjustments made for the natural movement of the population and migration.

With the formation of the Central Statistical Committee in 1858 a new system was introduced for the determination of the population to replace the revizii which were discontinued. The basis for the new method of calculating the population was three independent all-Russian registrations of the population, carried out in 1858, 1863, and 1884-1885, and one general census of the population in 1897. The collection of materials in the general registrations was entrusted to the urban and rural police according to units of administration. The provincial statistical committees processed the materials and checked them with results of the calculations made by the governors and with the data from the previous registration. The final compilation of all the information thus received and the correction of errors was entrusted to the Central Statistical Committee.

Aside from the greater efficiency and improved accuracy of these latter registrations, their principal advantage over the revizii was that they enumerated simultaneously all the classes in the population, that is, the nalichnoe naselenie, rather than each class separately.[2] As in the previous period, however,

---

[1] Kabuzan, Narodonaselenie Rossii v XVIII-pervoi polovine XIX v., p. 77.

[2] Ibid., p. 92.

calculations of the population between the general registrations and after the 1897 census were based on annual adjustments of the data from the registrations with information on natural movement and migration supplied by the Church and police respectively.

Inasmuch as the collection and compilation of statistical materials on the population and its composition, particularly for the periods between the revizii and registrations and after the census of 1897, depended to a large extent on local mediums, primarily the dioceses of the Orthodox Church, the district police, the rural communal administration, the provincial statistical committees and the governors, the accuracy of the materials thus collected depended on the competency with which these agencies fulfilled their functions. Unfortunately, their performance in this regard, on the whole, cannot be judged very favorably.[1]

The data provided by the Church on vital statistics were largely unreliable during the first part of the century and although they improved considerably during the second half, they still were by no means complete. The principal deficiencies in the records of the Church were the incomplete registration of births and especially deaths, less accurate records on females as compared with males, and incomplete information regarding persons of non-Orthodox faiths as well as of dissenting sects within the Orthodox Church.

The records maintained by the local civil authorities were also subject to various deficiencies. Distinctions between the population on hand at a given time, the nalichnoe naselenie, and the permanent (postoiannoe) or enscribed (pripisnoe) population were not always maintained by the local authorities. Calculations of the latter were often submitted when in fact the number of the former category had been requested. Double counting was also a common occurrence and became a particular problem during the second half of the century when the volume of migration and emigration rose substantially.[2] Between the general registrations migrants would often be counted twice: once at the place where they were last registered for purposes of taxation and another time at their new place of residence.

Finally, the provincial statistical committees and governors did not always fulfill their functions and when they did, it was

---

[1] Kaufmann, pp. 475-476.

[2] Rashin, Naselenie Rossii za 100 let, p. 20.

often in a negligent manner. The provincial statistical committees
were in reality, "administrative and learned societies," rather
than permanent bureaucratic institutions.[1] The quality of work
accomplished by these committees varied enormously. The performance of the statistical functions of the governors depended
generally on the initiative, enthusiasm, and competency of the
individual. For the most part, however, the governors did not
view the compilation of statistics as one of their primary functions.

In light of the deficiencies described above together with
various other shortcomings, the statistical information that was
finally compiled and published by the Tsarist government should be
viewed with caution. Nevertheless, while not as accurate and reliable in all instances as one would desire, the data do provide,
in varying degrees, a reasonable approximation to reality upon
which general trends and developments can be analyzed.

Population Growth in the Russian Empire

The population of the Russian Empire during the 19th century
grew very rapidly. From approximately 41,000,000 inhabitants in
1810, the population of the Empire increased nearly fourfold, or
by some 120,000,000 persons, reaching a total of 161,000,000 inhabitants in 1910. This large increment in population was largely
the result of a relatively high and rising rate of natural increase,
although territorial annexations also added sizeable numbers to the
total population of the Russian Empire during the 19th century.

In the first half of the 100-year period, 1810-1910, the
population of the Russian Empire increased by 82 per cent, or at
an average rate of 1.2 per cent per year. These figures, however,
are considerably distorted upward by major territorial acquisitions,
particularly Tsarist Poland, Bessarabia, and portions of the Caucasus and Central Asia. As seen from Figure 3 the average annual
rate of increase by decade declined steadily from a high of 1.8
per cent in the decade of the Napoleonic Wars to a low of 0.8 per
cent during the 1850's. The large increase in the population of
the Empire in the first decade was due mostly to territorial annexations which more than compensated for the negative effects of the
Napoleonic Wars on the population of Russia. In the ensuing four
decades, especially the decades between 1840 and 1860, the effects
of frequent crop failures, epidemics of cholera, and several wars

---

[1]Kaufman, p. 474.

FIGURE 3
GROWTH OF POPULATION IN THE RUSSIAN EMPIRE, 1810-1910

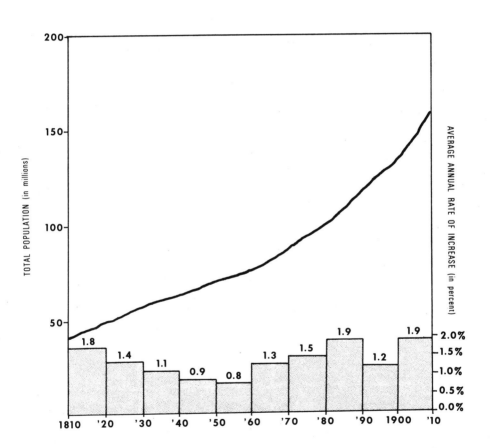

contributed substantially to the very low rates of growth experienced during this period.[1]

The second half of the period under study was one of rather rapid growth in the population. Between 1860 and 1910 the population of the Empire increased 117 per cent or by nearly 87,000,000 persons, from 74,000,000 to 161,000,000 inhabitants. The average annual rate of increase during this period was 1.6 per cent. In the first three decades of this period the rate of population growth sharply increased, partly because of territorial acquisitions, while in the following decade the rate dropped abruptly in part because of crop failures and general economic depression. In the last decade the rate of population growth sharply increased again, reaching the same high level of 1.9 per cent per year as in the 1870's. For the entire period of the study, 1810-1910, the average annual rate of increase was 1.4 per cent.

Population Growth in European Russia

The growth in the population of European Russia during the 19th century resembled closely the pattern of the entire Empire. Figure 4 shows the pattern of population growth for European Russia from 1811 to 1910. During this ninety-nine-year period the population increased 1.8 times and grew at an average annual rate of 1.1 per cent. The analysis of the trends in the growth of population in the first half of the period, however, is hampered by the lack of sufficient data for all but a few years. For the first 29 years the population in European Russia increased by only 19 per cent or at an average rate of 0.6 per cent per year. This was considerably below the growth rate of the entire Empire. During the next thirty years the rate of population growth increased somewhat to 0.9 per cent, which was similar to the rate of growth for the entire Empire in this period.

During the period between the liberation of the serfs and the beginning of the First World War the population grew considerably faster than in the previous period. Following the emancipation of the serfs the rate of population growth rose abruptly during the period 1870-1885, but declined markedly between 1885-1897. In the last three years of the 19th century and the first decade of the 20th century the rate of population growth sharply rose again, reaching the highest level during the entire ninety-nine-year period.

[1]V. M. Kabuzan, Narodonaselenie Rossii v XVIII - pervoi polovine XIX v. (Moskva: Izdatel'stvo Akademii Nauk SSSR, 1963), p. 90.

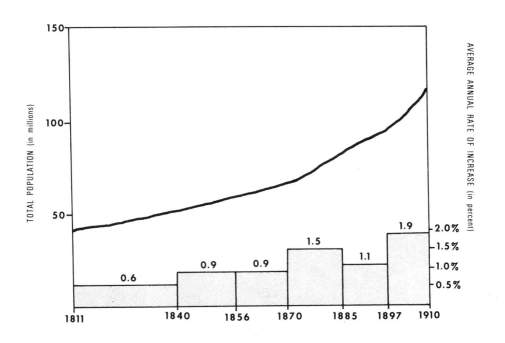

FIGURE 4
GROWTH OF POPULATION IN EUROPEAN RUSSIA, 1811-1910

The average annual rate of increase in the population of European
Russia, during the last forty years of the period under study, was
more than double the rate for the first 45 years, 1.5 per cent and
0.7 per cent respectively.

The regional variations in the growth of the population for
European Russia by guberniia between 1811 and 1914 are shown in
Figures 5 and 6. Throughout the 52-year period from 1811 to 1863
the population of the 49 guberniias of European Russia increased
by only 46 per cent. The guberniias with the lowest rates of increase form a broad band running from Poland and the Baltic Sea
in the west to the bend in the upper Volga in the east (Figure 5).
This belt consisted of the historic core of Russian settlement centered around Moscow from which the Russian Empire expanded from the
16th century onward, the area of Belorussia centered around Minsk
which was acquired in the latter quarter of the 18th century during
the partitions of the Kingdom of Poland, and the guberniias bordering on the Baltic Sea. St. Petersburg and Moscow guberniias stand
out from this zone of low population increase by virtue of the
growth in population of their capital cities.

Surrounding this zone of low growth is an arc of guberniias
with intermediate growth rates. These guberniias, particularly in
the southwest and southeast, were areas of intensive colonization
throughout the 18th century.[1] During the 19th century they became
the main reservoirs of population, supplying the immigrants who were
settling the recently acquired lands further south and in the southeast. These two latter areas, in turn, were the fastest growing regions in European Russia. The nine guberniias which make up these
two regions accounted for 35 per cent or about 6,756,000 persons, of
the total increase in the population of European Russia during this
period, and together with Viatka and Perm guberniias in the northeast, they accounted for 46 per cent of the total growth in population in European Russia.

In the fifty-year period following the emancipation of the
serfs the pattern of population growth in European Russia underwent
several prominent changes. The most dramatic change in the pattern
of population increase, as shown in Figure 6, was the shift in the
area of slowest population growth from the west-central part of
European Russia to the northern and north-central regions.

---

[1]V. K. Iatsunskii, "Izmeneniia v razmeschchenii naseleniia
Evropeiskoi Rossii V 1724-1916 gg.," Istoriia SSSR, I (Mart-Aprel'
1957), p. 197.

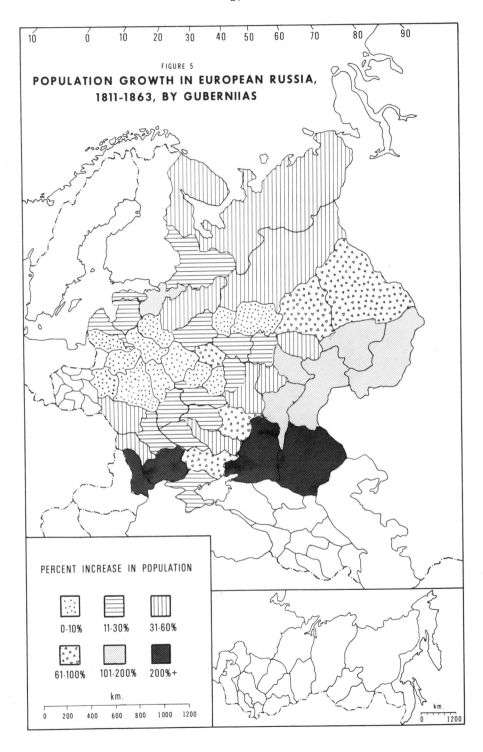

FIGURE 5

POPULATION GROWTH IN EUROPEAN RUSSIA,
1811-1863, BY GUBERNIIAS

PERCENT INCREASE IN POPULATION

0-10% 11-30% 31-60%

61-100% 101-200% 200%+

km.

0 200 400 600 800 1000 1200

km.

0 1200

The western or Belorussian guberniias, which were among the slowest growing guberniias in the earlier period, were now among the most rapidly growing ones. Beginning in the northwest from St. Petersburg and Vitebsk guberniias, a broad arc is formed consisting of guberniias which more than doubled their populations. The arc embraces all the guberniias on the right bank of the Dnepr River to the south, the southern steppe guberniias from the Black to the Caspian Seas, and the Trans-Volga guberniias in the northeast. An inner arc of guberniias with intermediate rates of increase is formed which separates the core of lowest growth from the periphery of highest growth.

The main reason accounting for the regional differences in the increase of the population in European Russia was the regional variation in the levels of the natural growth of the population.[1] During the last half of the period under study, for which reliable data are available, the rate of natural growth in the population of European Russia increased as a consequence of the more rapid decline in death rates than in birth rates. Although birth and death rates both declined, they still remained at comparatively high levels through 1910. Table 1 shows the movement of births and deaths by five-year averages from 1861 to 1913. During this period the birth rate declined from an annual average of 50.7 births per 1,000 inhabitants in the early 1860's to 45.8 during the last five years of the first decade of the 20th century. The comparable decline in death rates was from 36.5 to 29.5 per 1,000 population. The average annual rate of natural increase over the five decades was nearly 15 persons per 1,000 inhabitants.

The pattern of the average annual rate of natural increase in the population of European Russia by guberniias between 1863 and 1913 is shown in Figure 7. Compared with Figure 6, showing the per cent increase in total population, there is a striking similarity in basic patterns. The main differences between the two patterns reflect the role of migration.

Although the status of the sources prevents an accurate determination of the dimensions of migration during the 19th century, there is no doubt that migration in the latter part of the century was notably larger than in the earlier period.[2] With the abolition of serfdom in 1861 the major institutional barrier to movement was

[1] Ibid., p. 218.

[2] Ibid., p. 211.

TABLE 1

NATURAL MOVEMENT OF THE POPULATION IN THE
FIFTY GUBERNIIAS OF EUROPEAN RUSSIA,
1861-1913

Period	Birth Rate Per 1,000 Inhabitants	Death Rate Per 1,000 Inhabitants	Natural Increase Per 1,000 Inhabitants
1861-1865	50 7	36.5	14.2
1866-1870	49.7	37.4	12.3
1871-1875	51.2	37.1	14.1
1876-1880	49.5	35.7	13.8
1881-1885	50.5	36.4	14.1
1886-1890	50.2	34.5	15.7
1891-1895	48.9	36.2	12.7
1896-1900	49.5	32.1	17.4
1901-1905	47.7	31.0	16.7
1906-1910	45.8	29.5	16.3
1911-1913	43.9	27.1	16.8
Average Annual Rate, 1861-1913	48.9	34.0	14.9

Source: A. G. Rashin, Naselenie Rossii za 100 let, p. 54.

removed. This did not mean, however, that there were no other obstacles to movement. The presence of the peasant _mir_ and numerous legal restrictions attached to the conditions of emancipation continued to hinder the flow of migration throughout the remainder of the century. As an indication of the general dimensions of migration during the latter part of the 19th century some 15 per cent of the total population of the Russian Empire in 1897 no longer resided in the same _uezd_ or city of their birth.

Figures 8 and 9, based on the analysis by Leasure and Lewis of place of birth data in the 1897 census, show the general patterns of inter-guberniia migration during the latter part of the 19th Century in the Russian Empire. In-migration was a relatively unimportant factor in the growth of the population of the major part of the long-settled regions of European Russia, except for the more highly urbanized guberniias of St. Petersburg and Moscow and the Baltic and Polish guberniias where urban in-migration was an important factor. In-migration into this part of European Russia accounted for less than seven per cent of the total population. The main regions of in-migration were the southern steppe, the North Caucasus Foreland, and Siberia. In these regions in-migrants generally accounted for more than 15 per cent of the total population. Western Siberia had the highest per cent of new arrivals with over 26 per cent of its population consisting of in-migrants. Migration to the Trans-Caucasus and the Central Asian guberniias was comparatively insignificant.

Out-migration, on the other hand, was very pronounced from European Russia, particularly from the central Russian guberniias. In the sixteen contiguous guberniias in central Russia out-migration totaled 4,591,000 persons or 41 percent of the total number of out-migrants recorded in 1897 for the entire Russian Empire.[2] The Polish and Baltic guberniias were also regions of heavy out-migration, with the number of out-migrants being equal to more than 12 per cent of the total population born in these areas. In the rest of the Russian Empire, particularly in Central Asia and Eastern Siberia, migration was less important.

---

[1] J. William Leasure and Robert A. Lewis, "Internal Migration in Russia in the Late Nineteenth Century," _Slavic Review_. XXVII (No. 3, 1968), p. 377.

[2] Ibid., p. 380.

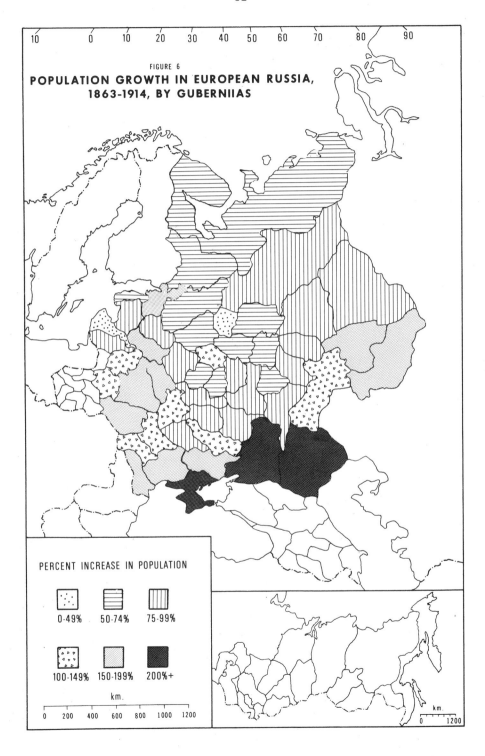

FIGURE 6
**POPULATION GROWTH IN EUROPEAN RUSSIA,
1863-1914, BY GUBERNIIAS**

PERCENT INCREASE IN POPULATION

0-49%   50-74%   75-99%

100-149%   150-199%   200%+

km.

0   200   400   600   800   1000   1200

km.

0   1200

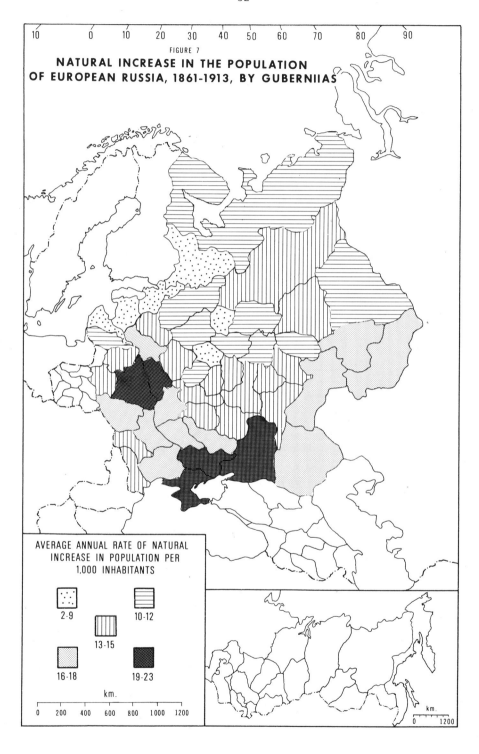

FIGURE 7

NATURAL INCREASE IN THE POPULATION
OF EUROPEAN RUSSIA, 1861-1913, BY GUBERNIIAS

AVERAGE ANNUAL RATE OF NATURAL
INCREASE IN POPULATION PER
1,000 INHABITANTS

2-9   10-12

13-15

16-18   19-23

km.

0   200   400   600   800   1,000   1200

km.

0   1200

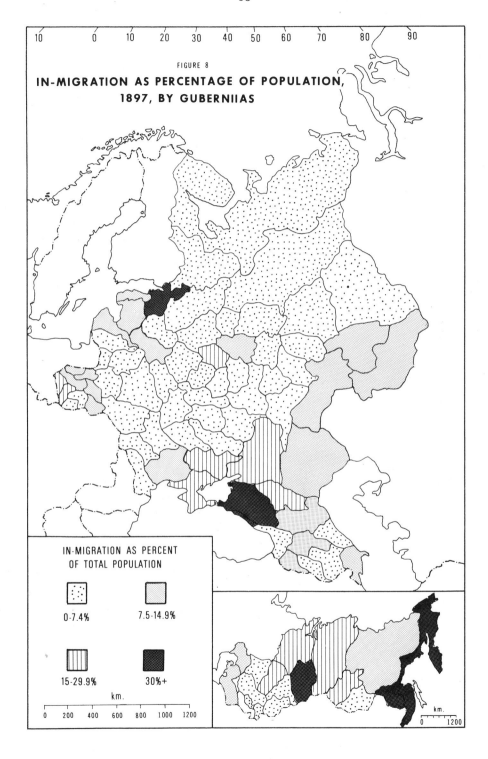

FIGURE 8

IN-MIGRATION AS PERCENTAGE OF POPULATION, 1897, BY GUBERNIIAS

IN-MIGRATION AS PERCENT
OF TOTAL POPULATION

0-7.4%

7.5-14.9%

15-29.9%

30%+

km.

0   200   400   600   800   1000   1200

km.

0   1200

34

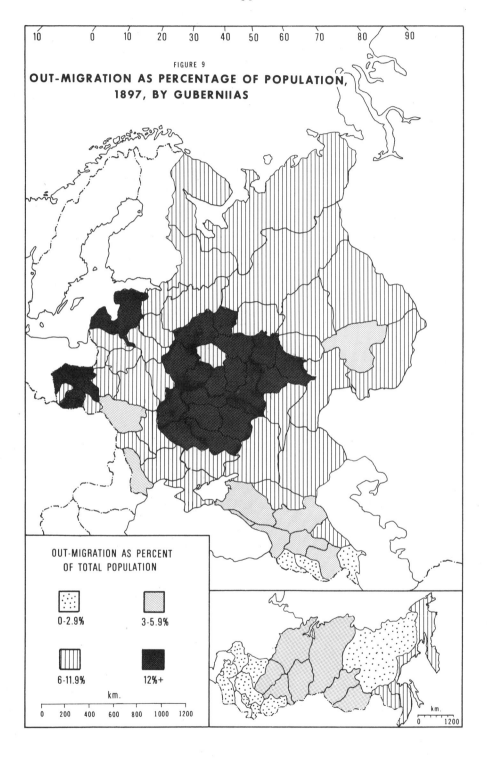

FIGURE 9
OUT-MIGRATION AS PERCENTAGE OF POPULATION, 1897, BY GUBERNIIAS

OUT-MIGRATION AS PERCENT
OF TOTAL POPULATION

0-2.9%   3-5.9%

6-11.9%   12%+

km.

0   200   400   600   800   1000   1200

km.

0   1200

Population Growth in the Peripheral Regions of the Russian Empire

In Tsarist Poland, united dynastically with Russia after the Congress of Vienna in 1815, the population increased 2.5 times or by an average annual rate of 1.4 per cent during the ninety-year period from 1820 to 1910. Figure 10 shows two very distinct patterns in the growth of the population during this period. Between 1820 and 1856 the population increased by only 36 per cent or by an average annual rate of 0.8 per cent. The period between 1840 and 1856, in particular, was one of virtual stagnation in the population as it increased by less than five per cent or at an average rate of 0.3 per cent per year.

Thereafter, however, the rate of population growth increased sharply and remained at high levels throughout the last half of the period. In the forty-year period from 1870 to 1910 the population nearly doubled, increasing from 6,079,000 to 12,129,000 inhabitants. The first decade of the 20th century, as was true for all of Russia, was one of very rapid increase. The population grew at an average annual rate of 2.0 per cent during these ten years.

In the remaining portions of the Russian Empire, the Caucasus, Siberia, and Central Asia, the rate of population growth was greater than in the European part (see Table 20 for population figures). During the last forty years of the period under study the population of these three regions together increased by 1.6 times or at an average annual rate of 1.9 per cent. The Caucasus and Siberia, regions of intensive Slavic immigration during this period, grew at approximately identical rates of 1.8 per cent per year.

In the Caucasus, migration from central Russia to the North Caucasus Foreland was a particularly significant factor in the growth of its population. Between 1870 and 1910 the population of the three North Caucasus Foreland guberniias, Kuban, Stavropol', and Terek, increased from 1,518,900 to 5,039,600, or 2.3 times, while the remaining nine guberniias only doubled their populations from 3,244,400 to 6,695,500 inhabitants.[1] The average annual rates of growth for these two parts of the Caucasus respectively were 2.4 per cent and 1.5 per cent.

In contrast to the Caucasus, where the highest rates of growth occurred in the earlier part of this period, i.e., between 1870 and

[1] Based on calculations from: Russia. Tsentral'nyi statisticheskii komitet. Statisticheskii vremennik Rossiiskoi Imperii. Seriia II, Vypusk desiatyi. Naselenie Aziatskoi Rossii po uezdam. 1870. (Sanktpeterburg, 1875) and Russia. Tsentral'nyi statisticheskii komitet. Statisticheskii ezhegodnik Rossii 1910 g. (S.-Peterburg, 1911).

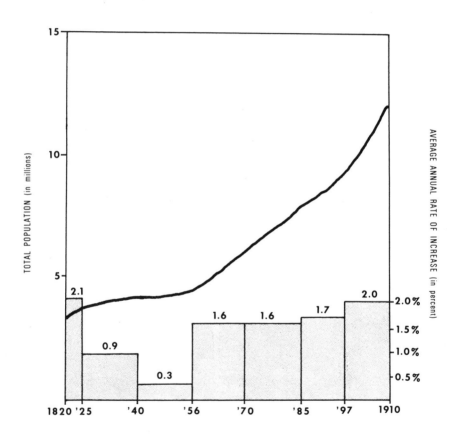

FIGURE 10
GROWTH OF POPULATION IN TSARIST POLAND, 1820-1910

1890, the greatest growth in the population of Siberia took place during the latter part.[1] After 1885 the flow of immigrants into Siberia began to increase sharply. Although precise figures for Siberia are not available, Figure 11 gives an indication of the volume of the migration movement into Siberia and the northern steppe guberniias of Central Asia. Beginning in the 1880's with an annual average flow of about 25,000 persons, the stream of migration increased to more than 100,000 persons per year by 1900 and to more than 200,000 by 1910. The peak year of immigration was 1908 when nearly 760,000 persons were recorded entering Asiatic Russia, while the period of lowest migration was during the Russo-Japanese War when fewer than 50,000 persons were registered. Between 1897 and 1910 the population of Siberia increased by 42.7 per cent or at an average annual rate of 2.5 per cent. For the entire ninety-nine-year period the population of Siberia grew 4.5 times from 1,485,700 in 1811 to 8,220,100 inhabitants in 1910[2]. The average annual rate of increase in the population was 1.7 per cent.

In Central Asia continual territorial expansion lasting into the final decade of the 19th century was a main factor in the high recorded increase in its population within the Russian Empire. Between 1870 and 1910 the population increased nearly threefold and grew at an average annual rate of 2.2 per cent. In the four guberniias of the northern steppe the population increased 1.1 times or by some 1,704,500 inhabitants during the last forty years of the period under study. Nearly half of the growth in population, however, took place in the last thirteen years of the period when the flow of migration beyond the Urals was at its peak.

---

[1]A. G. Rashin, "Sdvigi v territorial'nom razmeshchenii naseleniia Rossii v XIX i v nachale XX v.," Voprosy Geografii, XX (1950), pp. 112, 114.

[2]Ibid., p. 111.

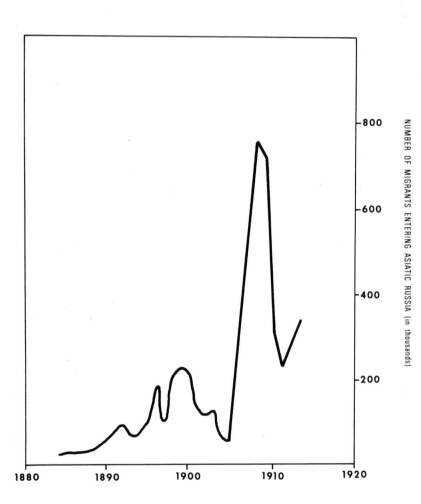

FIGURE 11

**ANNUAL VOLUME OF GROSS MIGRATION
INTO ASIATIC RUSSIA, 1885-1913**

CHAPTER III

URBAN DEVELOPMENT IN THE PRE-REFORM PERIOD,
1811-1856

The Growth in Urban Population and in the Number of Cities
1811-1910

During the 19th century and the first decade of the 20th
century the urban population of the Russian Empire grew very
rapidly. Between 1811 and 1910 the urban population increased
by 20,773,246 persons, from 2,780,337 in 1811 to 23,553,583 persons in 1910 (Table 20). This represented an increase of 7.5
times or an average annual rate of growth of 2.2 per cent. This
substantial increase in the urban population, however, was due
not only to the growth in the size of cities already existing in
the Empire at the beginning of the period, but also to the entry of
many new cities.

During the period under study the number of cities increased
by 65 per cent, from 570 cities in 1811 to 932 cities in 1910.
The addition of 362 new entries was brought about by the establishment of new cities, particularly in the frontier regions, by the
administrative change in the status of existing settlements, primarily in European Russia, and by a real expansion of the country
and the consequent annexation of existing cities. Of these three
factors the last one, territorial annexation, was the most significant.

In 1910 the population of these 362 entries accounted for
7,788,455 persons, or about 33 per cent of the total urban population in the Russian Empire. The significance of new entries in
the growth of the urban population, as seen in Table 2, was greatest during the periods 1811-1825 and 1856-1870 when they constituted nearly one-third and two-fifths respectively of the growth in
urban population during these two periods. The population of the
original 570 cities, on the other hand, as seen in Table 3, increased from 2,780,337 in 1811 to 15,765,128 in 1910, by 4.7 times,
or by 12,984,791 persons, during the period under study, representing an average annual rate of growth of 1.8 per cent.

An analysis of the pattern of urban growth between 1811 and

1910 is conveniently divided by the period coinciding with the emancipation of the serfs in 1861. Prior to the emancipation, as seen in Figure 12, urban growth was comparatively slow and erratic. Between 1811 and 1856 the total urban population of the Empire slightly more than doubled, increasing from 2.8 million to 5.8 million. This represented an average annual rate of increase in the urban population of 1.6 per cent. During the post-reform period, however, the urban population grew at a substantially faster rate. During the forty-year period between 1870 and 1910 the growth in the urban population amounted to nearly 15 million persons as the population of the cities grew from 9 million persons to nearly 24 million. The average annual rate of increase during this period was 2.5 per cent. The temporal and spatial pattern of urban growth during the entire period under study, however, varied considerably as the factors which influenced or retarded the growth of cities underwent substantial change.

TABLE 2

PER CENT OF THE TOTAL GROWTH IN URBAN POPULATION IN THE
RUSSIAN EMPIRE BETWEEN 1811-1910 ATTRIBUTABLE
TO NEW ENTRIES

Period	Absolute Increase in Urban Population in Russian Empire	Number of New Entries	Population of New Entries at Time of Entry	New Entries as a Percentage of Total Growth	Total Growth Without New Entries
1811-1825	694,602	54	211,003	30.4	483,599
1825-1840	1,426,183	44	280,759	19.7	1,145,424
1840-1856	867,079	14	64,996	7.5	803,083
1856-1870	3,152,640	132	1,228,679*	39.0	1,923,961
1870-1885	4,082,969	81	569,505	14.0	3,513,464
1885-1897	3,881,409	23	121,549	3.1	3,759,860
1897-1910	6,668,364	14	44,248	0.6	6,624,116
1811-1910	20,773,246	362	2,520,739	12.1	18,252,501

*Of which number 978,322 were from the inclusion of Tsarist Poland and 145,641 from annexations in Central Asia, or a total of 1,123,963 persons from changes in the area of reporting.

Source: Based on data in Appendix I.

TABLE 3

GROWTH IN THE POPULATION 1811–1910 OF THE
ORIGINAL 570 CITIES IN THE RUSSIAN EMPIRE
AS OF 1811

Year	Total Population	Absolute Growth	Per Cent Increase	Average Annual Per Cent Increase
1811	2,780,337			
1825	3,263,951	481,614	17.3	1.1
		1,058,875	32.4	1.9
1840	4,322,826	692,585	16.0	0.9
1856	5,015,411	1,655,046	33.0	2.0
1870	6,670,457	2,579,614	38.7	2.2
1885	9,250,071	2,245,516	24.3	1.8
1897	11,495,587	4,269,541	37.1	2.5
1910	15,765,128			
1811–1856		2,233,074	80.3	1.3
1870 1910		9,094,671	136.3	2.2
1811–1910		12,984,791	467.0	1.8

Source: Based on data in Appendix I.

FIGURE 12

URBAN GROWTH IN THE RUSSIAN EMPIRE, 1811-1910, BY MAJOR PERIODS

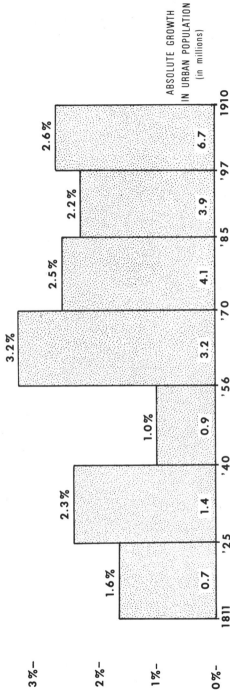

Urban Growth, 1811-1825

In the fourteen years between 1811 and 1825 urban growth was
very slow, reflecting in part the havoc and destruction caused by
the Napoleonic Wars, especially the burning of Moscow. The urban
population during this period, as shown in Table 4, increased by
only 694,602 persons, including some 211,003 persons ascribable to
the entry of new cities. The two capital guberniias, St. Petersburg and Moscow, together accounted for 30 per cent of the total
growth in urban population. Much of this growth was in St. Petersburg guberniia, in which the urban population increased by 41 per
cent, or by some 144,000 persons. The growth here was caused primarily by an unusually heavy influx into St. Petersburg of nobility
and their retinues, civil servants, and military personnel, many of
whom left Moscow following its burning by Napoleon and its subsequent rebuilding.[1]

Another 30 per cent of the growth was accounted for by the
guberniias in the regions of the Left and Right Banks of the Dnepr
River and in the region of the Southwestern Steppe. The growth in
the urban population of these eight guberniias reflected in part
the continued movement of colonists into the steppe as well as the
widespread administrative practice of granting the privilege of
transferring permanently into the cities to several categories
of the population, particularly Jews and members of the Polish
szlachta.[2] This practice continued into the following periods and
was an important factor in the growth of the urban population in
these regions. The only other region which experienced a substantial increase in urban population was the Northwest region consisting of Viatka and Perm guberniias. Although new entries represented a considerable portion of the nearly seven per cent of the
total growth in urban population which this region accounted for,
the great expansion of the gold mining industry in the Urals during
this period contributed significantly to the growth of the cities
in these two guberniias. In most of the remaining guberniias of
the Empire the urban population either declined absolutely or grew
only slightly.

---

[1] A. G. Rashin, Naselenie Rossii za 100 let, p. 127.

[2] P. G. Ryndziunskii, Gorodskoe grazhdanstvo doreformennoi
Rossii (Moskva: Izdatel'stvo Akademii Nauk SSSR, 1958),
pp. 367-368.

[3] L. E. Iofa, Goroda Urala. Chast' pervaia. Feodal'nyi
period (Moskva: Gosudarstvennoe Izdatel'stvo Geograficheskoi
Literatury, 1951), pp. 293-294.

TABLE 4

ABSOLUTE GROWTH AND PER CENT OF TOTAL GROWTH IN
URBAN POPULATION BY REGION IN RUSSIAN EMPIRE,
1811-1856

Region	1811-1825 Absolute Growth	Per Cent of Total	1825-1840 Absolute Growth	Per Cent of Total	1840-1856 Absolute Growth	Per Cent of Total	1811-1856 Absolute Growth	Per Cent of Total
Capitals	209,023	30.1	204,174	14.3	50,820	5.9	464,017	15.5
Central Industrial	14,206	2.1	61,534	4.3	37,914	4.4	113,654	3.8
Southern Industrial	10,202	1.5	65,927	4.6	22,288	2.6	98,417	3.3
Black Earth	10,593	1.5	111,915	7.9	49,650	5.7	172,158	5.8
Northwest	17,638	2.5	34,776	2.4	6,496	0.8	58,910	2.0
Baltic	22,400	3.2	52,151	3.7	15,184	1.8	89,735	3.0
West-Central	16,469	2.4	48,534	3.4	31,989	3.7	96,992	3.2
Western	26,341	3.8	81,481	5.7	69,416	8.0	177,238	5.9
Right Bank Dnepr	61,209	8.8	115,989	8.1	74,406	8.6	251,604	8.4
Left Bank Dnepr	41,581	6.0	88,464	6.2	38,936	4.5	168,981	5.7
Southwestern Steppe	100,187	14.4	247,311	17.4	140,332	16.2	487,830	16.3
Southeastern Steppe	11,486	1.7	57,618	4.0	10,267	1.2	79,371	2.7
Middle Volga	-21,037	-3.0	39,814	2.8	52,789	6.1	71,566	2.4
Lower Volga	12,218	1.8	49,183	3.5	78,458	9.1	139,859	4.7
Trans Volga	2,026	0.3	20,967	1.5	344	0.0	23,337	0.8
Pre-Caucasus	12,952	1.9	9,620	0.7	38,303	4.4	60,875	2.8
Caucasus	41,974	6.0	30,626	2.2	37,921	4.4	110,521	3.7
Caspian Sea	9,843	1.4	57,435	4.0	33,060	3.8	100,338	3.4
North	12,615	1.8	-4,763	-0.3	13,515	1.6	21,367	0.7
Northeast	47,810	6.9	19,223	1.4	26,032	3.0	93,065	3.1
Western Siberia	8,393	1.2	14,461	1.0	16,561	1.9	39,415	1.3
Eastern Siberia	8,768	1.3	13,831	1.0	12,844	1.5	35,443	1.2
Central Asiatic Steppe	17,711	2.6	5,907	0.4	9,553	1.1	33,171	1.1
Total	694,602	100.0	1,426,183	100.0	867,079	100.0	2,987,864	100.0

Source: Based on data in Appendix I.

Urban Growth, 1825-1840

In the following fifteen-year period, 1825-1840, the urban
population of the Empire registered a very significant increase.
The growth of cities during this period coincided with a rather
considerable economic upsurge throughout all of Russia. Domestic
commerce, particularly in the form of periodic fairs and bazaars,
greatly expanded. Industry, which grew very slowly in the previous
period in part as a consequence of the war and the liberal tariff
policies pursued after the war, began to develop rapidly following
the erection of a protectionist tariff in 1822.[1] Between 1825 and
1840 the number of factories increased by 31 per cent, reaching a
total of 6,863 in 1840, and the number of workers slightly more
than doubled, numbering 435,788 by the end of the period.[2] The
economic prosperity of this period continued into the first half of
the 1840's, but came to an abrupt halt with the onset of a severe
economic crisis in 1847.

Reflecting primarily the greatly expanded volume of domestic
commerce, in which the cities acquired an increasingly important
role as the intermediary points of commodity exchange, the urban
population of the Empire grew by some 1.4 million persons. This
represented an increase of 41 per cent in the urban population and
an average annual rate of growth of 2.3 per cent. Although new
entries continued to play an important role in the growth of the
urban population, their contribution declined to about 20 per cent
of the total growth in urban population in this period. Most of
the new entries during this period resulted from the new inclusion
of Bessarabia and parts of the trans-Caucasus in the official
statistics.

The regional distribution of the growth in urban population
during this period contrasted with the previous period in several
respects. The most notable change was the sharp decline, from 30
per cent to 14 per cent, in the proportion of the growth in urban
population accounted for by the two capital guberniias. In fact,
as seen in Table 4, the absolute growth in the numbers of urban
population in these two guberniias declined from 209,023 in the
former period to 204,174 persons during the period under study.
Moreover, in contrast with the previous period, it was the growth
in the urban population of Moscow guberniia that constituted most
of the increase in urban population in these two guberniias. The

---

[1]S. G. Strumilin, Ocherki ekonomicheskoi istorii Rossii
i SSSR (Moskva: Izdatel'stvo "Nauka", 1966), pp. 377-378.
[2]Ibid., p. 376.

growth in the population of the cities of Moscow guberniia accounted
for nearly two-thirds, or 129,891 persons, of the total growth in
urban population in these two guberniias.

Whereas the attraction of population to the cities in the capital guberniias declined, the cities in the guberniias of the central and southeastern regions of European Russia experienced a large
influx of population. The seven guberniias of the Southern Industrial region and the Black Earth region increased their share of
the urban growth from 3 per cent in the previous period to 12.5 per
cent, while the seven guberniias in the Volga River area, which experienced a net decline in urban population in the former period,
accounted for nearly 8 per cent of the growth in urban population.
In absolute terms the population of the cities in these fourteen
guberniias increased by 287,806 persons during the period 1825-1840,
compared to an increase of only 14,002 persons in the preceding
period, 1811-1825. The abrupt surge in the growth of the urban population in these two regions reflected on one hand the increasing
commercialization of agriculture and commodity exchange of these
regions with the Central Industrial region, and on the other hand
the continuation of the internal process of migration to the Lower
and Trans-Volga regions.[1]

The flow of migrants into the cities of the four southern
regions of European Russia continued at a high rate, as 374,309
persons, excluding the growth in urban population by the addition
of Bessarabia, were added to the populations of these cities. In
the regions of the Left and Right Banks of the Dnepr River the
rapid growth of the cities was based primarily on their increasingly important roles as nodal points in the well-organized network
of periodic fairs and bazaars which emerged in the Ukraine. It was
essentially through these fairs, at which the total volume of commercial turnover greatly expanded during this period, that the exchange of the agricultural products of the south for the manufactured goods of the Central Industrial region was effected. The
growth in the population of the cities in the two Southern Steppe
regions, on the other hand, was based more on their strategical and
military significance, as Russia sought to expand her influence in
the Middle East and in the Balkans. At the same time the port
cities of the Black and Azov Seas, especially Odessa, acquired
added commercial importance as the primary outlets for the increasing volume of grain exports from Russia, the overwhelming bulk of

---

[1]Ryndziunskii, _Gorodskoe grazhdanstvo_ . . . , p. 343.

which, for reasons of transportation and accessibility, was shipped through the southern ports during the pre-reform period.[1] The Baltic and Western guberniias also increased slightly their portion of the total growth in urban population during this period, while in the remaining peripheral regions, the North, Northeast, the Caucasus, and Siberia, the share of the growth in urban population declined from 23 per cent in the preceding period to only 10 per cent during the period under consideration.

Urban Growth, 1840-1856

In the final period preceding the emancipation of the serfs the rate of growth of the urban population abruptly declined. Between 1840 and 1856 the urban population in the Russian Empire increased by only 867,079 persons, or by 18 per cent. The average annual rate of increase during this period declined to only one per cent, the lowest rate during the entire ninety-nine-year period under study. This sharp decline in the growth of the urban population was associated with a general economic recession which began to set in during the middle of the 1840's, the effects of which, however, persisted into the following decade, and also with a number of natural disasters which struck Russia.

Curtailment of production in several branches of industry, particularly in the linen and woolen industries, began in 1846. During the next two years nearly all branches of industry were affected and declines in their production and employment levels were noted.[2] The effects of the economic crisis of 1847 were clearly reflected in the progression of employment in industry. Between 1840 and 1847 industrial employment rose from 435,800 to 532,100 persons, but then declined sharply thereafter to 465,000 workers by 1851. During the following five years employment grew gradually and reached 518,700 workers in 1856.[3] In general, the textile industries were the most strongly affected by the economic crisis and were also the slowest to recover.

---

[1] M. L. de Tegoborski, Commentaries on the Productive Forces of Russia (London: Longman, Brown, Green, and Longmans, 1856), II, p. 302.

[2] Strumilin, Ocherki ekonomicheskoi istorii Rossii i SSSR, pp. 422-423.

[3] P. A. Khromov, Ekonomicheskoe razvitie Rossii v XIX-XX vekakh (Moskva: Gosudarstvennoe Izdatel'stvo Politicheskoi Literatury, 1950), pp. 436-439.

The stagnation in the industrial sector of the economy was compounded by a period of a high frequency of below-average harvests. During the thirteen years between 1839 and 1851 the harvests in five years were considered failures and in another four years were deemed poor.[1] Finally in 1848 an epidemic of Asiatic cholera broke out and swept over the country. As a consequence of the epidemic and the ravages of scurvy which engulfed nearly the entire country between 1848 and 1849, it was estimated that over one million persons perished.[2] Entire factories ceased operations during this period. And in the cities, many of which were particularly hard hit by the epidemic, thousands of people perished and many more fled from them and sought refuge in the countryside.

The impact of the economic decline and the natural disasters which beset Russia during this period was felt most keenly in the capital guberniias. Their portion of the growth in the urban population of the Empire declined precipitously to only 5.9 per cent. The growth in the populations of the capital cities virtually ceased. During this period St. Petersburg gained only 20,606 inhabitants, while Moscow grew by a mere 19,697 persons. The Central Black Earth, the Southern Industrial, the Baltic, and the Northwest regions also experienced sharp declines in the growth of their urban population. These four regions together with the capital guberniias and the Central Industrial region accounted for only a little more than one-fifth of the growth in the urban population as compared to nearly two-fifths in the previous period.

The three regions to the west of the Dnepr River, the Western, the Right Bank of the Dnepr, and the Southwestern Steppe, accounted for nearly one-third of the growth in the urban population. The growth in the population of the city of Odessa alone, although considerably slower than in the preceding period, slightly exceeded the combined growth in the populations of the two capital cities. The two regions to the east of the Dnepr River, however, experienced a sharp decline in the growth of urban population, as they accounted for only half as much of the growth in urban population in the Empire as in the previous period.

The most spectacular increase in urban population took place in the Middle and Lower Volga regions. Their proportion of the growth in urban population increased from 6.3 per cent to 15.2

---

[1] Rashin, Naselenie Rossii za 100 let, pp. 36-37.

[2] Strumilin, Ocherki ekonomicheskoi istorii Rossii i SSSR, p. 367.

per cent. The share of the growth in urban population in the remaining peripheral regions, in general, also increased significantly.

The very substantial alteration in the pattern of urban growth during this period, that is, the stagnation of the urban population in the central and northwestern parts of the country and the continued growth in the peripheries, reflected above all the desire of the peasantry to escape from the economic and natural hardships of the former regions in search of better conditions in the latter ones.

Summary: Patterns of Urban Growth, 1811-1856

The distribution of urban growth by guberniia in relative and absolute terms for the entire period from 1811 to 1856 is shown in Figures 13 and 14. The basic contrast in the regional pattern of urban growth between the comparatively slow growth in the population of the cities in the northern and central portions of European Russia and the rapid increase in the urban population of the surrounding peripheral zone is readily apparent in Figure 13. With the exceptions of Moscow and Riazan' guberniias, where the urban population more than doubled, and a tier of guberniias where the increase in the urban population was less than 50 per cent, a fairly large and compact area is discernable in central European Russia consisting of guberniias in which the relative increase in the urban population was more than 50 per cent but less than 100 per cent. Enclosing this area on three sides is a nearly continuous crescent, beginning in the northwest and stretching south and southeastward along the Dnepr River to the Sea of Azov and then extending east and northeastward along the Volga River, composed of guberniias in which the urban population more than doubled between 1811 and 1856. With the exception of the western tier of guberniias, where part of the movement of population into the cities was a somewhat artificial result of administrative fiat, this area was, for the most part, the main recipient of a continuous stream of migration from the central regions, which went on during the entire period. The rapid growth of the cities in these regions took place largely on the basis of serving the needs of the increasing population and expanding agriculture and commerce.

51

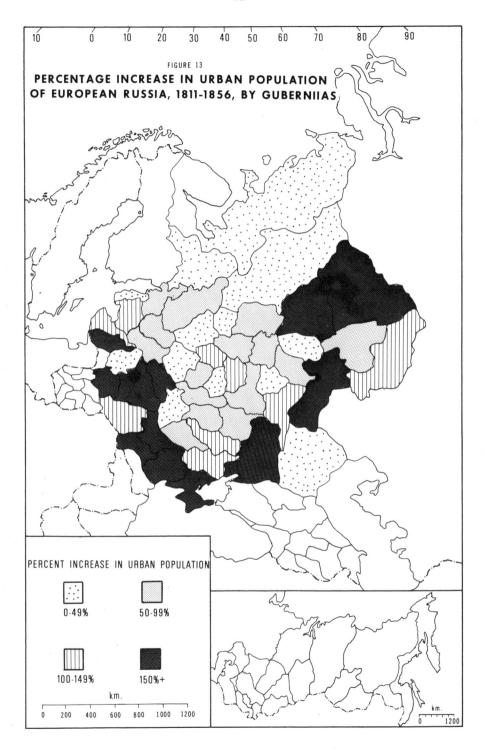

FIGURE 13

PERCENTAGE INCREASE IN URBAN POPULATION OF EUROPEAN RUSSIA, 1811-1856, BY GUBERNIIAS

PERCENT INCREASE IN URBAN POPULATION

0-49%

50-99%

100-149%

150%+

km.

0   200   400   600   800   1000   1200

km.

0   1200

Figure 14, on the other hand, shows the great disparity in the distribution of absolute growth in the urban population. The three guberniias of St. Petersburg, Moscow, and Kherson alone in the Capitals and Southwestern steppe regions accounted for nearly 23 per cent, or 680,225 persons, of the total growth in the urban population between 1811 and 1856. Furthermore, much of the growth was in the three cities of St. Petersburg, Moscow, and Odessa. Three guberniias in the south, Kiev, Khar'kov, and Tavrida, together with Saratov guberniia, accounted for an additional ten per cent of the growth in urban population. Consequently, one-third of the growth in urban population during this forty-five-year period was concentrated in only seven guberniias, much of it in the seven largest cities of these guberniias. The remainder of the growth in urban population was distributed fairly evenly among the guberniias, with the northern, Asiatic, and most of the guberniias in the Caucasus registering only small amounts of growth.

The resulting shift in the distribution of the urban population during the pre-reform period was such that the share of the eight, long-settled regions of the central and western portions of European Russia, which accounted for 61 per cent of the urban population in 1811, accounted for 51.5 per cent by 1856. The southern regions and parts of the Caucasus increased their share of the urban population.

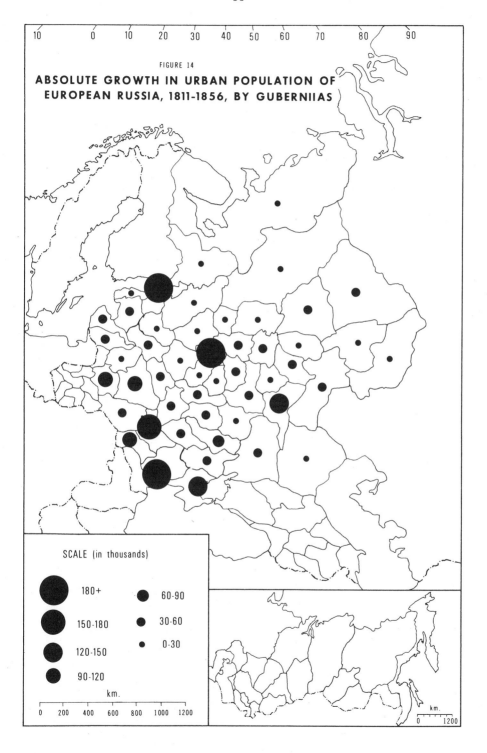

FIGURE 14

ABSOLUTE GROWTH IN URBAN POPULATION OF EUROPEAN RUSSIA, 1811-1856, BY GUBERNIIAS

SCALE (in thousands)

180+

150-180

120-150

90-120

60-90

30-60

0-30

km.

0   200   400   600   800   1000   1200

km.

0   1200

CHAPTER IV

FACTORS OF URBAN GROWTH IN THE PRE-REFORM PERIOD, 1811-1856

The growth of cities in the first half of the 19th century was not premised on any single cause, but rather was conditioned by a complex array of many circumstances. This period, in essence, can be viewed as one in which the institutional and environmental forces which for centuries had severely restricted the growth of cities were slowly becoming ameliorated.

The growth in the total population of the Empire provided a greatly expanded potential market for commodities, but the perpetuation of serfdom, albeit in a decaying state, prevented this potentiality from being fully realized. For the most part the rural population remained self-sufficient both in agricultural and manufactured goods. Furthermore, the exploitative character of serfdom continued to restrict the purchasing power of the rural population, the consequence of which was that manufactured goods could not and did not find a broad market among the peasantry.[1]

Territorial expansion and colonization were also important factors in the development of cities. With the spread of population over a greater area, the number and size of cities expanded in order to provide security for the new settlers, to administer to their religious, social, and political needs, and to satisfy their minimal requirements for manufactured products and implements. Likewise, the annexation and colonization of new regions fostered a greater inter-regional division of labor that was accompanied by the expansion of domestic commerce, especially in the form of periodic fairs, and by the growth of industry. To this end the cities performed an increasingly important role as the intermediaries in the exchange of commodities. Consequently, the further development of market relationships and the expansion of commerce were the most important economic factors influencing the rate and the pattern of city growth in the first half of the 19th century.

---

[1]M. K. Rozhkova, "Torgovlia," Ocherki ekonomicheskoi istorii Rossii pervoi poloviny XIX veka, ed. M. K. Rozhkova (Moskva: Izdatel'stvo Sotsial'no-Ekonomicheskoi Literatury, 1959), p. 260.

Periodic Fairs and the Growth of Cities

The most striking feature of the growth in trade and commerce
was the great role played by periodic fairs, or iarmarki, and bazaars. The great expanse of the Empire, the relatively low density
of population, the inadequacies of transportation and communication,
and the absence of an effective system of credit contributed to
making the fairs the primum mobile of domestic commercial turnover
in the Empire.[1]

By the end of the second decade of the 19th century there were
over 4,000 fairs of various significance in forty of the fifty-five
guberniias in the Empire.[2] The overwhelming majority of these
fairs, both urban and rural, were small and served only the needs
of the surrounding locality. Sixty-four fairs, however, were considered large, having a trade turnover exceeding one million rubles
annually, while ten of these were of all-Russian significance having a trade turnover of more than ten million rubles. The largest
fair in the Empire was at Nizhnii Novgorod where annually the value
of goods exchanging hands exceeded one hundred million rubles.[3]

Nearly one-half of the fairs in the Empire were located in
southern Russia, including twenty-three of the large fairs. The
great abundance of fairs in this region was the consequence primarily of the lack of sizeable markets for the sale of grain due to the
existing inadequacies of land and water transportation. The peasants and nobles here disposed of their grain production primarily
at the small rural markets to purchasers who in turn took the commodities to the large urban fairs which connected the south with the
rest of Russia. The largest and most important fairs were in the
region of the Left Bank of the Dnepr River. Here there were nearly
1,000 fairs with four large fairs at Khar'kov, three at Kremenchug,
and two each at Sumy, Starodub, and Romny. On the Right Bank of
the Dnepr River, Kiev and Berdichev possessed fairs of all-Russian
importance.

The Central Black Earth region, the Western region, and Siberia
also were important centers of fair activity. At these fairs,
especially in Siberia, goods from all over Russia and from foreign
countries were brought and exchanged. Merchants from the Central

---

[1] Tegoborski, Commentaries . . . , II, p. 155.

[2] M. K. Rozhkova, "K voprosu o znachenii iarmarok vo vnutrennei
torgovle doreformennoi Rossii," Istoricheskie Zapiski, LIV,
p. 299.

[3] Ibid.

Industrial region, from Central Asia, as well as from Western Europe, brought with them manufactured articles, primarily textiles and small metal goods and implements, and exchanged these for the commodities of the rural economy, especially food stuffs and livestock products.

During the latter decades of the pre-reform period the role of fairs in domestic commerce began to decline, except in the peripheries of the Empire. In the long-settled and densely populated Central Industrial region, which was notable for the absence of large fairs, the importance of seasonal fairs yielded at an early date to the development of permanent forms of trade in the larger cities. In Rostov, for example, the site of the largest fair in the Central Industrial region after Nizhnii Novgorod, the value of sales steadily declined from 4.6 million rubles in 1817 to only 1.3 million rubles in 1861.[1] In Moscow, there did not exist a single important fair, but instead the city had a number of markets which operated the year round. Of these permanent markets the gostinnyi dvor, or the merchant's courtyard, was the most important one at which more than 6,000 shops, booths and stalls were housed under long, pillared, glass roofed arcades.[2]

The gradual displacement of periodic fairs by permanent urban markets also began to take place in the south. In Khar'kov, for instance, on the site of four large annual fairs, warehouses began to be constructed to store goods for sale at forthcoming fairs, and merchants were finding it more convenient to register in the city for permanent residence rather than make numerous trips to the city.[3] Shops began to stay open the whole year instead of just during the fairs. By 1850 in Kiev wholesale receipts were nearly one half those of the various fairs held there.[4] With the expansion of the railway network the significance of fairs, especially urban fairs, began to decline rapidly. Nevertheless, by the beginning of the 1860's there were still some 1,127 urban fairs and 4,768 rural fairs in the 48 guberniias of European Russia.[5]

---

[1]Ibid., pp. 307-308.

[2]William L. Blackwell, The Beginnings of Russian Industrialization, 1800-1860 (Princeton, N.J.: Princeton University Press. 1960), pp. 76-77.

[3]Ibid., p. 76.

[4]Rozhkova, "K voprosu o znachenii iarmarok . . . , p. 312.

[5]P. A. Khromov, Ekonomicheskoe razvitie Rossii. Ocherki ekonomiki Rossii s drevneishikh vremen do velikoi oktiabr' skoi Revoliutsii (Moskva: Izdatel'stvo "Nauka", 1967), p. 188.

The Rise of Peasant Trade

The upsurge in the volume of trade and commerce that took place during the pre-reform period in a large degree was due to the increased activity of peasants in the market. Forced to increase their income to satisfy the growing demands made upon them by the state in the form of the poll tax and by their masters who increasingly were shifting the obligations of the peasantry from barshchina, or labor, to obrok, or cash payments, the peasants began to appear in greater numbers on the local markets with their agricultural products or with manufactured articles produced in their households or workshops.

The increase in the activity of small peasant traders was also stimulated by the easing of restrictions on their movement and activity by the government.[1] In 1801 the peasants were given the freedom to trade with foreign countries, while in 1814 persons of all estates received the right to trade at the fairs and bazaars. Four years later, in 1818, both state and private serfs were granted, with the agreement of the local authorities and the owners, the right to establish factories and plants with the condition of the payment of a tithe. Other measures which eased the restrictions of movement and the establishment of residence in the cities and the transfer into the urban estate, either in the meshchanstvo, or petty bourgeoisie estate, or in the merchantry were also passed during the course of the pre-reform period. Most closely associated with the expansion of small trade and industry were the state peasants, who possessed considerably more freedom than the seignoral peasantry, and serfs who had been shifted to obrok.[2]

The growth of small peasant trade was not without consequences to the existing guilded merchantry. During the first half of this period the number of persons belonging to the merchant guild did not increase.[3] Only in the latter part of the period, when many restrictions on the entry of peasants into the guild were removed, did the number of guilded merchants grow significantly.

Likewise, the growth in petty trade was not always viewed as advantageous to the prosperity of the cities. The alarm expressed by many officials and city residents on the deleterious effects of peasant trade on the economy of the cities and the prosperity of

---

[1] Ibid., pp. 185-186.

[2] Ibid., p. 186.

[3] Ryndziunskii, Gorodskoe grazhdanstvo . . . , p. 97.

the merchant and petty bourgeoisie classes was summed up in the
following quote from a report of the then Minister of Finance,
Count Kankrin to Nicholas the First:

> "Some measures were taken for the gradual reduction
> of petty trade in the cities and in the country in
> order, on the one hand, to concentrate industry in the
> cities, and on the other hand that people without capi-
> tal would occupy themselves more with productive activ-
> ities, especially in factories, rather than with worth-
> less petty trade. It is well known that from the time
> that the peasants intensified their trading, our cities
> began to decline noticeably. Ancient Russia had better
> cities, for then the peasants had freedom to become
> real city residents, not uniting agriculture with trade.[1]

The peasants, of course, were by no means limited to petty
trade. With the passage of time many peasants moved into wholesale trade and managed to accumulate great sums of capital. This
trend, however, was blurred by the fact that as peasants acquired
sufficient capital many of them, especially state peasants, were
able to transfer into one of the urban estates, primarily the meshchanstvo. But there is no doubt that the increased activity of
peasants on the market, particularly on the urban market, contributed significantly to the growth of commerce and trade and eventually to the economic development of many towns and cities.

Industrial Expansion and Urban Development

Although a significant industrial expansion took place in
Russia during the first half of the 19th century, it was still
essentially a locally limited phenomenon and had little direct
effect on the growth of all but a few cities. What little industry
was found in the cities was still primarily in the pre-manufacturing
stage of development with a predominance of small commodity production and handicrafts. Factories were found in comparatively few
cities, and still rarer, almost in the form of an exception, was
factory industry developed to any degree of significance in the
cities. [2]

Between 1811 and 1860, as seen in Table 5, the number of factories and plants increased 2.3 times from 2,921 to 9,562, and the

---

[1] Cited in: Walter McKenzie Pintner, Russian Economic
Policy under Nicholas I (Ithaca, N.Y.: Cornell University Press,
1967), pp. 58-59.

[2] Ryndziunskii, Gorodskoe grazhdanstvo . . . , p.379.

number of workers grew 2.7 times from 138,042 to 505,395. The growth of factory industry, however, was limited primarily to a few regions. Cotton and woolen textiles, metal processing, and beet sugar refining accounted for nearly 90 per cent, or some 328,404 persons, of the total growth in employment in manufacturing. Of these four industries, only textiles provided some impetus to urban growth.

Beet Sugar Refining

The refining of beet sugar, which developed rapidly with the decline in grain prices and the imposition of a high tariff on imported sugar cane in 1822, was carried out primarily on the gentry estates in the south-central guberniias of European Russia.[1] In 1860, over 80 per cent of the production came from the two regions of the Left and Right Banks of the Dnepr River. The difficulty of transporting the raw material, the availability of cheap labor in the form of serfs, and the availability of capital among the landed gentry limited production to the rural estates. On the eve of the reforms over sixty per cent of the 85,000 persons employed in industry in the south were accounted for by this industry.[2]

Metallurgical Industry

In the metallurgical industry, over 80 per cent of the production of iron by 1860 was concentrated in the Urals, primarily in Perm and Orenburg guberniias.[3] An old industry, dating from the time of Peter the Great, and almost wholly dependent on serf labor, it remained virtually stagnant through the first four decades of the 19th century. Beginning in the 1840's, however, the industry underwent a rejuvenation. In response to a growing domestic market stimulated in part by the initiation of railroad construction and increased military requirements, especially during the period of the Crimean War, the production of pig iron rose from 11.3 million poods in 1840 to 20.5 million poods by 1860.[4]

The iron industry as a whole, however, remained generally in a backward state. The protection afforded it by the government in the

---

[1]R. S. Livshits, Razmeshchenie promyshlennosti v dorevoliutsionnoi Rossii (Moskva: Isdatel'stvo Akademii Nauk SSSR, 1955), p. 115.

[2]Ibid., p. 121.

[3]Ibid., p. 128.

[4]Ibid., p. 123.

TABLE 5

GROWTH IN THE NUMBER OF FACTORIES AND WORKERS
IN EUROPEAN RUSSIA, 1811-1860

Industry	1811	1825	1835	1852	1860
Woolen	(209) 36,547	(324) 63,603	(456) 69,425	(657) 106,651	(706) 120,025
Cotton	(201) 13,703	(484) 47,021	(711) 90,539	(911) 140,635	(1,200) 152,236
Linen	(236) 36,612	(196) 26,832	(186) 26,801	(181) 15,735	(117) 17,284
Silks	(216) 10,265	(205) 10,709	(243) 13,420	(544) 16,078	(393) 14,287
Rope	(57) 2,129	(98) 2,503	(125) 2,942	(160) 3,526	(166) 5,385
Hattery	(42) 995	(69) 954	(81) 3,167	(37) 462	(18) 412
Paper	(68) 6,701	(94) 8,552	(137) 13,278	(211) 16,105	(207) 12,804
Leather	(1,226) 8,262	(1,784) 8,001	(1,728) 10,425	(2,081) 14,818	(2,515) 14,151
Tallow, Soap	(269) 834	(1,023) 5,105	(1,149) 6,717	(1,203) 8,690	(1,827) 12,122
Sugar	(10) 123	(47) 1,374	(69) 2,840	(408) 46,151	(467) 64,763
Tobacco	(6) 102	(35) 342	(113) 848	(345) 4,861	(343) 6,059
Potash	(116) 1,354	(228) 2,215	(177) 1,140	(199) 1,709	(263) 1,531
Chemicals	(45) 312	(59) 433	(108) 1,250	(110) 2,773	(135) 3,440
Nitrates	-- --	(40) 884	(102) 1,585	(130) 4,469	(101) 3,467
Crystal & Glass	(131) 5,497	(164) 5,765	(190) 8,592	(189) 11,650	(195) 11,464
Ceramics & Pottery	(12) 1,199	(45) 1,685	(57) 1,194	(43) 1,976	(55) 2,629
Iron Products	(39) 12,737	(170) 22,440	(364) 33,272	(495) 45,438	(693) 54,832
Copper Products	(38) 670	(104) 1,713		(156) 4,396	(161) 8,504

Totals					
Factories	(2,921)	(5,169)	(5,996)	(8,060)	(9,562)
Workers	138,042	210,131	287,435	466,123	505,395

Source: A. G. Rashin, Formirovanie promyshlennogo proletariata v Rossii, pp. 26-27, 30-31.

form of high tariffs on imported iron and by military purchases, the
dependence on serf labor, and the high costs of transporting the
product from the Urals to markets continued to hinder the introduction of technological improvements. Although some rather large
factory settlements grew up on the basis of iron production, such as
at Nizhnii Tagil, where in 1850 some 21,000 workers were employed,
production remained seasonal and took place in small-scale works located in rural areas where the serf labor and raw materials, especially fuel in the form of timber for making charcoal, were available.[1]
The cities of the Urals, with the exception of Ekaterinburg, remained virtually unaffected by the development of the metallurgical
industry.

Textile Industry

Textiles, and in particular cotton textiles, alone among growing factory industries had an important impact on the economic development of some cities. On the eve of the reforms the bulk of
production in the textile industries came from the peasant households and from factories located in rural settlements. These two
aspects of the industry were closely related since the practice of
"farming out" work from the factory to the peasant households for
preparation of further processing was widespread.[2] Most textile
production was concentrated in the Central Industrial region, especially in Moscow and Vladimir guberniias, where rural handicrafts
and factories had existed for a long time and where the distribu-
tional network was firmly established.[3] Also St. Petersburg and
Lifliand guberniias emerged as new centers, though not very large,
on the basis of imported raw materials and technology.

Although the woolen industry grew substantially, it for the
most part remained technologically backward and located primarily
in the countryside. A large share of the production of woolen textiles came from the estates of the gentry working with serf labor.[4]

[1] Iofa, Goroda Urala . . . , p. 379.

[2] Mikhail I. Tugan-Baranovskii, The Russian Factory in the 19th
Century, translated from the 3d Russian edition by Arthur Levin and
Claora S. Levin (Homewood, Illinois: Richard D. Irwin, Inc., 1970),
pp. 174-175.

[3] I. F. Rybakov, "Nekotorye voprosy genezisa kapitalisticheskogo
goroda v Rossii," Voprosy genezisa kapitalizma v Rossii, ed. V. V.
Mavrodin (Leningrad Izdatel'stvo Leningradskogo Universiteta,
1960), p. 230.

[4] V. K. Iatsunskii, "Krupnaia promyshlennost' Rossii v
1790-1860 gg.," Ocherki ekonomicheskoi istorii Rossii pervoi
poloviny XIX veka, ed. M. K. Rozhkova (Moskva: Izdatel'stvo
Sotsial'no-Ekonomicheskoi Literatury, 1959), p. 189.

This aspect of the industry was sustained largely by state purchases of cloth and was particularly important in the Black Earth and Middle Volga regions. Alongside this phase of the industry during the middle of the 1840's the manufacture of smooth woolen cloth, especially worsteds, grew up on the basis of imported machinery. This growing industry was based almost solely on hired labor and housed in large-scale factories, many of which were located in or near Moscow.[1] St. Petersburg and Riga also shared in this growth, though to a far lesser extent than Moscow.

The silk industry, which grew very slowly, and the linen industry, which experienced a sharp decline with the loss of foreign markets and from the competition of cheaper cotton cloth, were notable both for the lack of any significant technological progress and for the unimportance of gentry-owned enterprises working with serf labor. Virtually all the manufacture of silk was accounted for by factories in Moscow and by village handicraftsmen located primarily around Moscow and in adjacent districts of Vladimir guberniia.[2] The linen industry was at the same time both the most valuable of the Russian textile industries and the most backward. Although the introduction of mechanical and steam equipment began in the late 1850's, the linen industry remained essentially a peasant one with production originating primarily from the countryside.[3]

Of all the industries cotton textiles had the greatest impact on the growth of Russian cities. Between 1811 and 1860 cotton textiles accounted for nearly half of the growth in industrial employment in the Empire. The distribution of the cotton textile industry was basically similar to the other textile industries, but with a greater concentration in Moscow and Vladimir guberniias, and to a lesser extent in St. Petersburg guberniia.

In contrast to the woolen and linen industries, the growth in cotton textiles was based primarily on the increase in the demand of the domestic market for a cheap, durable material, although the industry was also aided by stringent protectionist policies, and at a very early period became virtually wholly dependent on free, hired labor.[4] Furthermore, this industry was the quickest to adopt the latest available technology, mainly imported from England, which fostered a trend towards comparatively large-scale enterprises. By the end of the 1850's some of the world's largest cotton spinning

---

[1] Blackwell, p. 49.

[2] Tugan-Baranovskii, pp. 193-194.

[3] Blackwell, p. 52.

[4] Iatsunskii, "Krupnaia promyshlennost' Rossii . . . ," p. 181.

factories were found in and around Moscow and St. Petersburg.[1]
The industry was also noted for the large proportion of privately
owned factories and for the emergence of a significant number of
entrepreneurs from the peasantry.

The development of this industry went through two distinct
stages. Up until the 1840's the Russian cotton textile industry
was devoted primarily to the weaving of imported British thread and
printing of imported cloth. Although most production still was in
the rural factories and households, several cities began to emerge
as centers of the industry. Most notable were Ivanovo, a privately owned village during this period, Shuia, St. Petersburg, and,
of course, Moscow.[2]

After 1842, with the removal of the British restrictions on
the export of machinery, the spinning of raw cotton grew extremely
rapidly. The number of cotton spindles in Russia increased from
350,000 in 1843 to 1.5 million in 1860.[3] Although cotton weaving
and finishing continued to be done principally at home and in small
rural establishments, cotton spinning began to develop into a factory industry with increasing specialization of production taking
place in large-scale plants. Notable also was the growth of factories which combined all three stages of cotton textile production
under a single roof. St. Petersburg had become the center of the
modern cotton spinning industry at an early date, but by the end of
the pre-reform period Moscow began to rival St. Petersburg in this
regard. Despite the great importance of the textile industries in
Russia on the eve of the emancipation of the serfs, it still had
little direct effect on the life of the cities besides the two capitals and perhaps a dozen or so smaller cities.

Impact of Industrial Expansion on Urban Development

The process of the formation of urban industrial centers
during the first half of the 19th century in Russia, as has been
shown in the foregoing sections, proceeded very slowly. The relative insignificance of manufacturing in the economic development
of the cities during this period is attested to by the small number
of industrial workers present even in the so-called, "industrial
centers" of Russia at this time, Moscow and St. Petersburg. In

---

[1]Blackwell, p. 47.

[2]Rybakov, p. 235.

[3]Iatsunskii, "Krupnaia promyshlennost' Rossii . . . ,"p. 178.

1853 there were approximately 48,000 persons in Moscow engaged in industry, which represented about 13 per cent of the total population.[1] In St. Petersburg there were only some 19,300 workers representing about 6 per cent of the population of the city by 1862.[2] On the eve of the reforms the number of persons engaged in industry accounted for about 4.5 per cent of the population in Kazan, 2.6 per cent in Nizhnii Novgorod, 1.8 per cent in Samara, and less than one per cent in Kiev.[3] Although many of the smaller cities in Moscow and Vladimir guberniias had a significantly larger percentage of their populations employed in manufacturing, chiefly in textiles, like Ivanovo, Shuia, and others, these cities for the most part experienced little growth during the period under study.

That the role of the development of manufacturing was of little consequence in the growth of most cities during the pre-reform period is attested to by the fact that the regions of the most rapid growth in industry were also among the slowest growing regions in terms of urban growth. In Vladimir guberniia, for example, which was second only to Moscow guberniia in terms of industrial development, the total number of persons employed in industry in 1854 was almost equal to the total urban population in the guberniia in 1856, 74,508 and 75,821 respectively. Yet the former figure represented 16.2 per cent of the total industrial labor force in the country, while the latter represented only 1.4 per cent of the total urban population in Russia. Moreover, while Vladimir guberniia accounted for 15 per cent of the growth in industrial employment between 1815 and 1860, it accounted for only 1.2 per cent of the growth in urban population between 1811 and 1856. During the forty-five-year period, 1811-1856, the per cent of the population in Vladimir guberniia residing in cities increased from 4 per cent to only 6 per cent. Some 38 per cent of the total growth in industrial employment between 1811 and 1860 took place in the Central Industrial region, including Moscow guberniia, while between 1811 and 1856 it accounted for only about 23 per cent of the total growth in urban population in the Empire.

---

[1]Ryndziunskii, Gorodskoe grazhdanstvo . . . , p. 426.

[2]A. I. Kopanev, Naselenie Peterburga v pervoi polovine XIX veka (Moskva: Izdatel'stvo Akademii Nauk SSSR, 1957), p. 58.

[3]Rybakov, p. 234.

Urban Handicraft Industry

By the end of the pre-reform period industry in the cities was present primarily in the form of handicrafts and small commodity production with only a few large manufacturing enterprises. Aside from handicraft work, the main factories consisted of tanneries, tallow boileries, soap and candle production, brickworks, tobacco processing, and other such similar operations. In the central regions of the country some cities also possessed small textile operations. It is clear, however, that the overwhelming proportion of manufacturing in the cities appeared essentially as an adjunct to the rural economy. The small scale of operation, technological backwardness, lack of mechanical or power equipment, and little division of labor characterized most of the manufacturing which was found in the cities. Towards the end of the period, however, the embryo of a machine construction industry, especially textile and agricultural machinery, began to appear in some cities. As late as 1848, there were only some twenty machine construction enterprises in the Russian Empire, but by 1861 there were more than one hundred such establishments.[1] The majority of these enterprises were constructed in the cities and some in the near vicinity of cities. St. Petersburg and Moscow were the most important centers of this growing industry, but other cities, like Lugansk, Orel, Konotop, and Kremenchug participated in this development.

Even the handicraft industry, which was the predominant form of industry in the majority of cities, was poorly developed. Although the guild and shop system was introduced from Western Europe into Russia by Peter the Great, it never functioned as the highly organized, quality control system as in Western Europe. In fact, guild lines were weakly conceived and persons could easily engage in practically any trade or craft they desired. In addition, the "irregular work habits, carelessness and negligence, low time horizons, and frightening dishonesty," which were characteristic of the trades and crafts in Russia, constituted persistent handicaps to economic progress in the cities.[2]

---

[1] Ibid., p. 230.

[2] Alexander Gerschenkron, "City Economies--Then and Now," Continuity in History and Other Essays, Alexander Gerschenkron, (Cambridge, Mass.: The Belknap Press of Harvard University Press, 1968), p. 251.

Administrative and Military Importance of the City

Despite the growth of commerce and trade and, to a lesser extent, manufacturing, most of the cities in Russia owed the limited degree of prosperity that they had attained, "solely to their being the seats of authority, and to the public establishments, which gave them somewhat of the appearance of a city."[1] Thus the capital and guberniia centers, and to a lesser extent the uezd centers, as foci of the administrative-military-police network of the empire, tended to attract a large number of civil officials, military personnel, and nobility. The nobility increasingly became attracted to the city partly for its "divertissements," few as they were, and for the satisfaction of their variegated needs.[2] Life in the city was often far preferred to that in the countryside. To these three groups of service people must also be included the large number of dvorovye liudi, or household serfs, who generally accompanied their masters to the cities. In St. Petersburg, for instance, these four groups, with the addition of the clergy, constituted 48 per cent of the population of the city in 1821.[3] This figure, however, was partially exaggerated due to the influx of nobility and officials into St. Petersburg following the Napoleonic Wars and the burning and subsequent rebuilding of Moscow. By 1857 this figure had declined to 28 per cent.[4] Similarly, in many of the cities in the south the proportion of military-administrative personnel in the urban population was very high. In Odessa, Kerch, and Tagonrog, for instance, nearly 30 per cent of the urban population consisted of these service elements.[5] These examples were by no means extraordinary. On the contrary, they were quite representative of the social structure of the urban population in general.

---

[1] Tegoborskii, Commentaries . . . , p. 102.

[2] P. G. Ryndziunskii, "Gorodskoe naselenie," Ocherki ekonomicheskoi istorii Rossii pervoi poloviny XIX veka, ed. M. K. Rozhkova (Moskva: Izdatel'stvo Sotsial'no-Ekonomicheskoi Literatury, 1959), p. 289.

[3] Kopanev, p. 25.

[4] Ibid.

[5] Ryndziunskii, Gorodskoe grazhdanstvo. . . , p. 283.

In 1858 these service estates constituted the following per-
centages of the total urban population in the Empire: nobility and
officials, 5.2 per cent; clergy, 1.6 per cent; military personnel,
14.1 per cent.[1] Together these estates represented 21 per cent of
the total urban population. To this figure must also be added the
household serfs who can be estimated to have constituted approximately 3 per cent of the urban population. The importance of these
elements in the population of the cities is not only attested to
by the nearly one-fourth share of the urban population they represented, but also by the fact that their presence in the cities must
have contributed to the maintenance of a significant portion of the
remaining, productive population of the cities. Of the remaining
population, peasants, including household serfs, constituted about
20 per cent, while the urban estate proper, the petty bourgeoisie
and merchant classes, represented about 55 per cent of the population in the cities.[2] Foreigners, intellectuals, and other groups
constituted the remainder of the urban population.

The City and the Peasant

The main cause of the growth in the population of the cities
during the pre-reform period was the departure of the peasant from
the village to the city in search of economic betterment. This was
not the only reason, however, for industry was comparatively widespread and well developed for the time in the countryside also.
But to secure a better economic position the peasant, in the final
analysis, had to secure his freedom from the owner, or the pomeshchik, and the rural administration. Although there were other
means of securing freedom from serfal dependency, the city afforded
the only significant avenue to liberty. The city, therefore,
attracted to itself the rural population not only as a center of
trade and industry, but by its very form and way of life. Thus the
peasants who transferred themselves to the city became fully libera-
ted from serfal dependency when they were able to change their
estate status and receive the rights of the urban citizenry.

Although the state closely regulated the movement of peasants
to the city by means of passports and tickets, it did promulgate a
number of measures which facilitated the acquisition of permanent

---

[1]Russia. Tsentral'nyi statisticheskii komitet. Statisticheskiia tablitsy Rossiiskoi Imperii. Vypusk 2. Nalichnoe naselenie
Imperii za 1858 god. A. Bushen (Sanktpeterburg, 1863), pp. 316-317.

[2]Ibid.

residence in the cities for peasants. In the guild reforms of
1824 one measure provided for the removal of the double taxation
of state peasants which had for a long time been a financial barrier
for peasants wanting to transfer into the urban estate.[1] Up until
then, when a peasant moved to the city he was taxed at the rate
both of his status as a peasant and that of his aspiring status,
the urban estate. Only when the following reviziia, or enumeration came, which often was more than a decade, was he then enrolled
officially as a member of the urban estate either as a petty bourgeoisie or merchant.

A number of other decrees, enacted in 1827 and 1848, granted
the right to state serfs to own a house in a city. In 1849 another
law was passed that forbade the village communal organization from
preventing the departure of a peasant from his village provided
that his tax obligations were fulfilled. At the same time this law
prohibited the town organization of the petty bourgeoisie and merchants from refusing to admit a state serf into their estate if
the latter had paid the required entrance fees.[2]

Although the records of the period do not allow one to make an
exact calculation of the volume of movement of peasants into the
urban estate, and thereby gaining permanent residence in the cities,
some estimates have been made. According to the calculations of
Ryndziunskii, it was estimated that between 1826 and 1851 some
726,000 state peasant taxed souls and approximately 66,000 privately owned, or pomeshchik, serfs were admitted into the urban estate.[3]
When one considers that between 1825 and 1856 the population of the
cities in the Empire increased by about 2.3 million persons, then
the importance of this process, the movement of peasants into the
urban estate, in the growth of the urban population during this
period is placed in proper perspective.

Not all of the peasants who came to the cities and transferred
into the urban estate pursued commercial or industrial occupations.
During the pre-reform period when the city's boundaries still em-
braced a considerable amount of open pasture and cultivated lands,
many peasants, especially in the Black Earth and southern regions,

---

[1]Ryndziunskii, Gorodskoe grazhdanstvo . . . , p.83.

[2]Pinter, p. 237.

[3]P. G. Ryndziunskii, "Krest'iane i gorod v doreformennoi
Rossii," Voprosy Istorii, IX (1955) . . . , p. 37.

who managed to enroll into the ranks of the city's meshchanstvo or even the merchantry class, turned to these lands for a livelihood, no longer as feudally dependent persons, but as free cultivators of the land.[1] Agriculture as an occupation still remained fairly important in the economic life of not a few cities in the Russian Empire.

All of the regulations aimed at facilitating the movement of peasants into the cities referred to above, however, pertained only to the state peasantry, which accounted for approximately half of the serfs in Russia, and did not affect the private serfs who were the unchallenged property of their masters. Consequently, about the only recourse open to the private serfs, and one frequently resorted to by the state serfs, was to flee. The unlawful flight of serfs from the village was a fairly widespread phenomenon in Russia. One of the primary regions to which the flow of fugitive serfs was directed was New Russia, or the Southern Steppe guberniias. Here the settling of fugitive serfs as permanent residents was partially overlooked and even allowed by the government as it attempted to colonize and bring the steppe into agricultural production. At the same time the less rigid social structure existing in this region also facilitated the movement of fugitives into the cities and even into the urban estate.[2]

Fugitive serfs belonging to various dissenting religious sects also played an important role in the growth of the population of many cities and in their economic development. Many such dissenting sects, generally called "old-believers," through their frugality and tight communal organization managed to accumulate large amounts of capital, which were frequently channelled into various industrial ventures. Wielding considerable economic power, these dissenting religious communities were often able to offer shelter from the authorities to many fugitive serfs and provide them with work in return for their fidelity to the precepts and organization of their community.[3] Moscow was the most important center of the "old believers," but in other cities like Ekaterinburg, Ivanovo-Voznesensk, Saratov, and Nizhnii Novgorod the old believers formed an important element of the population.

---

[1]Ryndziunskii, "Gorodskoe naselenie," pp. 292-293.

[2]Ryndziunskii, "Krest'iane i gorod v doreformennoi Rossii," p. 38.

[3]Blackwell, pp. 219-220.

Consequently, the "liberating" significance of the city contri-
butes to an explanation of the growth of many cities in the Russian
Empire during the pre-reform period when that growth was still
largely independent of industrial development and in no way indicated the separation of industry from the rural economy.

CHAPTER V

URBAN GROWTH DURING THE REFORM PERIOD

The Emancipation of the Serfs

The ascension to the throne of Alexander II in 1855 following
the death of his father, Nicholas I, signaled in many respects the
beginning of a new era in Russia history, for shortly after his
coronation the new tsar initiated the proceedings which led to the
abolition of serfdom in 1861.

The act of emancipation, though replete with numerous deficiencies, had far-reaching implications for Russia. The disappearance
of an institution which perhaps more than anything else served to
distinguish the historical development of Russia from that of the
West, "inevitably acted as a strong stimulus to the further westernization of economy and society, and this to a large extent
meant rapid industrial development."[1]

The release of millions of serfs from personal bondage provided a greatly enlarged potential reservoir of labor and entrepreneurs for industrial development and at the same time extended
the range of opportunity for occupational and social mobility of
many of the former serfs. The increasing flexibility of Russian
society, in turn, made it more receptive to new ideas and advanced
technology, so necessary to the process of modernization. Of particular importance was the impetus provided by the abolition of
serfdom toward the expansion of a market economy. The varied market mechanisms, and with them monetary rewards, acquired greater
relevance in the economy as the new fiscal responsibilities thrust
upon the peasants as a result of the emancipation forced them to
seek out new means of increasing their cash incomes. The act of
emancipation, moreover, rather than satisfying the need for social
and economic reform, stimulated it. New institutional arrangements
were required not only to replace those that had crumbled with the
reforms, but also to cope with emerging situations resulting from

---

[1] Alexander Gerschenkron, "Russia: Agrarian Policies and Indus-
trialization, 1861-1914," Continuity in History and Other Essays,
Alexander Gerschenkron (Cambridge, Mass.: The Belknap Press of
Harvard University Press, 1968), p. 208.

the processes of economic and social change that were either initiated or furthered by the emancipation.

Although the abolition of serfdom represented a significant alteration in the legal status of the peasantry, the conditions of the emancipation provided little opportunity for the mass of the peasantry to improve their economic position. The peasants in general received inadequate land allotments, did not receive the actual ownership of the land, and were hopelessly burdened by excessive redemption payments for the land they hoped to own eventually.[1] Moreover, the conditions of the emancipation, by confining the peasants within the communal structure of the village under circumstances that made permanent departures nearly as difficult as before the emancipation which prevented a mass exodus from the countryside from fully materializing. The subsequent development of the cities in the Russian Empire, as a consequence, was affected directly by the curtailment of potential migration and indirectly by the effect that the relative immobility of labor had on the nature and pattern of industrialization.

Pattern of Urban Growth during the Reform Period, 1856-1870.

The period from 1856 to 1870, coinciding with the preparations and implementation of the Great Reforms, was marked by industrial quiescence on the one hand and by a tremendous upsurge in the growth of the urban population on the other. The agrarian legislation of the early 1860's was not immediately followed by any significant industrial development. On the contrary, many industries experienced a period of virtual stagnation while others, especially those which had previously been dependent on the use of serf labor, met with sharp declines.[2] The manorial industries of the gentry, especially woolen textiles, were the most adversely affected, while the iron industry of the Urals, which was heavily dependent on serf labor, experienced an abrupt decline, from which recovery was very slow. The cotton textile industry also suffered a setback because of the temporary disruption of the importation of raw cotton during the civil wa in the United States. On the other hand, the first decade after the reforms witnessed the further growth of small-scale industry and handicraft production. Only towards the end of

---

[1] N. A. Rozhkov, Gorod i derevnia v Russkoi istorii. Kratkii ocherk ekonomicheskoi istorii Rossii (S.-Peterburg, Knizhnyi Sklad "Zemlia," Izdanie tret'e, 1913), p. 105.

[2] A. G. Rashin, Formirovanie rabochego klassa Rossii. Istoriko-ekonomicheskie ocherki (Moskva: Izdatel'stvo Sotsial'no-Ekonomicheskoi Literatury, 1958), pp. 108-110.

the decade, under the impetus of an upsurge in railroad construction, was there any notable expansion of factory industry.

Although the impact of the reforms on industrial development was delayed for more than a decade, the effects on the growth of cities was readily apparent. During this fourteenth-year period more than two million persons were added to the urban population of the Empire, excluding an additional 1.1 million persons from the annexations of Tsarist Poland and parts of Central Asia. This represented an average annual rate of growth of 2.2 per cent which was more than twice the rate of the previous period and only slightly less than the rate over the succeeding forty years.

The addition of 2,027,379 persons to the population of the cities during this fourteen-year period represented a numerical increase of slightly more than two-thirds of the total growth in urban population which had taken place during the previous 45 years. In sixteen guberniias, shown in Figure 15, situated primarily to the south and southeast of the central part of European Russia, the absolute increase in urban population during this period exceeded their total growth of the previous 45 years, while in twenty-three other guberniias the increase represented more than half of the growth in urban population which had taken place in the previous four and one-half decades.

The attraction of peasants to the capital guberniias in search of employment was particularly intense. The population of the main cities of these two guberniias grew by more than 330,000 persons, as seen in Table 6, in contrast to the previous period, 1840-1856, when the urban population of these two guberniias increased by only 50,820 persons. This growth reflected rural to urban migration. A similar rural exodus took place in the two regions, the Left Bank of the Dnepr River and the South-Eastern Steppe, situated to the east of the Dnepr River and south of the Black Earth region. Compared to the addition of only 49,203 persons to the population of the cities in these six guberniias between 1840 and 1856, slightly more than 300,000 persons sought to improve their economic status in these cities during the period of the reforms. The substantial flow of persons into the cities of the two regions west of the Dnepr River, especially in the guberniias of Kiev and Kherson, continued unabated as in the previous periods. Together these five regions accounted for nearly half, or about 940,000 persons, of the total increase in the urban population during the reform period.

74

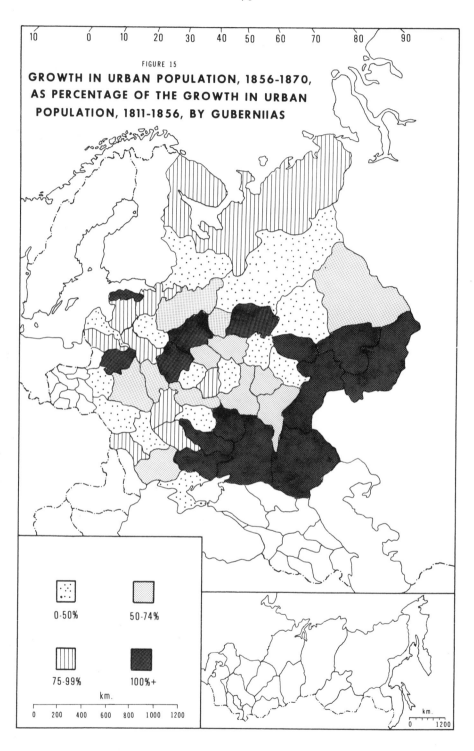

FIGURE 15

GROWTH IN URBAN POPULATION, 1856-1870,
AS PERCENTAGE OF THE GROWTH IN URBAN
POPULATION, 1811-1856, BY GUBERNIIAS

0-50%

50-74%

75-99%

100%+

km.

TABLE 6

ABSOLUTE GROWTH AND PER CENT OF TOTAL GROWTH IN URBAN POPULATION BY REGION IN
RUSSIAN EMPIRE WITH AND WITHOUT TSARIST POLAND AND CENTRAL ASIA, 1856-1870

Region	Without Tsarist Poland and Central Asia 1856-1870		With Tsarist Poland and Central Asia 1856-1870	
	Absolute Growth	Per Cent of Total	Absolute Growth	Per Cent of Total
Capitals	331,282	16.4		10.5
Central Industrial	53,293	2.6		1.7
Southern Industrial	18,677	0.9		0.6
Black Earth	111,275	5.5		3.5
Northwest	67,397	3.3		2.1
Baltic	68,897	3.4		2.2
West-Central	96,015	4.7		3.1
Western	111,544	5.5		3.5
Right Bank Dnepr	119,617	5.9		3.8
Left Bank Dnepr	157,039	7.8		5.0
Southwestern Steppe	187,223	9.2		5.9
Southeastern Steppe	144,866	7.2		4.6
Middle Volga	61,006	3.0		1.9
Lower Volga	110,581	5.5		3.5
Trans Volga	64,517	3.2		2.1
Pre-Caucasus	46,479	2.3		1.5
Caucasus	70,629	3.5		2.2
Caspian Sea	42,953	2.1		1.4
North	11,871	0.6		0.4
Northeast	40,990	2.0		1.3
Western Siberia	40,388	2.0		1.3
Eastern Siberia	30,214	1.5		1.0
Central Asian Steppe	39,644	2.0		1.3
Central Asia	--	-	147,921	4.7

TABLE 6--Continued

Region	Without Tsarist Poland and Central Asia 1856-1870		With Tsarist Poland and Central Asia 1856-1870	
	Absolute Growth	Per Cent of Total	Absolute Growth	Per Cent of Total
W. Tsarist Poland	--	--	691,085	21.9
E. Tsarist Poland	--	--	287,237	9.1
Total	2,026,397	100.0	3,152,640	100.0

Source: Based on data found in Appendix I.

The Rural Out-Migration Following the Emancipation

The substantial increment in the urban population of the Empire during this period can only be ascribed to the direct effects of the emancipation. Although the conditions of the emancipation did not significantly increase the mobility of the overwhelming majority of peasants, they did release a substantial number of persons from the bondage of the villages and the manors. As a direct consequence of the emancipation it was estimated that approximately three million serfs were rendered landless.[1] The dvorovye liudi, or household serfs, constituted the single largest element of the landless peasantry. Although these serfs became entirely free at the end of a two-year transitional period following the emancipation, they received no land unless they had held holdings as of March 2, 1858.[2] This was the date of an ukase that forbade the further conversion of agricultural serfs into domestics, a device resorted to by many owners as the emancipation became imminent in order to avoid turning land over to their peasants. This group of peasants, in particular, was literally pushed out of the countryside as a result of the emancipation:

> "Unless they desired to remain as domestic servants, and unless their former owners desired them to remain, they were practically obliged to resort to the towns for employment. They were not accustomed to field labor, and employment otherwise in the country was not to be obtained. They had as a rule no capital for the cultivation of rented land, nor had they any allotments even had they desired to become cultivators. Many of them were skilled artisans, and these thus provided immediately upon their emancipation a large landless class ready for industrial employment."[3]

Another important group who became landless following the emancipation were the possessional serfs whose primary, if not sole, occupation was working in a factory or mine. On the basis of an 1840 law such serfs, upon the liquidation of the enterprise, had the option of enrolling into one of the urban estates, which

---

[1] Peter I. Liashchenko, History of the National Economy of Russia to the 1917 Revolution, translated by L. M. Herman (New York: The MacMillan Company, 1949), p. 418.

[2] Jerome Blum, Lord and Peasant in Russia from the Ninth to the Nineteenth Century (Princeton, N.J.: Princeton University Press, 1961. First Princeton Paperback Printing, 1971), p. 593.

[3] James Mavor, An Economic History of Russia. (London: J. M. Dent and Sons, Limited, 1914) II, pp. 361-362.

appeared to be the preference of the majority, or of becoming state peasants.[1] In addition to the three million landless peasants, there were an estimated one million additional serfs who received extremely small land allotments.[2] Consequently, it was basically this mass of landless and near landless peasants that formed the "invisible population" which began to flow into the cities and industries during this and subsequent periods.

Growth in Urban Population of the Empire due to Territorial Annexations

A very substantial addition to the total urban population of the Empire represented the annexations of the Kingdom of Poland and parts of Central Asia, particularly Tashkent. Although the Kingdom of Poland was united dynastically to Russia following the Congress of Vienna in 1815, it still was considered, like the Grand Duchy of Finland, as an autonomous part of the Russian Empire. As a consequence of the uprising in Poland between 1830 and 1831, she was stripped of a considerable amount of her autonomy, but still remained nominally independent. This status was changed in 1864 following the abortive Polish rebellion of 1863. The territory of the Kingdom of Poland was annexed as an integral part of the Russian Empire and underwent a territorial-administrative reorganization as provinces of the Empire. At the same time an administrative reorganization of the status of urban settlements resulted in a decline in the number of such settlements from 452 to 172.[3] Consequently, a comparative analysis of the changes in urban population in the territory of the Kingdom of Poland prior and subsequent to 1864 is rendered most difficult because of the changing legal definition and status of cities and other types of urban settlements. The urban population of the "Vistula provinces", as the territory of the former Kingdom of Poland was now referred to, amounted to 978,322 persons residing in 103 cities by the end of this period.

The territorial annexations in Central Asia, which continued over the next several decades, added ten new cities with a combined population of 147,921 during this period. Finally, some 102,436

---

[1]Tugan-Baranovskii, p. 107.

[2]Liashchenko, p. 419.

[3]Russia. Tsentral'nyi statisticheskii komitet. Statisticheskii vremennik Rossikoi Imperii Seriia II Vypusk 1 Ekonomicheskoe sostoianie gorodov (Sanktpeterburg, 1871) , pp. 195-196.

persons were added to the urban population of the Empire from the entry of nineteen newly designated cities. Consequently, the urban population of the Russian Empire, including annexations and other new entries, increased by 55 per cent or by some 3,152,640 persons during the period of the reforms. Of this total, new entries of all types accounted for 39 per cent, or 1,228,679 persons of the total growth in urban population.

CHAPTER VI

ECONOMIC DEVELOPMENT IN THE POST-REFORM PERIOD, 1870-1910

The last three decades of the 19th century were distinguished by a substantial upsurge in the industrial and commercial growth of the Russian Empire. The rapid tempo of railroad construction and the emergence of a modern heavy industrial base were the most spectacular and at the same time the most unstable aspects of this economic upsurge, but the tremendous growth in domestic and foreign commerce, the rapid expansion of capital and credit, and the continued growth of light industry, particularly cotton textiles, all contributed to fostering a period of unparalled economic development in the Empire. In the early part of the period the growth of industry was gradual, but as the effects of the expanding railroad network began to be felt throughout the economy, the development of industry rapidly gained momentum, culminating in the brilliant outburst of industrial growth during the last decade of the century.

Expansion of the Railroad Network

At the heart of the industrial and commercial expansion which took place in the latter part of the century was railroad construction. Although the first railroad made its appearance in Russia in 1838, it was not until the middle of the 1860's that Russia embarked on a massive program of railroad construction that resulted in the expansion of the railroad network from a mere 5,038 km. in 1867 to 66,581 km. in 1910.[1] The pattern of railroad construction, however, was highly cyclical, alternating between periods of intense activity and sharp cutbacks, all of which had their repercussions on the rest of the economy. Figure 16 clearly depicts the roller-coaster-like pattern of railroad construction between 1860 and 1910. Coinciding with the two broad waves of construction between 1868-1878. and 1893-1901, and the smaller one of 1883-1888, were periods of general industrial expansion, while recession and stagnation followed closely on the heels of the troughs in railroad construction.

---

[1] Khromov, Ekonomicheskoe razvitie Rossii v XIX-XX vekakh, p. 462.

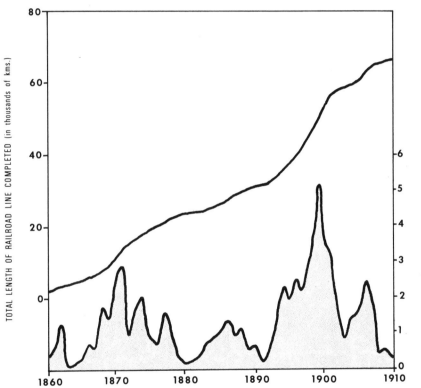

FIGURE 16

**EXPANSION OF THE RAILROAD NETWORK
IN THE RUSSIAN EMPIRE, 1860-1910**

The expansion of the railroad network, moreover, was accompanied by a tremendous growth in the labor force needed to construct, operate, and maintain the railroads. As shown in Figure 17, employment in railroad transportation increased from approximately 11,000 workers in 1860 to nearly 772,000 workers in 1910. Reflecting primarily the fluctuations in railroad construction, the growth in the labor force was also irregular. Slightly more than 40 per cent of the total growth in employment took place during the decade of the 1890's when some 306,000 persons were added to the labor force.[1]

The first wave of railroad construction, 1868-1878, was aimed at drawing into commercial circulation with the rest of the country the agricultural regions of Russia. This had the dual objective of increasing the supply of agricultural foodstuffs, especially grain, both for export and for the growing demands of the internal market, and of opening up the rural markets to the manufactured goods of the central and Baltic industrial regions.[2] Most of the construction activity during this period centered on connecting the grain-producing regions of the Ukraine with the ports of the Azov and Black Seas in the south and with the Baltic ports in the northwest, and the Volga region with the industrial markets of the central part of the country and the Baltic Sea ports.

The intermediate wave of construction during the middle of the 1880's saw the emphasis shift to serving the needs of industry, particularly the emerging heavy industrial base of the south. Of particular significance during this period was the opening of the Ekaterinoslav line which joined the coal of the Donets basin with the iron ore of Krivoi Rog.[3] The last and greatest wave of activity, which reached a peak at the turn of the century, was notable for the construction of the Trans-Siberian and Central Asian lines. Although military considerations strongly motivated the construction of these lines, they did provide a strong stimulus to the economic development of these two outlying regions of the Empire.[4]

---

[1] Rashin, Formirovanie rabochego klassa v Rossii, p. 117.

[2] V. K. Iatsunskii, Transport SSSR. Istoriia ego razvitiia i sovremennoe sostoianie v sviazi s kratkimi svedeniiami po ekonomike transporta (Moskva: NKPS: Transpechat', 1926), p. 34.

[3] Edward Ames, "A Century of Russian Railroad Construction, 1837-1936," The American Slavic and East European Review, VI, No. 18-19, (1947), p. 67.

[4] Iatsunskii, Transport SSSR . . . , pp. 54-56.

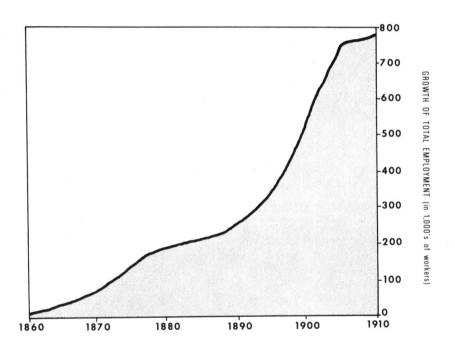

FIGURE 17

FIGURE 17

**GROWTH IN TOTAL EMPLOYMENT IN RAILROAD TRANSPORTATION,
1860-1910**

84

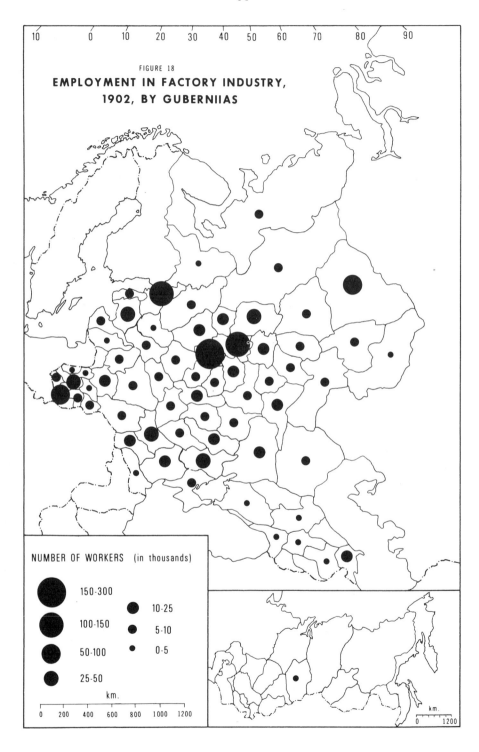

FIGURE 18

EMPLOYMENT IN FACTORY INDUSTRY,
1902, BY GUBERNIIAS

NUMBER OF WORKERS (in thousands)

150-300

100-150

50-100

25-50

10-25

5-10

0-5

km.

0   200   400   600   800   1000 1200

km.

0   1200

The Central Asian lines became especially important for the movement of raw cotton to the textile industry of the central industrial
region.

Throughout the entire period, however, Moscow remained the
focus of much of the railroad construction activity as the radial
network which developed around it was expanded to reach all the
regions of the Empire. The growth of the railroad network around
Moscow contributed greatly to expanding the markets for the manufactured goods of the old capital as well as for the central industrial region in general, while simultaneously extending the sources
of the raw materials for the region's growing industry and of foodstuffs for her rapidly increasing urban and industrial population.

The railroads played a most important role in the economic
development of the Russian Empire during the post-reform period.
By providing the necessary connecting linkage in the growing commercial exchange among the various regions of the Empire, the railroads made possible the rapid expansion of the volume, size, and
turnover of the domestic as well as the foreign commerce of the
Empire. At the same time, however, the appearance of the railroads
ruined many of the old overland highways, diverted freight from
some wharves while expanding the hinterland of others, and eliminated the commercial role of many former overland and riverine re-
loading, redistributing, and transit centers, rendering them un-
necessary as these functions were shifted to the railroad depots
and sidings.[1]

Expansion of Domestic and Foreign Commerce

With the expansion of the railroad network the very significant role of periodic fairs in the commercial turnover of the
country began to decline relatively, yielding its place in the
economy to permanent forms of trade. The number of fairs increased
in European Russia from 6,496 in 1868 to 15,910 in 1894. The value
of goods brought and sold at the fairs increased from 459 million
rubles and 305 million rubles respectively to only 573 million rubles and
460 million rubles respectively.[2] The value of commercial turnover
at the fairs reached its peak around 1881 and thereafter the importance of fairs in the Russian economy steadily declined.[3] Only the

---

[1] Liashchenko, p. 512.

[2] Khromov, Ekonomicheskoe razvitie Rossii v XIX--XX vekakh,
p. 245.

[3] Tugan-Baranovskii, p. 253.

fairs at Nizhnii Norgorod, Khar'kov, and Irbit continued to play a prominent role in the economy, but at the same time they increasingly acquired the character of commodity exhibitions rather than retail and wholesale market places.

. With the decline of periodic fairs the importance of commodity and stock exchanges, or birzhy, also rose. From about a half dozen such exchanges located primarily in the largest cities of the Empire at the time of the reforms, there were several dozen by the end of the century, including many specialized ones such as for grain, coal, livestock, timber, and other commodities.[1] These commodity exchanges became the centers of wholesale trade in the Empire and at the same time promoted the centralization of commodity turnover in Russia.

Simultaneously with the expansion of the domestic market there took place a very sizeable growth in foreign trade. Between 1860 and 1910, as shown in Table 7, the total value of foreign trade increased by nearly six and one-half times. Reflecting the government's policy of maintaining a positive trade balance, exports grew slightly faster than imports over this fifty year period. The sharp decline in imports during the 1880's was directly associated with the introduction of a number of highly protectionist tariffs aimed particularly at the importation of iron, steel, and coal.[2] From the time of the reforms until the beginning of the 1880's, Russia pursued a comparatively liberal tariff policy, including the duty-free importation of materials needed in the construction of the railroads. The nearly complete reversal of these policies was of great importance in stimulating the rapid development of Russia's iron and steel and coal industries during the last two decades of the century.

Throughout the entire period Russia remained primarily an exporter of agricultural products and raw materials and an importer of manufactured goods. The export of grain played a particularly important role in Russia's foreign trade since it provided the main source of foreign currency earnings. The proportion of the value of exported grains to total exports rose from nearly 40 per cent in 1860 to 52 per cent in 1910. During individual years this proportion declined to as low as 31 per cent in 1864 and rose to as high as 61 per cent in 1877. Timber, flax, hemp, oil seeds, and, especially after 1885, petroleum constituted the bulk of the remain-

---

[1]Khromov, Ekonomicheskoe razvitie Rossii v XIX-XX vekakh, pp. 246-247.

[2]Tugan-Baranovskii, p. 291.

der of exports. On the import side, machinery of all kinds and
metals accounted for between one-fourth and one-third of all the
imports, while raw cotton and tea were the next most important items.

Growth of Heavy Industry

The impact of railroad construction on the economy of Russia
was most vividly reflected in the spectacular growth of heavy industry, particularly during the last decade of the century. Great
quantities of iron, steel, coal, timber, brick, cement, and other
materials were needed to build and operate the railroads. At first
production from domestic industries was wholly inadequate to meet
the material demands of railroad construction and Russia was forced
to acquire nearly all of the rails, rolling stock, and other acces-
sory equipment from abroad.[1] This undesirable situation together
with the change in tariff policies promoted the organization of a
new metallurgical base in the south.

Prior to 1887, there were only two metallurgical factories in
the south. By the end of the century, however, there were seventeen
full-cycle iron and steel plants in the south with twenty-nine blast
furnaces in operation and twelve more under construction.[2] The
majority of these plants worked chiefly on state orders, produced
primarily railroad materials, especially rails, and were built largely with foreign capital. Although most of the growth in heavy industry was centered in the interior of Ekaterinoslav guberniia, primarily in the Donets basin, a number of plants arose near the port cities
on the Sea of Azov. These latter plants were built largely to supply
the pipe and other metal requirements of the greatly expanding production of petroleum at Baku on the Caspian Sea.

The resulting regional shift in the production of iron and
steel during the post-reform period was dramatic. Whereas in 1860
there was no production of iron or steel in the south, by 1900 it
had accounted for nearly 58 per cent of the production of pig iron
and 48 per cent of iron and steel production in Russia, excluding
Tsarist Poland.[3] The growth of heavy industry in the south was
almost entirely at the expense of the Urals where production expanded at a comparatively slow rate. During the same period Tsarist
Poland also emerged as an important center of heavy industry, yield-

---

[1] Alexander Gerschenkron, "The Rate of Industrial Growth in
Russia Since 1885," The Journal of Economic History, VII
(Supplement, 1947), p. 144.

[2] Livshits, pp. 170, 172.

[3] Ibid., p. 70.

TABLE 7

GROWTH IN THE VALUE OF FOREIGN TRADE
1860-1910

Year	Imports	Exports	Total
		(in millions of rubles)	
1860	159.3	181.3	340.6
1870	335.9	360.0	695.9
1880	622.8	498.7	1,121.5
1890	406.7	692.2	1,098.9
1897	560.0	729.7	1,289.7
1910	1,084.4	1,449.1	2,553.5

Source: P. A. Khromov, Ekonomicheskoe razvitie Rossii
v XIX-XX vekakh, 1800-1917, pp. 468-471.

ing only to the south and the Urals in significance.

Table 8 shows the growth in production of the main branches of heavy industry between 1870 and 1900. Although the production of iron ore, pig iron, and iron and steel doubled during the first twenty years, it more than tripled during the last decade of the century. Coal production expanded very rapidly during the first two decades to meet the needs of the railroads and continued to expand at a rapid rate as the metallurgical base of the south was brought into production. The growth in the production of petroleum was meteoric and by the end of the century Russia was the world's leading producer of petroleum.[1] The domestic consumption of petroleum products, however, remained low and primarily in the form of lubricants. Consequently, much of the production was exported.

The construction of the railroads was also a strong impetus to the very rapid growth of the metal fabrication industry. The growing demand for steam engines, boilers, turbines, railroad rolling stock, and other equipment as well as the demand for textile and agricultural machinery provided a tremendous stimulant to the growth of this industry. Between 1861 and 1897 the number of factories in the metal-working industry increased from 106 to 682, while the corresponding increase in the labor force was from 12,400 persons to 120,300.[2] Production from this industry, moreover, tended to gravitate toward the large cities where a permanent and skilled supply of industrial labor was readily available. St.Petersburg emerged at an early date as the metal-working and machine-construction center of the Empire, with Moscow, Warsaw, Riga, Khar'kov, and Lugansk as other important centers.

Growth of Light Industry

Although overshadowed by the spectacular rise of heavy industry, the growth of light industry was no less significant. Throughout the last three decades of the century the growth in light industry was rather continuous and little affected by the periodic crises that struck heavy industry since the former's markets were based primarily on the peasantry and the steadily growing urban population. The cotton textile industry, after recovering from the disruption in the supply of raw cotton caused by the civil war in the United

[1]Khromov, Ekonomicheskoe razvitie Rossii. Ocherki . . . , p.302.

[2]Ibid., p. 294.

TABLE 8

GROWTH IN THE OUTPUT OF THE MAIN BRANCHES
OF HEAVY INDUSTRY, 1870-1900

Year	Iron Ore	Pig Iron	Iron and Steel	Coal	Petroleum
		(in 1,000's of tons)			
1870	829	374	262	766	33
1880	1,087	471	637	3,622	614
1890	1,919	997	874	6,631	4,352
1900	6,631	3,192	2,427	17,970	11,412

Source: Peter I. Liashchenko, History of the National
Economy of Russia to the 1917 Revolution, pp.
528-529.

States, entered into a period of rapid and sustained growth. The
consumption of raw cotton increased from 218 million poods in 1870 to
7.6 million poods in 1885, and reached 16 million poods by 1900.
The number of mechanical looms increased from around 11,000 during
the period of the reforms to over 87,000 by 1890.[2] Production during this period also became increasingly mechanized and concentrated
in larger establishments. Table 9 shows the growth in the value of
production and the increasing concentration of production between
1870 and 1897. Although the value of production from these three
branches of cotton textile industry nearly tripled, the number of
factories actually declined.

Nature of Industrial Development in Russia

The nature of the industrialization process which took place
in Russia during the post-reform period assumed distinctive
characteristics, particularly in regard to the productive and organizational structures of industry, which set it apart from the
West. In the conditions of backwardness in which Russia had found
herself by mid-century vis-a-vis the West, it was necessary before
the process of industrialization could be launched to overcome
certain obstacles which for so long had retarded Russia's industrial
development and to find substitutes for those factors which in the
more advanced countries had significantly facilitated industrial
growth but which were lacking in Russia.[3] The deficiency of
internal market for industrial goods, the quantitative and qualitative inadequacy of the labor supply, the scarcity of capital, and
the lack of a sufficient reservoir of managerial and entrepreneurial
talent were among the most serious conditions restricting economic
growth in Russia. Each of these obstacles, however, was overcome
in varying degrees and manners during the course of Russia's industrial upsurge during the latter part of the century. Consequently,
the pattern of industrialization in Russia during the last part of
the century was shaped largely by the responses made to overcome
the negative conditions of economic backwardness.

---

[1]Khromov, Ekonomicheskoe razvitie Rossii v XIX-XX vekakh,
Appendix, Table 4, pp. 452-455.

[2]Ibid., p. 183.

[3]Alexander Gerschenkron, "Russia: Patterns and Problems of
Economic Development, 1861-1958," Economic Backwardness in Historical Perspective. A Book of Essays, p. 123.

TABLE 9

GROWTH OF THE COTTON TEXTILE INDUSTRY,

1870-1897

Year	Cotton Spinning		Cotton Weaving		Cotton Printing	
	Number of Factories	Value of Production*	Number of Factories	Value of Production*	Number of Factories	Value of Production*
1870	44	48.4	744	48.0	130	30.7
1880	69	74.2	678	99.7	774	66.6
1890	66	106.6	349	136.3	413	91.1
1897	67	134.9	465	237.5	190	105.5

* In millions of rubles.

Source: Peter I. Liashchenko, History of the National Economy of Russia to the 1917 Revolution, p. 530.

Role of the State

In Russia, it was the government, primarily through its domestic and foreign fiscal policies, which became the prime mover of industrialization. It built a protective tariff wall around its industry, promoted foreign investment, supplied investment funds to industry by means of subsidies, tax exemptions, loans and other privileges, and it provided a market for a substantial portion of industrial output. Perhaps most important of all, the government, through its policies, helped to create an atmosphere of industrial promotiveness in Russia.

The restrictions upon the growth of output from the peasant sector of the economy and the consequent limitations upon the peasant's purchasing power for industrial goods made it improbable that this sector could exert a strong influence on industrial growth. Rather than attempting to stimulate this sector, a process that was thought to promise to bear uncertain results and to be gradual at best, the government itself assumed the task of stimulating industrial development by assuring a reliable and substantial market for industrial products. The primary mechanism at the government's disposal was the promotion, directly and indirectly, of the construction of railroads on a large scale. The construction of railroads, as well as ancillary industries of steel, iron, coal, and machinery, which supplied the former, however, required huge sums of capital investment. Apart from the creation of conditions favorable to attracting foreign investment, which played a considerable role in the development of heavy industry, and heavy borrowing from abroad, the government turned to the peasantry.

Once industrialization became an avowed goal of the state, what initially appeared as an obstacle to industrial development, the insufficient peasant demand for industrial goods, no longer was a prerequisite for stimulating and sustaining industrial growth. In fact, its curtailment became imperative since a reduced peasant consumption meant an increased share of national output would be available for investment.[1] Consequently, the government unrelentlessly increased the tax burden of the peasantry in order to help finance the industrialization of the country.

Advantage of Relative Backwardness

The very nature of Russia's backwardness also afforded notable advantages for industrial development. Instead of being required to go through a slow and costly process of trial and error in develop-

[1] Ibid., p. 125.

ing industry on her own, Russia was able to turn to the more
advanced and experienced West and borrow the latest industrial
technology available. This Russia did, but in a selective manner,
choosing what best met her objectives and adapting the innovations
to suit the conditions of the country. At the same time the introduction of modern technology meant a substitution of capital for
labor. As the technology of the 19th century became more advanced,
it also tended to become increasingly labor saving. Thus although
large amounts of labor were still required to operate the factories,
the assurance of a government demand for a large portion of the industrial output, together with the introduction of modern technology,
created a situation in which the qualitative and quantitative inadequacies of the labor supply could be neutralized and still allow
for a relatively high rate of industrial growth.[1]

Largeness of Plant Size

The technology of the 19th century, which became increasingly
capital intensive, also favored a greatly expanded scale of production. Thus bigness of both individual plant and individual enterprise size was a characteristic feature of the structure of Russian
industry. The increase in the scale of plant and enterprise size
was, in addition, a means by which the scarcity of managerial and
entrepreneurial talent was compensated for by spreading what was
available over a large part of the industrial economy.[2] The state,
moreover, in its promotion of industrial growth centered its attention on the output of basic industrial materials and on machinery
production while showing little interest in light industry. Consequently, because of the technological requirements of the former,
gigantomaniia pervaded the minds of the Russian bureaucracy as well
as the entrepreneurs, much to the detriment of small industry. The
growth in the number of large factories and the increasing concentration of workers in large factories in European Russia between
1879 and 1902 is shown in Table 10.

It is easily discernable from the table that the larger the
factory size, the more rapid was the growth in the number of factories and in the number of workers. Between 1879 and 1902 factories with more than 1,000 workers accounted for 61 per cent of the
total growth in the number of workers in factories with over 100
persons employed. The table also provides a good indication of the

---

[1]Ibid., p. 127.

[2]Ibid., p. 129

tremendous growth in factory industry that took place during this period, especially between 1894 and 1902.

In 1902, according to the calculations of A. V. Pogozhev, there were some 27,666 factories in the Russian Empire employing some 1,887,700 workers. The structural pattern of factory industry, however, was very uneven. As shown in Table 11, factories employing more than 100 workers accounted for only 10 per cent of the total number of factories, but employed nearly 79 per cent of the total factory labor force.

Moreover, the very large factories, employing more than 1,000 workers, while constituting only about one per cent of the factories in the Russian Empire, accounted for approximately 38 per cent of the factory labor force. The degree to which factory production became concentrated in large plants was very striking for the period. The relative significance of large factories in the structure of industry in the Russian Empire was even greater than in Germany at the time.[1]

Regional Concentration of Industry

While production was becoming concentrated in large-scale establishments, it also became increasingly concentrated in a few regions of the Empire. In 1897 three regions, the Capitals, Central Industrial, and Western Tsarist Poland accounted for nearly 36 per cent of the total employment in manufacturing (See Table 12). The remainder of employment was rather evenly distributed over the rest of European Russia. In the remaining peripheral regions, manufacturing was comparatively unimportant.

If one excludes handicraft and small-scale commodity production, however, and considers only factory industry, then the degree of the regional concentration of industry was even more pronounced. Nearly half of the total labor force in factory industry in 1902 was located in the Capitals, Central Industrial, and Western Tsarist Poland regions, and within these three regions, four guberniias, Moscow, St. Petersburg, Vladimir, and Piotrków, accounted for 77 per cent of the total. Figure 18 shows the distribution of the labor force in factory industry by guberniia for 1902. Nearly 44 per cent of the factory labor force was concentrated in only five guberniias, Moscow, St. Petersburg, Vladimir, Piotrków, and Perm, while Warsaw, Kostroma, Lifliand, and Kiev guberniias accounted for an additional 12 per cent.

---

[1] A. V. Pogozhev, Uchet chislennosti i sostava rabochikh v Rossii. Materialy po statistike truda (S.-Peterburg: Tipografiia Imperatorskoi Akademii Nauk, 1906), p. xvi.

TABLE 10

GROWTH OF LARGE FACTORY INDUSTRY IN EUROPEAN RUSSIA AND THE
CONCENTRATION OF EMPLOYMENT IN LARGE INDUSTRY

1879-1902

Year		Factory Size Category (According to Number of Workers)			Total
		100-499	500-999	1,000 and more	
1879	Number of Factories	(979)	(164)	(86)	(1,229)
	Number of Workers	219,400	113,900	163,000	496,400
1890	Number of Factories	(1,131)	(182)	(108)	(1,421)
	Number of Workers	252,100	120,900	226,200	599,200
1894	Number of Factories	(1,136)	(215)	(117)	(1,468)
	Number of Workers	252,700	143,500	259,500	655,700
1902	Number of Factories	(1,746)	(359)	(261)	(2,366)
	Number of Workers	386,200	245,900	626,500	1,258,600

Source: A. V. Pogozhev, Uchet chislennosti i sostava
rabochikh v Rossii, p. 42.

TABLE 11

DISTRIBUTION OF FACTORIES AND EMPLOYMENT
ACCORDING TO SIZE OF FACTORY IN THE
RUSSIAN EMPIRE FOR 1902

Size of Factory (Number of Workers)	Number of Factories	Number of Workers
2--4 workers	8,455	24,500
5--49	14,189	234,500
50--99	2,098	143,900
100--499	2,200	485,000
500--999	424	289,600
>1,000 workers	302	710,200
Total	27,666	1,887,700

Source: A. V. Pogozhev, Uchet chislennosti i sostava
rabochikh v Rossii, pp. 42, 43, and 51.

TABLE 12

DISTRIBUTION OF EMPLOYMENT IN MANUFACTURING IN 1897
AND EMPLOYMENT IN FACTORY INDUSTRY IN 1902
BY REGION

Region	Total Employment in Manufacturing 1897[1]	Per Cent of Total Employment	Total Employment in Factory Industry 1902[2]	Per Cent of Total Employment
Capitals	771,897	18.3	448,228	23.7
Central Industrial	372,218	8.8	269,042	14.2
Southern Industrial	160,360	3.8	55,642	2.9
Black Earth	205,898	4.9	63,389	3.4
Northwest	104,041	2.5	47,351	2.5
Baltic	161,792	3.8	75,393	4.0
West-Central	97,824	2.3	29,434	1.6
Western	204,219	4.8	41,101	2.2
Right Bank Dnepr	234,618	5.6	95,955	5.1
Left Bank Dnepr	192,789	4.6	72,483	3.8
Southwest Steppe	179,000	4.2	41,928	2.2
Southeast Steppe	155,861	3.7	82,818	4.4
Middle Volga	96,168	2.3	35,478	1.9
Lower Volga	106,146	2.5	30,652	1.6
Trans Volga	54,070	1.3	20,906	1.1
Pre-Caucasus	73,370	1.7	14,952	0.8
Caucasus	51,756	1.2	11,839	0.6
Caspian Sea	49,811	1.2	39,512	2.1
North	32,650	0.8	21,845	1.2
Northeast	153,298	3.6	127,713	6.8
W. Siberia	66,143	1.6	10,302	0.5
E. Siberia	47,013	1.1	11,397	0.6
C. A. Steppe	17,017	0.4	4,922	0.3
Central Asia	185,892	4.4	3,379[3]	0.2
W. Tsarist Poland	361,934	8.6	215,616	11.4
E. Tsarist Poland	93,318	2.2	19,127	1.0
Total	4,229,103	100.0 [4]	1,890,404	100.0 [4]

[1]Based on calculations from: Russia, Tsentral'nyi statisticheskii komitet. Pervaia vseobshchaia perepis' naseleniia Rossiiskoi Imperii 1897 g. Obshchii svod po Imperii rezul'tatov razrabotki dannykh Pervoi vseobshchei perepisi naseliniia, proizvedennoi 28 ianvaria 1897 goda. II. (S.-Peterburg, 1905), pp. 256-295. Also see Appendix II for the occupations included under manufacturing in 1897.

[2]Based on calculations from: A. V. Pogozhev, Uchet chislennosti i sostava rabochikh v Rossii (S.-Peterburg, 1906), Appendix, Table 1.

[3]No data for Ferganskaia and Zakaspiiskaia guberniias.

[4]Columns do not add exactly to 100.0 per cent because of rounding.

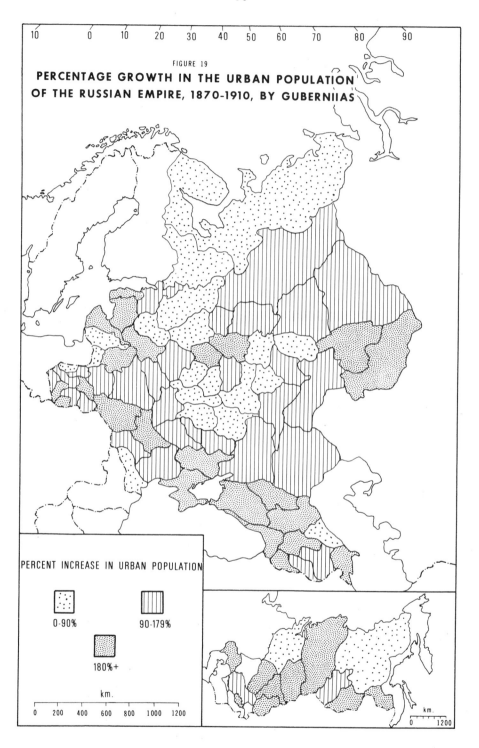

FIGURE 19

PERCENTAGE GROWTH IN THE URBAN POPULATION OF THE RUSSIAN EMPIRE, 1870-1910, BY GUBERNIIAS

PERCENT INCREASE IN URBAN POPULATION

0-90%   90-179%

180%+

km.

0   200   400   600   800   1000   1200

km.

0   1200

CHAPTER VII

PATTERNS OF URBAN GROWTH IN THE POST-REFORM PERIOD, 1870-1910

The last forty years of the period under study, 1870-1910, were characterized by an unparalleled growth in the population of the cities in the Russian Empire. During this period the growth in urban population amounted to nearly 15 million persons, representing about 72 per cent of the total growth in the numbers in urban population during the entire ninety-nine-year period of the study. The average annual rate of increase during this period was 2.5 per cent, compared to a rate of 1.6 per cent during the first four and one-half decades of the study (See Figure 12). Although this tremendous growth in urban population occurred simultaneously with the unprecedented expansion of industry, the basis of the growth of the former did not rest entirely on the significant advances of the latter.

Urban Growth, 1870-1885

During the first period following the emancipation, substantial industrial growth, particularly in light industry, and improved conditions in agriculture contributed to fostering a period of relative economic prosperity for the cities. Although the statistics for the first several decades following the reforms are so unsatisfactory as to preclude a detailed analysis of industrial growth, some indications of the volume of industrial growth during this period are available. According to Strumilin, the total value of production from fourteen leading branches on industry in European Russia grew from 284 million rubles in 1870 to 429 million rubles in 1885.[1] The latter figure, however, is somewhat low since Russia at this time was just emerging from the midst of an industrial crisis. According to other indices of industrial growth that have been made, it has been estimated that industrial production in the Russian Empire approximately doubled during this period. This would imply an average annual rate of growth in industrial output in the vicinity of five per cent.[2] Apart from coal mining, the growth of heavy

[1]Strumilin, Ocherki ekonomicheskoi istorii Rossii i SSSR, pp. 438, 442.

[2]Raymond W. Goldsmith, "The Economic Growth of Tsarist Russia, 1860-1913," Economic Development and Cultural Change, IX (April, 1961), pp. 462-463, 465.

industry was rather slow during this period, while the most significant advances were noted in textiles, especially in cotton textiles.

The urban population of the Russian Empire during this fifteen-
year period grew at an average annual rate of 2.5 per cent as
slightly more than four million persons were added to the populations of the cities. Although the growth of the urban population
in the two capital guberniias and the western guberniias of Tsarist
Poland, two of the most important industrial regions of the Empire,
was very significant, accounting for more than 20 per cent, or
867,697 persons, of the total growth in urban population, the guberniias situated primarily west of the Dnepr River, among the most
important commercial agricultural regions of the Empire, also grew
very rapidly (See Table 13). In the four regions consisting of the
Western, Left and Right Banks of the Dnepr River, and the Southwestern Steppe, the urban population grew by nearly 1.3 million
persons, which constituted nearly one-third of the growth in the
urban population of the entire Empire. A significant portion of
this growth was somewhat artificial, however, as the Jewish population residing in the villages of these guberniias, which made up a
large part of the Jewish Pale of Settlement, was compelled to leave
the countryside as the consequence of a number of laws promulgated
in 1882-1883 and move into the cities of these guberniias.[1] In the
remaining regions of the Empire the growth in urban population was
not particularly great, except in the Baltic region where the growing importance of foreign trade and the consequent attraction of
industry provided a great stimulus to the growth of the port cities,
and in the guberniias of the North Caucasian Foreland, where the
significantly increased volume of colonists provided an impetus to
the commercial development of the cities in this region. The sharp
increase in the urban population of Central Asia was due most of
all to the continued territorial annexations which took place during this period.

---

[1]S. M. Dubnow, History of the Jews in Russia and Poland From
the Earliest Times Until the Present Day. II. From the Death of
Alexander I Until the Death of Alexander II (1825-1894). Translated from the Russian by I. Friedlaender (Philadelphia: The
Jewish Publication Society of America, 1918), pp. 310, 318-319,
340-341.

TABLE 13

ABSOLUTE GROWTH AND PER CENT OF TOTAL GROWTH IN
URBAN POPULATION BY REGION IN THE RUSSIAN EMPIRE,
1870-1910

Region	1870-1885		1885-1897		1897-1910		1870-1910	
	Absolute Growth	Per Cent of Total	Absolute Growth	Per Cent of Total	Absolute Growth	Per Cent of Total	Absolute Growth	Per Cent of Total
Capitals	521,869	12.8	711,764	18.3	821,505	12.3	2,055,138	14.0
Central Industrial	91,942	3.9	144,465	3.7	190,812	2.9	427,219	2.9
Southern Industrial	26,410	0.7	117,150	3.0	27,861	0.4	171,421	1.2
Black Earth	119,959	2.9	166,427	4.3	87,277	1.3	373,663	2.6
Northwest	43,212	1.1	20,222	0.5	58,592	0.9	122,026	0.8
Baltic	160,920	3.9	216,229	5.6	184,802	2.8	561,951	3.8
West-Central	130,723	3.2	51,124	1.3	276,186	4.1	458,033	3.1
Western	294,229	7.2	99,672	2.6	216,055	3.2	609,956	4.2
Right Bank Dnepr	255,444	6.3	152,898	3.9	609,617	9.1	1,017,959	7.0
Left Bank Dnepr	297,124	7.3	27,382	0.7	323,751	4.9	648,257	4.4
Southwest Steppe	402,177	9.9	285,765	7.4	523,309	7.9	1,211,251	8.3
Southeast Steppe	120,573	3.0	232,576	6.0	360,115	5.4	713,264	4.9
Middle Volga	131,536	3.2	-18,078	-0.5	129,870	2.0	243,348	1.7
Lower Volga	137,826	3.4	15,018	0.4	271,033	4.1	423,877	2.9
Trans Volga	83,050	2.0	68,324	1.8	174,240	2.6	325,614	2.2
Pre-Caucasus	122,069	3.0	85,082	2.2	213,465	3.2	420,616	2.9
Caucasus	55,830	1.4	176,824	4.6	258,621	3.9	491,275	3.4
Caspian Sea	44,428	1.1	102,481	2.6	174,975	2.6	321,884	2.2
North	2,809	0.1	25,848	0.7	40,453	0.6	69,110	0.5
Northeast	49,421	1.2	58,274	1.5	67,929	1.0	175,624	1.2
W. Siberia	58,625	1.4	27,646	0.7	183,194	2.8	269,465	1.8
E. Siberia	57,745	1.4	112,693	2.9	341,732	5.1	512,170	3.5
Central Asiatic Steppe	57,703	1.4	61,519	1.6	130,990	2.0	250,212	1.7
Central Asia	358,445	8.8	221,145	5.7	298,387	4.5	877,977	6.0

Region	1870-1885		1885-1897		1897-1910		1870-1910	
	Absolute Growth	Per Cent of Total	Absolute Growth	Per Cent of Total	Absolute Growth	Per Cent of Total	Absolute Growth	Per Cent of Total
W. Tsarist Poland	345,828	7.8	611,143	15.8	576,670	8.7	1,533,641	10.5
E. Tsarist Poland	113,082	2.8	107,806	2.8	126,833	1.9	347,721	2.4
Total	4,082,969	100.0	3,881,409	100.0	6,668,364	100.0	14,632,742	100.0

Source: Based on data found in Appendix I. Columns do not add to exactly 100.0 per cent because of rounding.

Urban Growth, 1885-1897

The general economic expansion which took place in the Russian Empire during the 1870's gave way to an industrial recession and an agricultural crisis. Beginning in 1881-1882, partly as a result of short crops, but also as a reaction to an abrupt decline in railroad construction, and finally under the influence of an economic crisis in Western Europe in 1880, industrial growth was seriously disrupted and the entire economy entered into a period of stagnation which continued for nearly a decade and culminated in the catastrophic famine of 1891. Beginning shortly thereafter, however, an industrial revival was initiated which in the course of the remaining part of the decade produced results that virtually dwarfed the achievements of industry during the previous two decades. During the last decade of the century industrial output grew at an average annual rate of over seven per cent.[2] During the same time the total value of factory production doubled and factory employment increased by over 60 per cent.

Table 14 shows the growth in employment in the major branches of factory industry between 1887 and 1897. Over this ten-year period nearly 800,000 persons were added to the factory labor force in these industries, with four industries, textiles, mining and metallurgy, metal fabrication, and ceramics accounting for about 75 per cent of the total growth in employment in these industries.

The great spurt in the volume of railroad construction during this period was the primary stimulant to this unprecedented industrial growth. During the last seven years of the 19th century 18,740 km. of new track were completed, an amount exceeding the total amount of railroad line constructed during the previous twenty-one years. The importance of railroad construction to the growth of heavy industry during this period was evident by the fact that nearly 75 per cent of the output of iron and steel in the country was consumed by the railroads during this decade.[3]

---

[1]Liashchenko, p. 508.

[2]Goldsmith, pp. 464-465.

[3]Liashchenko, p. 508.

TABLE 14

GROWTH IN FACTORY EMPLOYMENT
BY MAJOR BRANCH OF INDUSTRY,
1887-1897

Industry	Number of Workers 1887	1897	Absolute Increase in the Number of Workers
Textiles	399,200	642,500	243,300
Food Products	205,200	255,400	50,200
Animal Products	38,900	64,400	25,500
Wood Processing	30,700	86,300	55,600
Paper Products	19,500	46,200	26,700
Ceramics	67,300	143,300	76,000
Chemical Products	21,100	35,300	14,200
Metal Fabrication	103,300	214,300	111,000
Mining and Metallurgy	390,900	544,300	153,400
Other	41,800	66,200	24,400
Totals	1,317,900	2,098,200	780,300

Source: A. G. Rashin, <u>Formirovanie promyshlennogo proletariata v Rossii</u>, pp. 112-113.

In spite of the tremendous industrial expansion which took place, especially during the latter part of this period, the rate of growth of the urban population between 1885 and 1897 declined somewhat to 2.2 per cent per annum as some 3.9 million persons were added to the populations of the cities in the Empire. This decline in the growth rate of the urban population must be ascribed primarily to the deterioration in the economic conditions of the countryside which was occurring at this time. Beginning in the early 1880's the prices of agricultural products began to decline rapidly in large degree as a result of a growing international crisis in agriculture brought about by the expansion of grain exports from Russia and from other countries.

At first the decline in prices affected mostly the peasant crops of rye and oats, but by the end of the 1880's the prices on wheat were also severely affected. By the middle of the following decade the prices of these commodities had dropped by nearly fifty per cent.[1] Although the crop failures of 1883 and 1891 temporarily boosted prices, they also contributed to the further economic impoverishment of the countryside. Consequently, the decline in the purchasing power of the peasants, a condition aggravated by the increasing tax burden placed on them to help finance industrialization and by a rapidly expanding rural population which, because of the restrictions on mobility, was forced to remain in the countryside, seriously affected the growth of many cities, especially in the agricultural regions, whose economic well being was based largely on servicing the needs of the peasantry and processing their products.

On the other hand, the crisis in agriculture had little effect on the growth of industry during this period since the nature of the industrialization taking place was largely oriented to heavy industry and as such was not heavily dependent on the peasant market. Consequently, the cities which participated in the industrial upsurge of the 1890's grew very rapidly. The urban population in the four most industrialized regions, the Capitals, the Central Industrial, the Baltic, and Western Tsarist Poland, grew by 1,683,601 persons which constituted about 43 per cent of the total growth in the urban population of the Russian Empire during this period.

The effects of these two counter trends, the rapid expansion of industry and the deterioration in agriculture, on the regional

---

[1] Ibid., p. 469.

pattern of the growth of cities is clearly depicted on Table 15. The rate of growth in the population of the cities in the four most industrialized regions mentioned above rose from an annual average of 2.4 per cent 1870-1885 to 3.1 per cent 1885-1897. On the other hand, the growth rate of the urban population in eleven selected regions which were predominantly oriented to commercial agriculture and whose cities had possessed considerable commercial importance, declined sharply from an average annual rate of 2.7 per cent in the former period to only 1.1 per cent in the period under consideration. Compared with the previous period 1870-1885 when the growth in the urban population of these eleven agricultural regions reached 2,010,472 persons, or nearly 50 per cent of the total urban growth in the Empire, only 895,215 persons, representing about 23 per cent of the total urban growth, were added to the urban population of these regions between 1885 and 1897.

Consequently, the impact of industrial growth was limited to the cities in only a few regions and was not great enough to overcome the deleterious effects of the crisis in agriculture on most of the remaining cities in the Empire. Hence, there resulted an overall decline in the rate of urban growth during this period.

Urban Growth, 1897-1910

The last period of the study was also the period of greatest urban growth. Between 1897 and 1910 the population of the cities grew at an average annual rate of 2.6 per cent as nearly 6.7 million persons were added to the urban population of the Empire. Unlike the previous period when industrial expansion played a leading role in the growth of the urban population, the importance of industry as a factor in the growth of cities declined as a severe and prolonged depression swept over the Empire.

Economic Crisis and Political Disorder

Beginning as a financial crisis in 1900, but also based on industrial over-production and the exhaustion of the tax-paying capacity of the peasantry, a severe depression broke out at the beginning of the 20th century and its effects on industrial output lasted to nearly the end of the decade.[1] Similar to the previous economic setbacks, this one affected heavy industry most of all, although by 1905 it had spread to light industry as well. Unlike the previous ones, however, the severity of the industrial crisis

---

[1]Khromov, Ekonomicheskoe razvitie Rossii. Ocherki . . . . , pp. 405-406.

TABLE 15

COMPARATIVE GROWTH OF THE URBAN POPULATION IN
SELECTED INDUSTRIAL AND AGRICULTURAL REGIONS
IN THE RUSSIAN EMPIRE BY MAJOR PERIODS,

1870-1910

	Growth of Urban Population				
Period	Four Industrial Regions[1]		Eleven Agricultural Regions[2]		
	Absolute Increase	Average Annual Per Cent Increase	Absolute Increase	Average Annual Per Cent Increase	
1870-1885	1,120,559	2.4	2,010,472	2.7	
1885-1897	1,683,601	3.1	895,215	1.1	
1897-1910	1,773,789	2.2	2,922,971	2.7	

[1]Consist of the Capitals, Baltic, Central Industrial, and
Western Tsarist Poland regions.

[2]Consist of Eastern Tsarist Poland, Northwest, West-Central,
Western, Right Bank of the Dnepr River, Left Bank of the Dnepr
River, Southwestern Steppe, Pre-Caucasus, Middle Volga, Lower
Volga, and the Trans Volga Regions.

Source: Based on data in Appendix I.

of 1900-1903, and the ensuing economic stagnation, was intensified
by a wave of internal political strife both in the cities and in
the countryside. Furthermore, the crushing defeat of Russia in the
war with Japan in 1904-1905 contributed greatly to the instability
of internal conditions.

At the base of this turmoil was the growth in unemployment
and strikes, brought about by the industrial depression, and the
outbreak of peasant disorders and riots in protest against their
hopelessly impoverished conditions. At first the government re-
acted with force, which only intensified the situation. Finally,
by the end of 1905, faced with the near economic paralysis of the
country brought about by a wave of general strikes and a danger-
ously rebellious mood among the population as well as in the armed
forces, the government moved to make political concessions, including the establishment of an elected representative assembly
or duma. At the same time the government also moved to calm the
agrarian disorders and problems by issuing a number of decrees in
1905 and 1906 which allowed the peasants to acquire actual ownership of the land, liquidated the land redemption payments which
were miserably in arrears, and finally granted the right to the
peasants of freely determining the place of their residence.[1]
These two measures went a long way in temporarily quelling the
internal strife and within a couple of years Russia was back on
the path of substantial economic growth which lasted into the
beginning of the First World War.

The effects of the economic depression and the internal disorders during the first six years of the 1900's, and the subsequent
industrial recovery during the last several years of the decade on
the growth of industrial employment are shown in Table 16.

Thus for the first half of the decade the number of workers
remained at a standstill, while a sharp reduction in the number
of factories took place. Consequently, one of the effects of the
crisis on the structure of industry was to further concentrate
production in larger plants by weeding out the smaller, weaker,
and less efficient enterprises. Most of the growth in factory
employment over the entire decade was accounted for by the cotton
textile industry which was comparatively little affected by the
crisis. Although experiencing a brief decline between 1903-1904,

---

[1] Geroid Tanquary Robinson, Rural Russia Under the Old Regime.
A History of the Landlord-Peasant World and a Prologue to the
Peasant Revolution of 1917 (Berkeley, California: University of
California Press, 1969. Originally Printed in 1932), pp. 208-209.

employment in cotton textiles grew by 45 per cent during this period, increasing from 391,000 workers to 501,000 workers by 1910.[1] In other industries, however, employment remained at a virtual standstill or even declined. In the ceramics industry employment grew by only 12,000 persons, while in the food processing industry employment declined by more than 3,000 persons, and in the metal fabrication industry it declined by over 6,000 persons.[2]

In heavy industry the picture was a mixed one. In the coal mining industry employment declined during the first half of the period but grew rather quickly afterwards for a net gain of about 40,000 persons.[3] Employment in this industry reached 158,000 persons by 1910. In the heavy metallurgical industry, although production levels of 1900 were recovered by 1910 following a sharp decline, employment actually remained below the 1900 levels. Between 1900 and 1911 employment declined by 72,000 persons, from 263,000 in 1900 to 191,000 at the beginning of 1911.[4]

Consequently, the effects of industrial development on the growth of cities were most notable at the beginning of the period, which followed the most intensive years of the industrial boom of the 1890's, and near the end of the period, when industry once again initiated a period of rapid expansion. These two brief periods, however, were not sufficient to overcome the effects of the industrial depression and stagnation during the intermediate period on the growth of cities. As seen from Table 15 again, the annual growth rate of the cities in the main industrial regions decline from 3.1 per cent in 1885-1897 to 2.2 per cent in 1897-1910 and their portion of the total urban growth declined from 43 per cent in the earlier period to only 22 per cent in the latter one. The effects of the industrial crisis on the growth of cities in the guberniias of Western Tsarist Poland were particularly severe, especially in Warsaw and in the textile center of Lodz, as the absolute growth in the urban population of this region decline to 576,670 persons in the latter period as compared to an addition of 611,143 persons in the previous period. Consequently, it was not so much the development of industry which stimulated the tremendous influx of persons into the cities of the Empire during this period as it

---

[1] A. G. Rashin, Formirovanie promyshlennogo proletariata v Rossii (Moskva: Gosudarstvennoe Sotsial'no-Ekonomicheskoe Izdatel'stvo, 1940), p. 147.

[2] Ibid., pp. 150, 151, 141.

[3] Ibid., p. 155.

[4] Ibid., p. 156.

TABLE 16

GROWTH IN THE NUMBER OF FACTORIES AND WORKERS
SUBORDINATED TO THE FACTORY INSPECTORATE,
1901-1910

Year	Number of Factories	Number of Workers
1901	18,729	1,692,300
1903	16,173	1,640,400
1905	14,615	1,660,700
1907	14,048	1,718,100
1910	14,438	1,793,400

Source: A. G. Rashin, Formirovanie promyshlennogo proletariata v Rossii, p. 133. Data do not include mining and heavy metallurgy.

was the push of the peasants from the countryside brought about
by other reasons.

Agrarian Reforms and Rural Out-Migration

Undoubtedly, many peasants took advantage of the internal
disorders of the first half of the decade to migrate with or
without passports to the cities, but this movement was miniscule
compared to the surge of migration from the countryside which
came about as a result of the agrarian legislation of 1906.

The basic aim of the legislation introduced by the prime
minister and former minister of the interior, P. A. Stolypin,
aside from restoring order in the countryside, was to rectify
the shortcomings of the Emancipation of 1861 by creating a new
class of small, independent landowners. Under the basic conditions of the reforms the village communes which had not reparti-
tioned their land during the previous twenty-four years were
declared as having shifted to a basis of household allotment land
tenure and all the landholdings of the individual peasants were
secured to them in personal ownership.[1] In the communes where
land had been periodically redistributed, every member could at
any time request that all the land to which he was entitled under
the conditions of the redistribution be granted to him in personal
ownership. Furthermore, the peasants were given the right to demand the consolidation of their holdings into one compact parcel
at any time.

Although the Stolypin reforms dealt a severe blow to the
institution of the obshchina, or village commune, they far from
destroyed it. The reforms did, nevertheless, put the principle
of communal association on a voluntary basis rather than a com-
pulsory one, and they opened the way for improvements to be made
on the land.

The explosive nature of the rush out of the village communes
on the part of those who had wanted to leave is clearly revealed
by the annual data on requests for land separation and withdrawal.
Of the 2,755,633 household heads, representing about 24 per cent
of the total number of household units, who requested separation
from the communes between 1907 and 1915, 62 per cent, or 1,701,902
did so between 1907 and 1909.[2] In relation to the total situation

---

[1] Alexander Gerschenkron, "Russia: Agrarian Policies and
Industrialization, 1861-1914," p. 240.

[2] Liashchenko, p. 748.

in agriculture, about 30 per cent of the number of heads of households in all village communes declared their intention of leaving
during this period, and almost 22 per cent were actually separated
out of the obshchina and became individual owners of their alloted
lands.[1] The corresponding percentage of lands owned by former
obshchina members was about 10 per cent. The discrepancy between
these two figures reveals the fact that the number of those who
had less than average allotments of land was considerable among
the departing obshchina members.[2]

The importance of the Stolypin reforms in regard to the growth
of cities rested on the abolition of the judicial power of the
village commune over the peasantry and the removal of the principal
legal barriers to free mobility. For the first time in modern
Russian history, a peasant, wishing to abandon his land and to
emigrate to the city or to another part of the empire, could sell
his land and acquire the means to finance his move away from the
village.[3] In this respect the effects of the Stolypin reforms
were similar to the land enclosures in Great Britain during the
18th and early 19th centuries.

Equally if not more important, however, were the changes
introduced concerning the issuance of passports, which were the
primary means for peasants to legally depart from the village in
order to seek employment in industry or move into the cities. In
receiving passports the peasants were no longer dependent on the
consent of the household or the village commune, nor was there any
longer a time limitation on the validity of passports.[4] The
village commune lost its right to recall at any time absent members of the commune. This removed the serious threat, one not
infrequently resorted to by communes and household heads as a
source of monetary extortion, to peasants with passports of being
recalled to the village or of becoming passportless outlaws and
being forceably deported back to the home village if they refused
to heed the recall. In essence, the peasantry received the right
to choose freely a place of permanent residence.

The effects of the Stolypin reforms on the growth of cities
were most apparent in the agricultural regions of the country, as

---

[1]Gerschenkron, "Russia: Agrarian Policies and Industrialization . . . ," pp. 242-243.

[2]Ibid., p. 243.

[3]Ibid.

[4]Ibid., p. 234.

a glance at Table 15 again will confirm. Compared to the average annual rate of growth of 1.1 per cent in the previous period, 1885-1897, the urban population in the eleven agricultural regions grew at average an annual rate of 2.7 per cent, 1897-1910, considerably higher than the industrial regions, as nearly three million persons were added to the cities. Thus the eleven selected agricultural regions received nearly 44 per cent of the total urban growth in the Empire.

The growth of the urban population was particularly intense in the regions of the Volga and Dnepr Rivers. In the three regions of the Volga River, the urban population increased by 575,143 persons during this period as compared to an increase of only 65,264 persons in the previous period. Likewise, the growth of the urban population in the Western, West-Central, Left and Right banks of the Dnepr River regions, which were also regions where the proportion of separated land to the total area of allotment land tenure was greatest, was very rapid.[1] Between 1897-1910 a total of 1,425,609 persons was added to the urban population as compared to an increase of 331,076 persons in the previous period.

In Siberia and the Steppe region of Central Asia the surge in the growth of the urban population resulted primarily from the construction of the Trans-Siberian Railroad. The urban population increased by nearly 656,000 persons between 1897-1910 as compared to an increase of 201,858 persons in the preceding period. Most of the increase in the urban population was accounted for by the growth of cities located on the railroad, especially where the railroad intersected with important waterways. Although the advent of the railroad tremendously facilitated migration into Siberia and promoted the growth of manufacturing in the cities, especially the food processing industry, it also contributed directly to the growth of the population of many cities by the attraction of a large cadre of transportation workers required in the construction and maintenance of the Trans-Siberian railroad.[2]

Summary: Pattern of Urban Growth, 1870-1910

Although the volume of urban growth during the post-reform period was tremendously larger than in the pre-reform period, the

[1]Liashchenko, p. 748.

[2]V. V. Pokshishevskii, Zaselenie Sibir. Istoriko-geografi-cheskie ocherki (Irkutsk: Oblastnoe Gosudarstvennoe Izdatel'stvo, 1951). pp. 137-138.

spatial pattern of urban growth remained substantially unaltered. Figure 19 shows the distribution of the percentage growth in the urban population by guberniia between 1870 and 1910. The guberniias which experienced the lowest increase in their urban populations form a core in the central part of European Russia, coinciding basically with the Black-Earth region, and a band stretching from Pskov to Arkhangel'sk guberniia in the northwestern part of European Russia. The urban population in these guberniias increased by less than 90 per cent during the post-reform period. Surrounding these two cores of low urban growth is a broad band of guberniias beginning in the west-central part of European Russia and extending southeastward to Astrakhan'guberniia and then northward into Vologda guberniia. The urban population in these guberniias increased between 0.9 and 1.8 times. The guberniias which experienced the largest increases in urban population, with the exception of Moscow and Vladimir guberniias, were located primarily on the periphery of European Russia. The urban population in these guberniias increased by more than 1.8 times. In contrast with the pre-reform period, the most notable changes took place in the Baltic guberniias and in Moscow and Vladimir guberniias, which experienced substantially larger increases in their urban population during the post-reform period than in the pre-reform period.

Figure 20, on the other hand, shows the distribution of the absolute growth in the urban population by guberniia during the post-reform period. In comparison with the pre-reform period, the distribution of the growth in urban population was relatively more concentrated in a few guberniias. In the two capital guberniias, St. Petersburg and Moscow, the urban population increased by 2,055,138 persons, which represented 14 per cent of the total growth in urban population. In the two southern guberniias, Kherson and Kiev, the urban population grew by 1,314,196 persons while in the two Polish guberniias, Piotrków and Warszawa, the increase in urban population amounted to 1,297,384. Together, these six guberniias accounted for nearly one-third, or 4,840,940 persons, of the total growth in the urban population of the Russian Empire between 1870 and 1910. On a regional basis, the southern part of European Russia accounted for a large share of the total growth in urban population. The urban population in the four regions of the south increased by 3,590,731 persons, representing nearly one-fourth of the total growth in urban population in the Empire during the last four decades of the study.

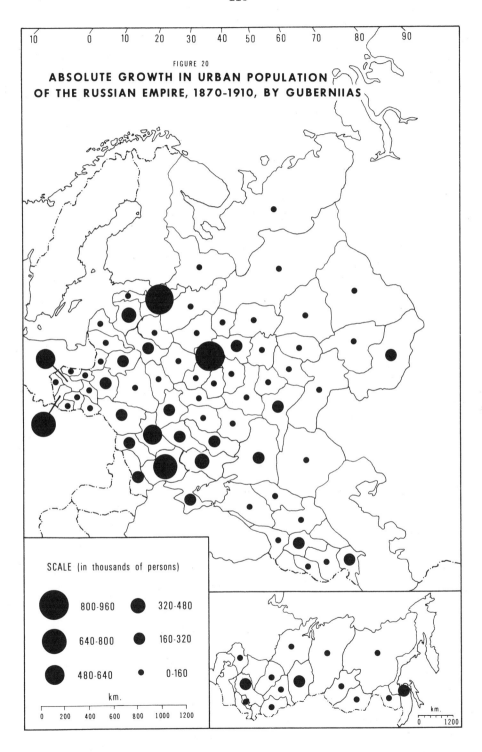

FIGURE 20

**ABSOLUTE GROWTH IN URBAN POPULATION
OF THE RUSSIAN EMPIRE, 1870-1910, BY GUBERNIIAS**

SCALE (in thousands of persons)

800-960   320-480

640-800   160-320

480-640   0-160

km.

0   200   400   600   800   1000   1200

km.

0   1200

CHAPTER VIII

URBAN GROWTH: NATURAL INCREASE AND MIGRATION

Rates of Natural Increase in the Urban Population

Although virtually all of the cities in the Russian Empire
had achieved a positive rate of natural increase by the last
quarter of the 19th century, the contribution to the growth in
the population of the cities from natural increases remained
comparatively small.   Consequently, the large increase in the
urban population that occurred during the post-reform period
was due primarily to mechanical movement, or in-migration.

Table 17 shows the average annual rate of natural increase
in the urban population for European Russia during two periods,
1859-1863 and 1909-1913, and the comparative rates for the rural
population.   For both periods, the rate of natural increase in
rural areas was approximately twice that of the cities.

TABLE 17

BIRTHS, DEATHS, AND NATURAL INCREASE OF THE
URBAN AND RURAL POPULATION IN EUROPEAN
RUSSIA, 1859-1863 AND 1909-1913
(Per 1,000 Inhabitants)

| | 1859-1863 | | | 1909-1913 | | |
	Births	Deaths	Natural Increase	Births	Deaths	Natural Increase
Urban	45.9	38.6	7.3	33.9	25.4	8.5
Rural	50.9	35.8	15.1	44.3	28.0	16.3

Source: A. G. Rashin, Naselenie Rossii za 100 let, p. 245.

rate of the urban population, which exceeded the rural rate at the
time of the reforms, declined by 34 per cent, the very sharp drop
in birth rates, nearly a 45 per cent reduction, contributed to
maintaining a comparatively low rate of natural increase in the
population of the cities. On the other hand, although the death
rate in the countryside also declined significantly, a high rate
of natural increase in the rural population was sustained
throughout the post-reform period because of the comparatively
slow decline in the rural birth rates.

In many of the large cities of the Empire the death rate of
the population remained high following the reforms while the birth
rate declined. Consequently, most of the large cities experienced
natural decreases in their population until towards the end of the
1880's. In St. Petersburg, for instance, a positive natural increase in its population was not registered until 1886. Even then
the rate of natural increase remained low, averaging 4.6 persons
per 1,000 inhabitants for the period 1886-1915.[1] Likewise in Moscow,
only from 1890 was there a definite, though very small, natural increase in the population. The same trends in the rate of natural
increase held true for Kostroma, Saratov, Samara, Nizhnii Novgorod
and many other large cities of the Empire.[2] The persistence of
high death rates in the large cities of the Empire was a testimony
to the arduous life endured by the majority of residents in their
struggle for economic survival and to the notoriously unsanitary
conditions found in many, if not most of the Russian cities at
the time. Nevertheless, the cities of the Empire continued to
attract an ever-increasing stream of migrants who viewed the city
as their main opportunity for improving their economic and social
status.

Urban In-Migration

During the post-reform period, in spite of the continued
restrictions on mobility, a significant amount of internal migration
took place in the Russian Empire. According to data from the 1897
census, nearly 15 per cent, or about 18.4 million persons, of the
total population of the Empire resided in an uezd or city at the

---

[1] Rashin, Naselenie Rossii za 100 let, p. 234.

[2] Ibid., pp. 240-244.

time of the census other than the one in which they were born.[1] Of
this amount, however, only about 42 per cent, or some 7.8 million
persons, chose to migrate to the cities of the Empire, as defined
in the 1897 census.

The distribution of the urban population in 1897 for the major
regions of the Russian Empire according to place of birth is shown
in Table 18. Of the total urban population in 1897 of 16.8 million
persons, slightly less than half, or 46.5 per cent, were not born
in the city in which they were residing. The proportion of native-
born city residents to the total urban population was highest in
Central Asia, nearly 74 per cent. In the long-inhabitated, predominantly Moslem guberniias of Central Asia, such as Fergana, Samarkand,
and Syr-Dar'ia, the growth in the populations of the cities was due
almost entirely to natural increase as in-migrants accounted for
slightly less than 20 per cent of the urban population. On the
other hand, the proportion of urban in-migrants to the total urban
population was highest in Siberia, accounting for 58 per cent of the
urban population. In Primorsk (Maritime) guberniia nearly 90 per
cent of the urban population consisted of new arrivals.

In European Russia urban in-migration was particularly large
in the two capital guberniias. In Moscow guberniia new arrivals
constituted 71 per cent of the urban population, while in St. Petersburg guberniia they constituted 69 per cent of the urban population.[2]
In ten other guberniias in European Russia, located primarily in the
Baltic and Southeastern Steppe regions, over fifty per cent of the
urban population had not been born in the city in which they were
residing at the time of the census.

The migrants who opted for the cities in search of better
economic opportunity were most likely to migrate to another guberniia
and to a large city. Urban in-migration in the Russian Empire was
predominantly inter-guberniia rather than intra-guberniia. Nearly
two-thirds of the total number of urban in-migrants came from another
guberniia, while only one-third moved into a city located in
the same guberniia in which they were born. St. Petersburg and
Moscow were the overwhelmingly preferred destinations of the urban

---

[1] Based on calculations from: Russia. Tsentral'nyi statisticheskii komitet. Pervaia vseobshchaia perepis' naseleniia
Rossiiskoi Imperii 1897 g. Obshchii svod po Imperii rezul'tatov
razrabotki dannykh pervoi vseobshchei perepisi naseleniia,
proizvedennoi 28 ianvaria 1897 goda. I, pp. 84-113.

[2] A. G. Rashin, "Dinamika chislennosti i protsessy formirovaniia gorodskoe naseleniia Rossii v XIX-nachale XX.," p. 71.

TABLE 18

DISTRIBUTION OF THE URBAN POPULATION IN THE RUSSIAN EMPIRE
IN 1897 ACCORDING TO PLACE OF BIRTH
BY MAJOR REGION

Region	Total Urban Population	Natives of the Same Uezd or City		Natives of Another Uezd or City in the Same Guberniia		Natives of Another Guberniia		Natives of Foreign Countries	
		Total	Per Cent	Total	Per Cent	Total	Per Cent	Total	Per Cent
European Russia	12,049,300	6,287,400	52	2,033,600	17	3,645,300	30	83,000	1
Tsarist Poland	2,158,700	1,185,400	55	337,100	16	603,700	28	32.500	2
Caucasus	1,200,200	640,600	53	137,000	11	372,400	31	50,200	4
Siberia	485,900	202,400	42	65,100	13	195,400	40	23,000	5
Central Asia	934,400	687,000	74	33,100	4	190,100	20	24,100	3
Total Empire	16,825,500	9,002,800	54	2,605,900	16	5,007,000	30	212,800	1

Source: Russia. Tsentral'nyi statisticheskii komitet. Pervaia vseobshchaia perepis'
naseleniia Rossiiskoi Imperii 1897 g. Obshchii svod po Imperii rezul'tatov razrabotki
dannykh pervoi vseobshchei perepisi naseleniia proizvedennoi 28 ianvaria 1897 goda,
I, pp. 84-113.

in-migrants. Together these two cities, with almost equal shares, attracted 1,675,000 persons, or about 22 per cent, of the total number of urban in-migrants.[1] Another 24 per cent of the urban in-migrants went to the seventeen other cities in the Empire with more than 100,000 inhabitants.

Although the flow of migration during the post-reform period in the Russian Empire was economically motivated, with people moving to areas having higher standards of living, the growth of manufacturing during this period did not appear to be a particularly strong attraction for migrants. In a study on the nature and pattern of internal migration during the post-reform period by Lewis and Leasure, based on data from the 1897 census, it was found that although migrants in general moved out of rural and urban guberniias into more urbanized and literate ones, they did not necessarily move into more industralized guberniias.[2] This relationship held true particularly for long-distance urban in-migration. The authors found that inter-guberniia urban in-migration was negatively correlated with the proportion of the urban labor force engaged in manufacturing by guberniia and was independent of the level of literacy as well.[3] The authors felt, however, that the inclusion of employment in handicrafts in the proportion of the urban labor force employed in manufacturing biased the data and therefore rendered this finding partially suspect. The finding was consistent, however, with the flow of migrants from the central and western, comparatively more industralized parts of European Russia to the less industrialized eastern and southeastern guberniias of European Russia and Siberia.

Intra-guberniia urban in-migration, on the other hand, was found to be positively correlated with the percentage of the urban labor force employed in manufacturing and with the degree of literacy, although even here the correlation with the former variable was less strong than with the latter one. This finding did tend to confirm, however, that people who lived in close proximity to urban centers migrated to them provided there was relatively more industry and a higher level of literacy.[4] Consequently, it may be concluded from the foregoing evidence that

---

[1] Obshchii svod po Imperii rezul'tatov razrabotki dannykh pervoi vseobshchei perepisi naseleniia, proizvedennoi 28 ianvaria 1897 goda , I, pp. 84-113.

[2] Leasure and Lewis, "Internal Migration in Russia in the Late Nineteenth Century," p. 389.

[3] Ibid., p. 392.

[4] Ibid.

while the growth of manufacturing in many cities attracted a substantial number of persons from the countryside, the employment
opportunities in other fields, especially in commerce and transportation, were equally, if not more attractive forces to migrants
and provided the basis for a large part of the growth in the population of the cities during the post-reform period.

CHAPTER IX

URBANIZATION AND THE GROWTH OF CITIES

Urbanization is one of the most important aspects of societal development in a country. It signals social change on a vast scale and brings about deep and irrevocable changes that alter all sectors of society.[1] The appearance and continuation of urbanization, therefore, is both a confirmation of changes already underway in society as well as an augury of future changes.

Increase in the Number and Size of Cities

Urbanization may be defined in a variety of manners. From a demographic point of view, urbanization can be defined as a tendency towards population concentration and the increase in the number and size of the points of concentration.[2] Urbanization thus conceived represents a societal process resulting in the formation and growth of cities.

One of the most salient features of urban development in the Russian Empire during the 19th century was the rapid growth in the number of large cities and the increasing degree of the concentration of the urban population in the large cities. In 1811 Russia was essentially a country of small provincial centers completely dominated by the two capitals. As shown in Table 19, 57 per cent of the urban population resided in cities with less than 10,000 inhabitants, while the two primate cities, St. Petersburg and Moscow, alone accounted for nearly 19 per cent of the urban population. Intermediate-size cities were weakly developed, with only three cities, Vil'no, Kazan', and Tula, having populations exceeding 50,000 persons, the largest of which was Vil'no with 56,314 inhabitants, and only two other cities, Astrakhan and Riga, having populations exceeding 30,000 inhabitants.[3] By 1910, however, only 11 per cent of the urban population was found in cities with less than 10,000 inhabitants, while the percentage of the urban population

---

[1] Reissman, p. 154.

[2] Tisdale, p. 312.

[3] Karl F. German, _Statisticheskiia issledovaniia otnositel'no Rossiiskoi Imperii. Chast' I. O narodonaselenii_ (S.-Peterburg, 1819), pp. 231-232.

accounted for by the two capital cities, which remained the largest cities in the Empire during the entire period, declined to about 13 per cent. Consequently, during the intervening period there was a substantial filling-in of the urban structure. The number of cities with over 50,000 residents, aside from the two capitals increased from 3 to 87, while the corresponding increase in the share of the urban population found in these cities rose from about 6 per cent to nearly 45 per cent.

In the first half of the period, prior to the reforms of 1861, the growth in the number of intermediate-size cities was the most characteristic feature of the structural pattern of urban growth. The significant expansion of domestic commerce during this period provided a broad basis for the growth of cities, but as long as transportation remained primitive, cities also remained comparatively small and the urban population fairly evenly distributed. Only two cities, St. Petersburg and Moscow, managed to achieve sizeable dimensions. Between 1811 and 1856, as seen again in Table 19, the number of cities with populations between 10,000 and 100,000 inhabitants increased from 34 to 130, while their share of the urban population rose correspondingly from 24 per cent to 44 per cent. The shares of the urban population found in the two extreme size categories declined during this period.

During the post-reform period, however, the importance of small cities in the urban structure became completely overshadowed by the emergence of a significant number of large cities. Between 1856 and 1910 the number of cities with more than 100,000 inhabitants grew from two to thirty, while the share of the urban population found in these cities increased correspondingly from about 17 per cent to nearly 40 per cent. Although the number of smaller cities with populations under 20,000 persons increased slightly from 639 to 698 during the same period, their share of the urban population declined sharply from 59 per cent in 1856 to only 23 per cent by 1910. The process of the concentration of urban growth in a comparatively small number of urban centers was fostered above all by the construction of railroads. The reduction in transport costs that accompanied the advent of the railroads tended to transform a dispersed, ubiquitous pattern of production and exchange into a more concentrated one, while simultaneously making possible a progressive differentiation and selection among sites with superior and inferior resources and accessibility to markets.

TABLE 19

GROWTH IN THE NUMBER AND SIZE OF CITIES AND THE DISTRIBUTION OF THE URBAN POPULATION

ACCORDING TO CITY SIZE,
1811–1910

Year	(City Size According to Number of Inhabitants)							Total Number of Cities
	>1,000,000	999,999–500,000	499,999–100,000	99,999–50,000	49,999–20,000	19,999–10,000	10,000	
	Growth in the Number and Size of Cities							
1811	0	0	2	3	9	22	534	570
1825	0	0	2	0	19	32	571	624
1840	0	0	2	5	26	70	565	668
1856	0	0	3	7	34	89	549	682
1870	0	0	4	12	57	132	608	814
1885	0	2	11	23	93	164	602	895
1897	2	1	15	36	113	177	574	918
1910	2	3	25	59	145	206	492	932
	Distribution of the Urban Population According to City Size in Per Cent							
1811	0	0	19	6	8	10	57	2,780,337
1825	0	0	20	0	16	12	52	3,474,939
1840	0	0	17	6	17	19	42	4,901,122
1856	0	0	17	7	17	20	39	5,768,201
1870	0	8	11	10	20	21	31	8,920,841
1885	0	12	15	11	22	18	22	13,003,810
1897	14	4	15	14	20	15	19	16,885,219
1910	13	8	19	18	19	12	11	23,553,583

Source: Based on data in Appendix I.

Increase in the Proportion of the Total Population Residing in Cities

Urbanization may also be viewed as a structural change affecting the patterning of the population and of its economic activities within a given territorial framework.[1] Urbanization in this sense normally signals the movement of people out of agricultural communities and occupations into other, generally larger non-agricultural communities and occupations. Consequently, a change in the urban population viewed in relation to a change in the rural population provides a meaningful index of societal development.

Viewed in the context of structural change, the urbanization of Russian society proceeded very slowly. The per cent of the population residing in the cities of the Russian Empire increased from 6.4 per cent in 1811 to only 14.7 per cent in 1910. Moreover, there appeared to be little variation in the rate of increase in the degree of urbanization over the entire period.

The levels and changes in the levels of urbanization in the Russian Empire and its major parts between 1811 and 1910 are shown in Table 20. Because of the comparative instability of the internal boundaries in the pre-reform and reform periods, and the inadequacy of data for the earlier period, including the non-simultaneous enumeration of the urban and total populations, an analysis of the regional pattern of urbanization is precluded. The table does show, however, that for the entire pre-reform period the level of urbanization in the Russian Empire rose by only 2.6 percentage points, from 6.4 to 9.0 per cent. An indication of the temporal variation in the pattern of urbanization during this period is given by the data for European Russia. A substantial advance in the urbanization of the population of European Russia took place between 1811 and 1840, while in the following period, 1840-1856, coinciding with a period of economic crisis and natural disasters, the level of urbanization remained stationary.

Between 1856 and 1910 the largest increment in the level of urbanization in the Russian Empire took place during the reform period. The per cent of the population residing in cities rose from 9.0 per cent in 1856 to 10.7 per cent in 1870, or by percentage points in 14 years. Undoubtedly, the annexation of Tsarist Poland,

---

[1]Eric E. Lampard, "The Evolving System of Cities in the United States: Urbanization and Economic Development," Issues in Urban Economics, eds. Harvey S. Perloff and Lowdon Wingo, Jr. (Baltimore: The Johns Hopkins Press, 1968), p. 116.

TABLE 20

TOTAL POPULATION, URBAN POPULATION, AND PER CENT URBAN FOR RUSSIAN EMPIRE AND ITS MAJOR REGIONS
1811-1910

Year	Russian Empire	European Russia	Tsarist Poland	Caucasus	Siberia	Central Asia
1910	160,748,400 23,553,583 (14.7%)	118,690,600 16,641,707 (14.0%)	12,129,200 2,859,684 (23.6%)	11,735,100 1,682,445 (14.3%)	8,220,100 1,008,609 (12.3%)	9,973,400 1,361,138 (13.7%)
1897	125,640,021 16,885,219 (13.4%)	93,442,864 12,278,280 (13.1%)	9,402,253 2,156,181 (22.9%)	9,289,364 1,035,314 (11.2%)	5,758,822 483,683 (8.4%)	7,746,718 931,761 (12.0%)
1885	106,610,814 13,003,810 (12.2%)	81,725,185 9,903,210 (12.1%)	7,960,304 1,437,232 (18.1%)	7,284,547 670,927 (9.2%)	4,313,680 343,344 (8.0%)	5,327,098 649,097 (12.2%)
1870	83,256,132 8,920,841 (10.7%)	65,704,559 7,033,996 (10.7%)	6,026,421 978,322 (16.2%)	4,763,309 448,600 (9.4%)	3,405,084 226,974 (6.7%)	3,356,759 232,949 (6.4%)
1856	63,861,997 5,768,201 (9.0%)	57,602,185 5,277,906 (9.2%)				
1840	-- 4,901,122 -	49,511,000 4,559,069 (9.2%)				
1825	-- 3,474,939 -	-- 3,264,772 -				
1811	43,484,900 2,780,337 (6.4%)	41,505,600 2,669,805 (6.4%)				

Sources: Urban population based on data in Appendix I.
For total population see Sources listed for Figure 4.

which was considerably more urbanized than the rest of the Empire, accounted for part of the size of the figure, but the growth of the cities, as pointed out previously, was very substantial during this period.

During the post-reform period, however, notwithstanding the large increase in the urban population, nearly 15 million persons, and the tremendous surge in industrial growth, the rate of increase in the degree of urbanization remained remarkably stationary at about 0.1 per cent per year: 1.5 per cent in the 15-year period 1870-1885, 1.2 per cent in the 12-year period 1885-1897, and 1.3 per cent in the 13-year period 1897-1910.

Spatial Variations in the Pattern of Urbanization

Regionally, the largest increment in the level of urbanization during the post-reform period took place in Tsarist Poland, 7.4 percentage points. The temporal pattern of the advance in urbanization, however, was very irregular. The greatest advance in the level of urbanization in Poland took place in the period 1885-1897, coinciding with the time of greatest industrial growth in Tsarist Poland, when it rose by 4.8 percentage points. This was the largest single increase in the level of urbanization during any period recorded by any of the major parts of the Empire during the post-reform period. In the last period, 1897-1910, however, urbanization virtually ceased in Tsarist Poland as the proportion of the population residing in cities rose by only 0.7 of a percentage point.

In European Russia, on the other hand, the level of urbanization not only rose the slowest of any major part of the Empire, with the exception of Central Asia, but the rate of increase of urbanization declined slightly during the period. The proportion of the urban population in European Russia increased by 1.4 percentage points between 1870-1885, by 1.0 percentage point between 1885-1897, and by only 0.9 of a percentage point during the last period, 1897-1910. Thus over the entire forty-year period the level of urbanization in European Russia rose by only 3.3 percentage points.

In contrast to the two regions of the Empire treated above, where the rate of urbanization was greatest during the earlier part of the post-reform period, the largest advances in the level of urbanization in the Caucasus and the Asiatic part of the Empire took place in the final period. Between 1897 and 1910 the level of urbanization increased by 3.1 percentage points in the Caucasus,

3.9 points in Siberia, and 1.7 percentage points in Central Asia.
The apparent increase of 5.8 percentage points in the level of
urbanization in Central Asia between 1870 and 1885 was the result
of the inclusion of cities in the 1885 figures which were not included in the 1870 ones.

Although at the national scale the rising levels of technology
and industrialization appeared to have little impact on the rate of
urbanization, with the possible exception of Tsarist Poland, at the
guberniia level a closer association between these factors appears
in several instances. Figure 21 shows the distribution of the increment in the level of urbanization by guberniia between 1870 and
1910. Perhaps the most striking feature of the map is the large
number of guberniias in which the level of urbanization rose very
slightly or even retrogressed. In thirteen guberniias the level of
urbanization actually declined during the post-reform period, while
in another twenty-nine guberniias the level of urbanization rose by
less than two percentage points. These guberniias, for the most
part, were areas where comparatively little commercial or industrial development took place and where the growth of the urban population was outstripped by the natural increases of the rural population, particularly in the western and central guberniias of European Russia, or by the growth of the rural population through in-
migration combined with high rates of natural increase as was true
especially for the eastern and southeastern guberniias of European
Russia.

Significant increases in the level of urbanization were limited
to only several groups of guberniias located primarily in the western part of the Empire. In Piotrków guberniia in Tsarist Poland
the remarkable rise in the level of urbanization, from 17 per cent
in 1870 to 42 per cent in 1910, was clearly associated with the
tremendous growth in industry, especially textiles, that took place
during the post-reform period. Also very significant was the sizeable increment in the level of urbanization, more than 10 percentage points, in the three Baltic guberniias. Substantial growth of
industry and commerce, particularly foreign commerce, which fostered a rapid growth in the urban population, together with low
rates of natural increase in the rural population, the lowest in
the Empire, contributed to the marked rise in the level of urbanization in these three guberniias.

In the central part of European Russia the proportion of the
population residing in cities increased noticeably in only three
guberniias. In Moscow guberniia the tremendous growth of industry

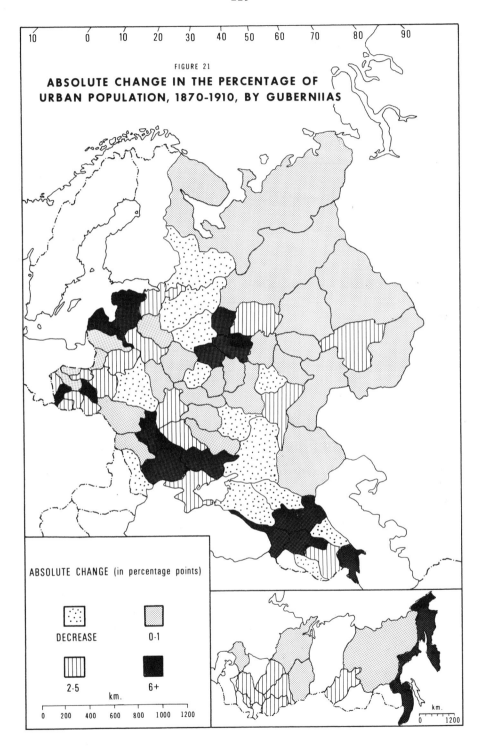

FIGURE 21

**ABSOLUTE CHANGE IN THE PERCENTAGE OF
URBAN POPULATION, 1870-1910, BY GUBERNIIAS**

ABSOLUTE CHANGE (in percentage points)

DECREASE   0-1

2-5   6+

km.

0   200   400   600   800   1000   1200

km.

0   1200

and commerce accounted for an increment in the level of urbanization of more than 10 percentage points. In Vladimir guberniia
industrial growth in the cities tended to attract a slightly greater proportion of the population, while in Iaroslavl' guberniia
rural out-migration coupled with some industrial growth in the
cities accounted for the rise in its level of urbanization.

In the south the expansion of domestic commerce in Kiev
guberniia and of foreign commerce in Kherson guberniia, particularly in Odessa, accounted for the advances in urbanization in
these two guberniias, while the increased urbanization of the
population of Ekaterinoslav guberniia was associated with the
rapid growth of the metallurgical industry in the Donbas. Of the
three guberniias, the largest increment in urbanization, 7.2 percentage points, took place in Kherson guberniia.

In the Caucasus the development of the petroleum industry
in Baku and, to a lesser extent, in Terek guberniia, together
with the growing commercial significance of the port cities along
the Black Sea coast promoted the growth of the urban population in
relation to the rural. The rapid growth of the city of Tiflis,
based primarily on commerce, was the sole factor responsible for
the rise in the level of urbanization in its guberniia.

The largest increments in the level of urbanization took place
in the guberniias located in the far southeastern part of Siberia,
bordering on China and the Pacific Ocean. The proportionately
greater increase in the urban population of these largely unpopulated guberniias was due primarily to the growth of a few cities
based on their strategical and military significance.

The pattern of the territorial variation in the levels of
urbanization by guberniia for 1910 is shown in Figure 22. Perhaps
the most salient feature of the pattern is the peripheral location
of the more highly urbanized guberniias. Of the fourteen guberniias with more than 20 per cent of their populations residing in
cities, only Moscow guberniia was not situated in the margins of
the Empire. This pattern would tend to suggest that the processes
of economic development proceeded more rapidly in those areas that
were readily accessible to the flow of international commerce and
modern technology on the Baltic or Black Seas and in Poland, and
were least constrained by the structure of the old social order.
In the Far East the weakness of the rural sector was doubtless a
factor in the high percentage of urban population. Intermediate
levels of urbanization predominated in the guberniias located in
the western part of European Russia, Tsarist Poland, and in Central

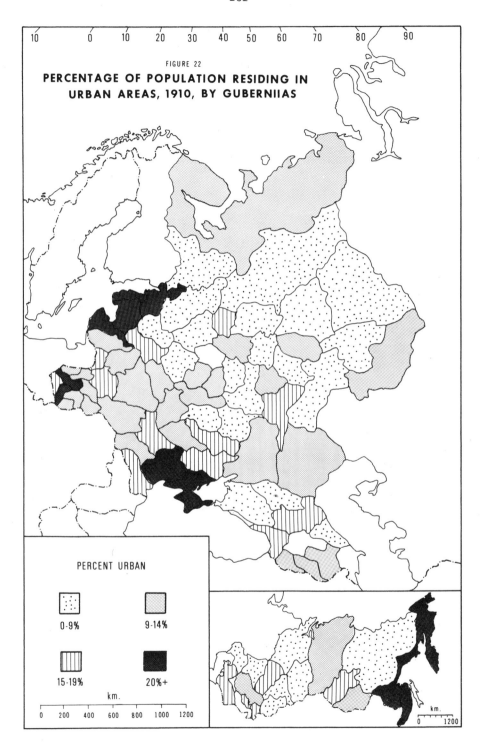

FIGURE 22

PERCENTAGE OF POPULATION RESIDING IN
URBAN AREAS, 1910, BY GUBERNIIAS

PERCENT URBAN

0-9%   9-14%

15-19%   20%+

km.

0   200   400   600   800   1000   1200

km.

0   1200

TABLE 21

COMPARATIVE GROWTH OF THE URBAN AND RURAL
POPULATION IN THE RUSSIAN EMPIRE,
1811-1856, 1870-1910, AND 1811-1910

Population	Per Cent Increase	Average Annual Per Cent Increase	Absolute Increase
		1811-1856	
Urban	108	1.6	2,987,864
Rural	43	0.8	17,389,864
		1870-1910	
Urban	164	2.5	14,632,742
Rural	85	1.5	62,859,526
		1811-1910	
Urban	747	2.2	20,773,246
Rural	233	1.3	95,990,254

TABLE 22

GROWTH RATES OF THE URBAN AND RURAL
POPULATION DURING THE POST-REFORM PERIOD
1870-1910

Population	Average Annual Per Cent Increase		
	1870-1885	1885-1897	1897-1910
Urban	2.5	2.2	2.6
Rural	1.5	1.3	1.8

Asia. Although predominantly agricultural, these regions possessed
a strong urban tradition with many of the cities pre-dating the
formation of the modern Russian state. The guberniias with the
lowest levels of urbanization, less than 9 per cent urban, were
situated primarily in the northern part of the Empire and in the
eastern part of European Russia. These regions were the least
accessible to the impulses of modernization. Constrained by the
marginality of agriculture, as in the northern guberniias, by the
deterioration of agriculture and the rigidity of the social system,
as in the southcentral region, or by the availability of land for
colonization as in the eastern part of European Russia, the cities
had a weak economic basis for growth.

Growth of the Urban Population Relative to the Rural Population

In view of the foregoing, the question naturally arises as
to why, in contrast to the pattern of economic and social development in the West, did the urban and industrial growth which took
place in the Russian Empire during the 19th century, especially
in the latter part, have so little impact on the level of urbanization? Since the urban population of the Russian Empire grew at
relatively high rates, comparable to and even greater than the
rates of urban growth in Western Europe, then part of the explanation must lie in the rapid growth of the rural population, and
equally important, in the barriers, legal and otherwise, to the
movement of population out of the countryside and into the cities.

The average annual gain in the urban population of the Empire,
as shown in Table 21, rose significantly from 1.6 per cent in the
pre-reform period to 2.5 per cent in the post-reform period. For
the entire ninety-nine-year period the urban population increased
at an average rate of 2.2 per cent per year. In comparison, in
nine European countries during their period of fastest urban population growth, mostly in the latter half of the 19th century, the
average annual rate of increase was 2.1 per cent.[1] On the other
hand, while the rate of rural population growth declined in most
European countries during the 19th century, and in several cases,
the rural population declined absolutely, in the Russian Empire
the rate of growth actually increased substantially, resulting in
a tremendous increment in the absolute number of the rural population. Whereas the rural population during the initial forty-five

---

[1]Kingsley Davis, "The Urbanization of the Human Population,"
Scientific American, CCXIII (September, 1965), p. 49.

years of the study, 1811-1856, increased at an average annual rate
of 0.8 per cent, the rate of growth was nearly twice as large, or
1.5 per cent, during the last forty years of the study, 1870-1910.
For the entire period the rural population grew at an average rate
of 1.3 per cent per year. The very sizeable increment in the rate
of rural population growth, consequently, was a fundamental factor
accounting for the very slow rise in the level of urbanization,
especially during the post-reform period. As Table 22 shows, the
difference between the urban and rural rates of growth, instead
of widening, actually diminished slightly. Between 1870 and 1910,
the rate of growth in the rural population increased from an
average of 1.5 per cent per year during the initial period 1870-1885
to 1.8 per cent during the last period 1897-1910, while on the
other hand, the corresponding increase in the annual rate of urban
growth rose only from 2.5 per cent between 1870 and 1885 to 2.6
per cent between 1897-1910.

For the entire period of study 1811-1910, while the urban
population increased 7.5 times, or by nearly 21 million persons,
the rural population increased by only 2.3 times, but this increase
represented a net addition to the rural population of nearly 96
million persons. Consequently, the absolute growth in the rural
population was so great that it retarded the growth in the proportion of the urban population.

Impediments to Rural Out-Migration

The tremendous growth of the rural population during the 19th
century was a function of the increasingly larger excesses of
births over deaths and of the barriers erected primarily by the
state that severely restricted movement out of the countryside
and into the cities. The principal barrier to movement was, of
course, the institution of serfdom. Promoted by the state in order
to guarantee a cheap labor force for its new class of servitors,
serfdom was confirmed as a legal institution with the publication
of the Sobornoe Ulozhenie, or the Assembly Code of 1649.[1] Under
its provisions, which continued to govern the relationships between
lord and serf, with few exceptions, until the Emancipation of 1861,
the seignorial peasantry, or those peasants who rented land under
contract from the upper classes, were deprived of the right to free
movement and were permanently bound to their seigniors. Besides

---

[1] Blum, p. 262.

the loss of their ability to move, save at the will of their masters,
the peasants were also deprived of their legal competence and stripped
of their right to full ownership of personal property. In essence,
the peasants became the chatel of their masters to do with as they
pleased.

Not all peasants, however, became seignorial serfs; many had
managed to remain free toilers of the soil. But during the 18th
century, particularly under Peter the Great and Catherine II, nearly
all of the remaining peasants who were not privately-owned serfs,
became bound to the state. The state peasantry received legal confirmation under Peter the Great. In his determination to ensure
that none of his subjects would escape performing duties to the
state, Peter formed the core of the state peasantry through a series
of decrees that imposed taxes, quitrents, and military conscription
upon one after another group of formally free peasants. In 1724
these newly obligated-to-the-state peasants were collectively referred to for the first time as "state peasants".[1] This category
of serfs, or actually state peasants, was enlarged by Peter's successors, particularly Catherine II, who incorporated the ecclesias-
tical serfs upon secularization of church lands in 1764, certain
types of peasants from the annexed territories of Poland and Turkey,
and various other groups of peasants who for one reason or another
came to live on state lands. By the time of the emancipation,
through administrative additions and natural increase, the state
peasants came to outnumber slightly the seignorial serfs.[2]

Once incorporated into the state peasantry, these various
groups of peasants tended to lose most of their former rights and
privileges, including the right to permanently change their place
of residence.[3] Similar to serfs, the state peasants were required
to obtain passports from the local civil authorities before they
could temporarily leave their district. These permits were usually
granted for only a limited period of time and then had to be renewed.
As a class, however, the state peasants tended to be slightly better
off economically and possessed considerably more freedom than the
privately owned serfs. Towards the end of the 18th century and

---

[1]Ibid., p. 475.

[2]Tsentral'nyi statistecheskii komitet. Statisticheskiia
tablitsy Rossiiskoi Imperii. Vypusk 2. Nalichnoe Naselenie Imperii
za 1858 god, p. 306. According to figures presented for 1858, there
were 27,397,289 state peasants, 22,846,054 proprietary serfs, and
2,072,285 independent peasants.

[3]Blum, p. 476.

during the first half of the 19th century the state moved to ease some of the restrictions on their personal freedom, including allowing them the right to own property, to engage in trade and industry, and even to gain permanent residence in the cities. These few concessions to the state peasantry, important as they were in the context of the period, should not, however, obscure the fact that the overwhelming majority of state peasants together with virtually all of the proprietary serfs remained rigidly secured to the villages. Movement to the cities, and especially the establishment of permanent residency, remained difficult for the state peasants and virtually impossible for the privately owned serfs.

While the Emancipation of 1861 represented a genuine advance in the legal and social status of the peasantry, it did not greatly alter the immobility of the overwhelming majority of the peasantry. Although the extremely unfavorable conditions of the emancipation imposed upon the peasantry, especially the inadequacy of the land allotments and the heavy financial obligations, created a potential situation in which many peasants might have abandoned agriculture and moved to the cities, the state's preservation and strengening of the role obshchina, or village commune, and its administrative counterpart, the mir, prevented a massive exodus out of the countryside from materializing.

The social and legal foundations of the mir rested on the principle of collective responsibility.[1] The mir was made responsible to the state for the payment of the redemption debt on land alloted to the village communes and for the collection and payment of taxes. Since these obligations were apportioned among the members of the commune on an egalitarian basis, departure of one or more members before their obligations were fulfilled meant that a greater burden fell upon the others. Consequently, while permanent departures were possible, they remained very difficult. Before a peasant could leave the mir he had to waive all rights to a share in the communal lands, to discharge all tax payments, and to secure the permission of his parents as well as from the mir.[2] Furthermore, even temporary absences from the village were difficult. Travel outside of one's district required a passport which was obtainable only with the consent of the mir and the head of the household. The regulations governing the system of passports

---

[1] Robinson, p. 67.

[2] Gerschenkron, "Russia: Agrarian Policies and Industrialization, 1861-1914," p. 194.

underwent little change until 1894, when most of the restrictions on the granting of passports were relaxed and the time limitation on the validity of a passport was extended from one to five years.[1] Consequently, although the act of emancipation allowed a greater volume of migration from the countryside into the cities than was possible under serfdom, it was not nearly enough to relieve the mounting additions in the rural population due to natural increase. Only with the Stolypin reforms of 1906 were the peasants finally granted the right to leave the countryside virtually unimpeded.

---

[1] Ibid., p. 196.

CHAPTER X

INDUSTRIAL DEVELOPMENT AND THE RUSSIAN CITY:
AN INTERPRETATION

The prevention of the movement of the peasants from the land
into the cities, effected by serfdom and later by the character of
the emancipation, had a profound impact on the nature and pattern of
industrial growth in the Russian Empire. Although other factors
played important roles, it was primarily the containment in the
countryside of the growth in the rural population that fostered the
emergence and expansion of industrial activity in rural localities
at the expense of the urban centers. Consequently, in the economic
development of the Russian Empire, especially during the 19th century, the cities, for the most part, did not evolve into the organizational centers of industrialization as they did in the West.

Certainly, industry was to be found in many cities, and its
expansion, particularly in the latter decades of the 19th century,
did become an important factor in the growth of a number of cities.
Some of the larger cities, like St. Petersburg, Moscow, Riga, Łodź,
and Ivanovo, even acquired an industrial character by the end of the
century. Nevertheless, because of the institutional barriers to
movement out of the countryside and also to the perpetuation of
conditions in the cities which were inimical to the attraction of
industrial activity, industry remained strongly attached to the
rural environment. The development of industry in the countryside,
in turn, also contributed to the slow progression in the levels of
urbanization since the creation of non-agricultural employment
opportunities in the countryside mitigated the need and the desire
of the peasantry to migrate to the cities.

In 1897 there were 4,224,130 persons occupied in manufacturing of all kinds in the Russian Empire, representing about 13 per cent of the population having a means of livelihood.[1] Of the total number of persons occupied in manufacturing, however, less than half, or about 48 per cent, were located in the cities of the Empire.

The proportion of those occupied in manufacturing located in the cities varied considerably according to guberniia as shown in Table 23. Seventy-two guberniias had more than 10,000 persons occupied in manufacturing; in only nineteen of them did the number occupied in manufacturing in the cities exceed the number so occupied in the countryside. In only three guberniias, St. Petersburg, Warsaw, and Kherson, did the cities account for more than 70 per cent of the total number of persons occupied in manufacturing in the guberniia.

Among the more industrialized guberniias several interesting contrasts appear in the proportion of the labor force in cities. The urban labor force in manufacturing in Moscow and St. Petersburg guberniias was nearly equal and the highest of any guberniias in the country. Only 57 per cent of those occupied in manufacturing in Moscow guberniia lived in cities, whereas 92 per cent of those occupied in manufacturing in St. Petersburg guberniia lived in cities. In Vladimir and Piotrków guberniias the contrast in the distribution of the labor force was even more interesting since most of the industry in both guberniias was related primarily to textiles. Yet in Vladimir guberniia 68 per cent of those occupied in manufacturing were located in the countryside, while in Piotrków guberniia 66 per cent were concentrated in the cities, particularly Łódź. The predominance of rural industry was also very notable among the more industrialized guberniias such as Perm, Nizhnii Novgorod, Kostroma, and Riazan', where over 75 per cent of those occupied in manufacturing were located outside cities.

The distribution of gainfully occupied in manufacturing also varied according to the type of industry. The more highly urbanized industries, as shown in Table 24, tended to be those which required a specialized skill or craft and catered to a select market-

---

[1] Based on calculations made on occupational data presented in: Tsentral'nyi statisticheskii komitet. Pervaia vseobshchaia perepis' naseleniia Rossiiskoi Imperii 1897 g. Obshchii svod po Imperii rezul'tatov razrabotki dannykh Pervoi vseobshchei perepisi naseleniia, proizvedennoi 28 ianvaria 1897 goda. II. (S.-Peterburg, 1905), pp. 256-325. Also see Appendix II for the occupations included under the category of manufacturing.

TABLE 23

PERSONS OCCUPIED IN MANUFACTURING IN THE RUSSIAN EMPIRE
IN 1897 BY GUBERNIIA AND PER CENT IN EACH GUBERNIIA
LOCATED IN CITIES

	Persons Occupied in Manufacturing			
Guberniia	Total	Per Cent in Cities of the Guberniia	Per Cent of Total for Entire Empire	Per Cent of Total in Cities for Entire Empire
1. Moscow	493,978	57	11.7	13.6
2. St. Petersburg	277,919	92	6.6	12.6
3. Vladimir	165,452	32	3.9	2.6
4. Piotrków	148,577	66	3.5	4.8
5. Warsaw	141,265	71	3.3	4.9
6. Fergana	111,743	54	2.7	2.9
7. Kiev	108,124	44	2.6	2.3
8. Lifliand	102,218	60	2.4	3.0
9. Perm	96,949	21	2.3	1.0
10. Kherson	96,442	76	2.3	3.6
11. Nizhnii Novgorod	79,432	20	1.9	0.8
12. Khar'kov	73,628	58	1.7	2.1
13. Kostroma	71,152	21	1.7	0.7
14. Riazan'	71,095	28	1.7	1.0
15. Voiska Don	68,067	43	1.6	1.4
16. Ekaterino- slav	67,092	43	1.6	1.4
17. Saratov	64,277	48	1.5	1.5
18. Volyniia	64,136	26	1.5	0.8
19. Chernigov	63,635	36	1.5	1.1
20. Podoliia	62 358	24	1.5	0.7
21. Orel	59,881	48	1.4	1.4
22. Tver'	59,796	44	1.4	1.3
23. Grodna	56,721	51	1.3	1.4
24. Viatka	56,349	24	1.3	0.7
25. Iaroslavl'	56,182	48	1.3	1.1
26. Minsk	55,681	40	1.3	1.1
27. Poltava	55,526	46	1.3	1.2
28. Tambov	50,508	40	1.2	1.0
29. Tula	50,043	62	1.2	1.5
30. Kovna	48,104	25	1.1	0.6
31. Vornonezh	48,017	35	1.1	0.8
32. Kursk	47,492	39	1.1	0.9
33. Vil'na	43,713	49	1.0	1.1
34. Kuban	43,387	33	1.0	0.7
35. Samara	41,869	32	1.0	0.7
36. Tavride	41,775	54	1.0	1.1
37. Syr-Dar'ia	41,159	43	1.0	0.9
38. Bessarabia	40,783	47	1.0	0.9
39. Kazan'	39,509	56	0.9	1.1

TABLE 23
(Continued)

PERSONS OCCUPIED IN MANUFACTURING IN THE RUSSIAN EMPIRE
IN 1897 BY GUBERNIIA AND PER CENT IN EACH GUBERNIIA
LOCATED IN CITIES

Guberniia	Persons Occupied in Manufacturing			
	Total	Per Cent in Cities of the Guberniia	Per Cent of Total for Entire Empire	Per Cent of Total in Cities for Entire Empire
40. Kaluga	39,222	30	0.9	0.6
41. Tomsk	36,178	27	0.9	0.5
42. Kurliand	34,689	48	0.8	0.8
43. Vitebsk	34,421	57	0.8	1.0
44. Mogilev	33,668	38	0.8	0.6
45. Kalisz	32,324	46	0.8	0.6
46. Lublin	30,999	35	0.7	0.5
47. Novgorod	30,827	24	0.7	0.4
48. Simbirsk	30,136	29	0.7	0.4
49. Tobol'sk	29,965	29	0.7	0.4
50. Smolensk	29,735	40	0.7	0.6
51. Tiflis	28,820	68	0.7	1.0
52. Ufa	28,027	30	0.7	0.4
53. Penza	26,523	42	0.6	0.5
54. Orenburg	26,043	36	0.6	0.5
55. Estliand	24,885	36	0.6	0.4
56. Baku	24,544	65	0.6	0.8
57. Radom	23,357	37	0.6	0.4
58. Astrakhan'	20,702	55	0.5	0.6
59. Siedlce	19,742	39	0.5	0.4
60. Samarkand	19,551	61	0.5	0.6
61. Vologda	17,637	34	0.4	0.3
62. Elisavetpol'	16,664	48	0.4	0.4
63. Enisei	16,567	30	0.4	0.2
64. Kielce	16,411	31	0.4	0.3
65. Płock	15,409	40	0.4	0.3
66. Łomża	15,406	32	0.4	0.2
67. Kutais	14,334	63	0.3	0.4
68. Irkutsk	13,870	35	0.3	0.2
69. Pskov	13,418	46	0.3	0.3
70. Terek	13,326	53	0.3	0.3
71. Stavropol'	12,913	26	0.3	0.2
72. Suwałki	12,122	35	0.3	0.2
73. Dagestan	8,603	20	0.2	0.1
74. Arkhangel'sk	8,545	33	0.2	0.1
75. Semirech'e	7,650	32	0.2	0.1
76. Erivan	6,792	77	0.2	0.3
77. Olonets	6,468	31	0.2	0.1
78. Zabaikal	6,385	31	0.1	0.1
79. Akmolinsk	6,253	66	0.1	0.2
80. Zakaspiisk	5,789	43	0.1	0.1
81. Ural'sk	5,869	52	0.1	0.2
82. Primorsk	5,444	63	0.1	0.2
83. Semipala-tinsk	4,052	54	0.1	0.1

TABLE 23
(continued)

PERSONS OCCUPIED IN MANUFACTURING IN THE RUSSIAN EMPIRE
IN 1897 BY GUBERNIIA AND PER CENT IN EACH GUBERNIIA
LOCATED IN CITIES

Guberniia	Persons Occupied in Manufacturing			
	Total	Per Cent in Cities of the Guberniia	Per Cent of Total Employment for Entire Empire	Per Cent of Employment in Cities for Entire Empire
84. Chernomorsk	3,744	38	0.1	0.1
85. Amur	3,187	74	0.1	0.1
86. Kars	1,810	63	–	–
87. Yakutsk	1,560	22	–	–
88. Turgai	843	57	–	–
Total	4,229,463	48	100.0	100.0

Source: Tsentral'nyi statisticheskii komitet. Pervaia
vseobshchaia perepis' naseleniia Rossiiskoi
Imperii 1897 g. Volumes 1-89 (S.-Peterburg,1899-
1904). Also see Appendix II for the occupations
included under manufacturing in 1897.

the literate, cultured, and wealthy stratum of Russian society.
On the other hand, those manufacturing industries requiring comparatively less highly skilled workers or close proximity to raw
materials were frequently located in rural areas.   These rural
industries included such highly mechanized concerns as the textile
industry where, for instance, many phases of production underwent
a significant technological transformation while remaining a rural
industry with close to 65 per cent of the 960,000 persons occupied
in processing fibrous materials being found in the countryside.
The garment industry which accounted for slightly more than one-
fourth of the total employment in manufacturing in the Empire,
occupied an intermediate position in regards to both the location
of its labor force and the nature of its productive technique.
The slightly larger proportion of the gainfully occupied in this
industry accounted for by the cities was attributable to a greater
demand on the part of the urban population for ready-to-wear
clothes.   Yet this industry, because of the relatively high degree
of the division of labor attained in the manufacturing process
and the comparative unimportance of mechanical or power equipment,
remained closely associated with handicraft forms of production.
Consequently, the data on the distribution of the labor force tend
to suggest that the more modern forms of manufacturing did not
necessarily gravitate to the cities of the Empire.

Although manufacturing of all types, including handicraft
production, became the single largest source of employment in the
cities by the end of the century it by no means dominated the
occupational structure of the urban population.   As shown in Table
25, manufacturing represented only one-fourth of the gainfully
occupied population in the cities in 1897.   Nearly 20 per cent of
the urban labor force found employment, often very temporary, in
such capacities as unskilled laborers, day laborers, and domestics,
while nearly 12 per cent were involved in trade and commerce.
Attesting to the political significance of cities in Russia, 10.6
per cent of the gainfully occupied population were members of the
armed forces while an additional 2.6 per cent were employed in
civil administration.

Within the manufacturing sector of the urban economy, employment was concentrated primarily in three industries.   The garment
industry alone, as shown in Table 26, accounted for nearly 32 per
cent of those occupied in manufacturing.   A distant second was the
textile industry with about 17 per cent of the labor force,
followed by the metal-working industry with 14 per cent.   Together

TABLE 24

PERSONS OCCUPIED IN MANUFACTURING IN THE RUSSIAN
EMPIRE IN 1897 BY TYPE OF MANUFACTURING
AND LOCATION IN CITIES

Type of Manufacturing	Number Occupied	Number in Cities	Per Cent in Cities
Tobacco and Related Products	31,485	29,728	94.4
Printing	82,397	71,500	86.8
Instruments (Physical, Optical, Surgical), Watches, etc.	23,391	17,988	76.9
Jewelry, Painting, Articles of Luxury, Culture, etc.	54,570	41,651	76.3
Manufacture of Carriages, Construction of Wooden Vessels	14,400	8,698	62.5
Production of Chemicals and Related Products	76,869	43,180	65.2
Preparation of Garments	1,158,865	645,180	55.7
Processing of Animal Products	154,221	76,340	49.5
Distillation, Brewing and Related Products	57,225	27,860	48.9
Processing of Metals	624,954	294,929	47.2
Processing of Vegetable and Animal Food Products	343,794	159,690	46.5
Processing of Wood	410,126	188,462	45.9
Processing of Fibrous Materials	959,584	341,382	35.6
Processing of Mineral Matter (Ceramics)	125,781	31,645	25.2
Not Included in Above or Undetermined	106,468	66,508	62.5
Total All Types of Manufacturing	4,224,130	2,044,741	48.4

Source: Tsentral'nyi statisticheskii komitet. Pervaia
vseobshchaiu perepis' naseleniia Rossiiskoi
Imperii 1897 g. Obshchii svod po Imperii rezul'
tatov razrabotki dannykh Pervoi vseobshchei
perepisi naseleniia, proizvednnoi 28 ianvaria
1897 goda, II (s.-Peterburg, 1905), pp. 256-
295.

these three industries employed about 62 per cent of all persons gainfully occupied in manufacturing in the cities.

Although the importance of manufacturing in the urban economy grew steadily during the 19th century, only a comparatively small number of cities acquired a predominantly industrial character by the end of the century. According to the data on occupation from the 1897 census, of the 334 cities in the Russian Empire containing 10,000 or more inhabitants, only 66 cities, or approximately one out of every five, as shown in Table 27, had 30 per cent or more of their gainfully occupied populations employed in manufacturing of all types, and only 33 cities, or about one out of every ten, had more than 40 per cent. Only 11 of the 66 cities with 30 per cent or more of their labor forces employed in manufacturing had populations of 50,000 or more inhabitants.

On the other hand, in only 5 of the 18 cities with 100,000 or more inhabitants and in only 6 of the 36 cities with a population between 50,000 and 100,000 persons, was 30 per cent or more of the labor force occupied in manufacturing. Two-thirds of the total number of cities with 10,000 or more inhabitants fell below the national average of 25 per cent of the gainfully occupied urban population employed in manufacturing.

The distribution of the urban labor force occupied in manufacturing, moreover, was concentrated in relatively few cities. One-fourth of the total number occupied in manufacturing in cities of the Empire were in Moscow and St. Petersburg. In only nine other cities, shown in Table 28, did the number occupied in manufacturing exceed 20,000 persons. These nine cities, together with the two capitals, accounted for nearly 43 per cent of the total urban labor force in manufacturing. In relation to the combined urban and rural population engaged in manufacturing, however, these eleven cities accounted for only about 21 per cent of the nation's manufacturing labor force.

Excluding handicraft industries which were particularly well developed both in the cities and in the countryside and considering only factory industry, the proportion of manufacturing employment found in cities was even smaller. According to the calculations by Pogozhev of factory industry for 1902, only 39 per cent of the 30,914 factories and 41 per cent of the 1,890,938 workers were located in the cities of the Empire.[1]

---

[1] Pogozhev, p. 56.

TABLE 25

OCCUPATIONAL STRUCTURE OF THE URBAN POPULATION
IN THE RUSSIAN EMPIRE IN 1987

Occupational Categories	Total Number of Persons Gainfully Occupied	Per Cent of Total
Administration	206,896	2.6
Armed Forces	861,173	10.6
Religious	96,367	1.2
Liberal Professions	220,689	2.7
Activity and Service as Domestics, Unskilled Labor, Day Labor, etc.	1,579,529	19.5
Income from Fixed Property, Capital, Birth, and Inheritance	401,223	5.0
Income from State, Social, and Private Institutions	337,344	4.2
Agriculture and Related Activity	412,951	5.1
Mining and Smelting	13,740	0.2
Manufacturing	2,044,741	25.2
Construction	281,588	3.5
Transport and Communication	377,519	4.7
Trade and Commerce	1,046,034	12.9
Others	222,501	2.8
Total	8,102,295	100.0
Total Urban Population	16,828,395	

Source: Tsentral'nyi statisticheskii komitet. _Pervaia vseobsh-chaia perepis' naseleniia Rossiiskoi Imperii 1897 g. Obshchii svod po Imperii rezul'tatov razrabotki dannykh Pervoi vseobshchei perepisi naseleniia, poizvedennoi 28 ianvaria 1897 goda_, II (S.-Peterberg, 1905), pp. 256-295. Also see Appendix II for the occupations included under each category.

TABLE 26

OCCUPATIONAL STRUCTURE IN MANUFACTURING
OF THE URBAN POPULATION IN 1897

Type of Manufacturing	Number Employed	Per Cent of Total
Preparation of Garments	645,180	31.6
Processing of Fibrous Materials	341,382	16.7
Processing of Metals	294,929	14.4
Processing of Wood	188,462	9.2
Processing of Vegetable and Animal Food Products	159,690	7.8
Processing of Animal Products	76,340	3.7
Printing	71,500	3.5
Production of Chemicals and Related Products	43,180	2.1
Jewelry, Painting, Articles of Luxury, Culture,	41,651	2.0
Processing of Mineral Matter (Ceramics)	31,645	1.5
Tobacco and Related Products	29,728	1.5
Distillation, Brewing, and Related Products	27,860	1.4
Instruments, (Physical, Optical, Surgical), Watches, etc.	17,988	0.9
Manufacture of Carriages, Construction of Wooden Vessels	8,698	0.4
Not Included in Above or Undetermined	66,508	3.3
Total All Types of Manufacturing	2,044,741	100.0

Source: Tsentral'nyi statisticheskii komitet. Pervaia
vseobshchaia perepis' naseleniia Rossiikoi Imperii 1897
g. Obshchii svod po Imperii rezul'tatov razrabotke
dannykh Pervoi vseobshchei perepisi naseleniia, proizvedennoi 28 ianvaria 1897 goda, II (S.-Peterburg, 1905),
pp. 256-295.

TABLE 27

DISTRIBUTION OF CITIES WITH ≥10,000 INHABITANTS BY SIZE
OF POPULATION AND PER CENT OF GAINFULLY OCCUPIED
POPULATION EMPLOYED IN MANUFACTURING IN 1897

	Number of Cities (City Size According to Number of Inhabitants)						
Per Cent of Gainfully Occupied Population Employed in Manufacturing	10,000–19,999	20,000–49,999	50,000–99,999	100,000–499,999	500,000–999,999	≥1,000,000	Total
<10	10	5	0	0	0	0	15
10–14	31	21	2	0	0	0	54
15–19	38	26	10	3	0	0	77
20–24	34	26	16	5	0	0	81
25–29	24	10	2	4	1	0	41
30–34	11	9	0	1	0	1	22
35–39	4	5	3	0	0	1	13
40–44	2	4	0	0	0	0	6
45–49	3	4	0	1	0	0	8
≥50	10	3	3	1	0	0	17
Total	167	113	36	15	1	2	334

Source: Tsentral'nyi statisticheskii komitet. Pervaia vseobshchaia perepis' naselennia Rossiiskoi Imperii 1897 g. Volumes 1–89 (S.-Peterburg, 1899–1904).

TABLE 28

CITIES IN THE RUSSIAN EMPIRE WITH MORE THAN
20,000 PERSONS OCCUPIED IN MANUFACTURING
IN 1897

City	Number Occupied in Manufacturing
Moscow	256,803
St. Petersburg	242,948
Warsaw	87,327
Łódź	67,387
Riga	50,655
Odessa	42,919
Kiev	28,402
Tula	26,073
Khar'kov	24,425
Ivanovo-Voznesensk	22,690
Kokand	21,067
Total	870,696
Total in All Cities of Empire	2,044,741
Total Empire	4,224,741

Source: Tsentral'nyi statisticheskii komitet.
Pervaia vseobshchaia perepis' naseleniia
Rossiiskoi Imperii 1897 g. Volumes 1-89
(S.-Peterburg, 1899-1904).

Even more striking was the dispersal of large-scale factory industry outside of the cities. As shown in Table 28, for factories employing 50 or more persons, as the size of the factory increased, the proportion of the number of factories and employment located in cities declined. Thus the percentage of factories located in cities declined from 54 per cent for those employing between 50 and 99 workers to only 38 per cent of the very largest factories, those employing 1,000 or more workers. The percentage of total employment located in cities declined from 54 per cent for factories employing 50-99 workers, to 44 per cent for factories employing 100-499 workers, to 41 per cent for factories employing 500-999 workers, down to 36 per cent in factories employing more than 1,000 workers. The low index of urban location for the latter category of factories was particularly significant in relation to the over-all distribution of industry since these factories, while numbering only 302, accounted for 710,219 workers, or about 38 per cent of the total factory labor force in the Russian Empire.

While the majority of the employment in factory industry was dispersed in the countryside, the distribution of the urban labor force was largely concentrated in a small number of cities. St. Petersburg and Moscow were by far the largest industrial centers of the Empire, as together they accounted for 30 per cent of the employment in urban-located factories. Only eleven cities, shown in Table 29, had more than 10,000 persons employed in factory industry, but they accounted for 474,200 workers, or nearly 61 per cent of the total urban factory labor force for the entire country. Only twelve other cities had between 5,000 and 10,000 persons employed in factory industry, representing an additional 12 per cent of the urban factory labor force. Thus nearly 73 per cent of the total employment in factories located in cities was concentrated in twenty-three cities. Nevertheless, in relation to the total distribution of factory industry, these twenty-three leading urban industrial centers contained only 30 per cent of the total factory labor force in the Russian Empire.

TABLE 29

DISTRIBUTION OF FACTORY INDUSTRY
BY SIZE CATEGORY AND LOCATION
1902

	Factory Size Category (By Number of Workers)						
	<10	10-49	50-99	100-499	500-999	≥1,000	Total
	Number of Factories						
Total Number of Factories	16,895	8,995	2,098	2,200	424	302	30,914
Number of Factories Located in Cities	5,407	4,156	1,126	1,013	176	115	11,993
Per Cent of Factories Located in Cities	32%	46%	54%	46%	42%	38%	39%
	Total Employment in Factories						
Total Employment	62,006	200,238	143,936	484,968	289,571	710,219	1,890,938
Employment in Cities	20,641	97,359	77,599	215,295	119,393	253,566	783,583
Per Cent of Total Employment in Cities	33%	49%	54%	44%	41%	36%	41%

Source: A. V. Pogozhev, Uchet chíslennosti í sostava rabochikh v
Rossii (S.-Peterburg, 1906), pp. 53-56.

TABLE 30

CITIES IN THE RUSSIAN EMPIRE WITH MORE THAN
5,000 PERSONS EMPLOYED IN FACTORY INDUSTRY
IN 1902

City	Number of Factories	Total Employment
St. Petersburg	488	129,200
Moscow	918	105,300
Łódź	475	62,000
Riga	287	40,000
Warsaw	426	32,900
Baku	179	28,000
Ivanovo-Voznesensk	41	27,100
Odessa	309	15,000
Iaroslavl'	41	13,800
Shuia	30	10,300
Tula	80	10,000
Khar'kov	88	9,400
Rostov-na-Donu	64	9,300
Ekaterinoslav	72	9,000
Egor'evsk	7	9,000
Kostroma	31	7,800
Częstochowa	53	7,600
Vladimir	7	7,600
Kiev	113	7,000
Revel'	34	6,900
Belostok	195	5,600
Astrakhan'	156	5,300
Vitebsk	275	5,300
Total		564,000
Total in All Cities of Empire		783,583
Total Empire		1,890,938

Source: A. V. Pogozhev, Uchet chislennosti i sostava rabochikh
v Rossii (S.-Peterburg, 1906), pp. 63-64.

The Legacy of Political Impotence

The inability of the cities to forge for themselves a greater role in the industrial development of the Empire was above all a reflection of their historically weak political position. The political development of cities in Russia suffered a severe set-back in the 13th century with the Mongol invasion. The Mongols laid waste to many flourishing cities and deprived others of their independence. Following the decline of Mongol suzerainty in the latter part of the 14th century, the cities for the most part were unable to regain their former status. As the Mongol yoke was lifted that of the Moscovite princes was imposed upon them. By the end of the 16th century even the most powerful Russian cities like Novgorod, Pskov, Suzdal', Tver', Kazan', and Astrakhan', "had lost any semblance of anti-princely power, and in most cases had taken from them the institution which symbolized their independence, the _veche_ or town council."[1] Thus as the power and dominion of the Moscow principality expanded from the 15th century onward, the cities were simultaneously reduced to servile, voiceless, and powerless instruments of the state. Incapable of asserting or even protecting their interests, the cities were unable to nurture the formation of a forceful and enterprising bourgeoisie or to attract sufficient reserves of labor to be able to provide the basis for the establishment and growth of industry.

In its early history the Russian city developed along a path similar to the city in Western Europe. Settlements of merchants and craftsmen, or _posady_, sprang up around the fortified seat of authority, the _detinets_, also referred to as the _kremlin_, and in time walls were also erected around the _posady_ for security and protection.[2] But the similarity of development ended here.

In Western Europe the market place and the public square eventually became one as the _faubourg_ of the merchants merged with, and often absorbed the _bourg_ of the lord or bishop. As the growth of the city proceeded the walls of the fortified noble or episcopal _bourg_ became useless artifacts of the feudal age and frequently were dismantled to provide space for new streets and residences.

---

[1]C. M. Foust, "Russian Expansion to the East Through the Eighteenth Century," _Journal of Economic History,_ XX (1961), p. 470.

[2]M. Tikhomirov, _The Towns of Ancient Rus_, translated from the second Russian edition by T. Sdobnikov (Moscow: Foreign Languages Publishing House, 1959), pp. 44-52.

In Russia, on the other hand, the _posad_, rather than merging with the _kremlin_, became its prisoner. Though the walls of the _posad_ might crumble with the passage of time, "never were the walls of the _kremlin_, that symbol of the authority of the state, allowed to fall into disrepair."[1]

The urban estates, like all other classes in Russian society, became subservient to the state. They were obligated to perform "loyal service" to the state and in return they were bestowed with certain commercial and industrial privileges.[2] The activity of the urban estates in these spheres, however, remained closely regulated by the state and seldom were they able to exceed, yet alone expand, the limits established by the state. The all-encompassing power of the Russian autocracy effectively stifled personal initiative and suffocated individual and class freedom in the cities.[3] Consequently, unlike Western Europe, where the development of urban society was substantially altered, "when the merchant became leader . . . ," and ". . . when the superiority of the landowner was eliminated," such a transformation never took place in Russia.[4] The course of the development of urban society in Russia was set not by the initiative and action of its constituent members, but instead, "was determined by the kinds of attitudes which the autocratic power had for state interests."[5] During the 18th century and well into the 19th century these interests tended to reflect and often coincided with those of the landed gentry. The foundations of power and prestige as well as the basis of class distinction continued to remain in Russia birth rather than wealth. The superiority of the landed gentry was never seriously threatened by the urban classes until the very end of the 19th century.

---

[1]Valentine T. Bill, The Forgotten Class: The Russian Bourgeoisie From the Earliest Beginnings to 1900 (New York: Frederick A. Praeger, Publishers, 1959), p. 68.

[2]Miliukov, pp. 231, 234.

[3]Ibid., p. 228.

[4]Robert S. Lopez, "The Crossroads Within the Wall," The Historian and the City, eds. Oscar Handlin and John Burchard (Cambridge, Mass.: The M.I.T. Press, Second Paperback Printing, 1967), pp. 33-34.

[5]I. Ditiatin, Ustroistvo i upravlenie gorodov Rossii, I. Goroda Rossii v XVIII stoletii (Sanktpeterburg, 1875), p. 109.

Urban-Industrial Development under Peter the Great

The appearance of manufacturing on a significant scale in Russia took place during the early part of the 18th century under the aegis of Peter the Great.[1] In his efforts to modernize Russia and at the same time to ensure an adequate and reliable domestic supply of materials needed to equip his armies, Peter promoted, directly and indirectly, the establishment of many industries and factories. Apart from the heavy metallurgical industry, much of the growth in manufacturing that took place in his period was largely concentrated in the cities.[2]

The cities offered certain initial advantages which, in relation to the nature of industrial growth under Peter, made them the preferred sites for the location of manufacturing. The sharp increases in industrial production demanded by Peter were effected through the establishment of comparatively, for Russia at the time, large-scale factories. This process, however, required large sums of capital and the presence of a sufficient supply of labor. Aside from the state, which directly owned many of the factories, most of the capital for the establishment of factories came primarily from members of the merchantry.[3] Since the merchantry by law resided in the cities, it was only natural that many of the merchants who did invest in industrial undertakings preferred to have them located near their place of residence.

An equally perplexing problem in the development of industry was the availability of labor. Until Peter sanctioned the use of serf labor in 1721, most of the factories remained dependent on hired labor. With the simultaneous expansion of serfdom and the military forces on one hand, and the growth of industry on the other, hired labor quickly became a scarce factor of production.[4] Consequently, the cities, by virtue of the presence of the only sufficiently large and readily available source of labor, became attractive sites for the location of industry.[5] Moreover, foreign entrepreneurs and craftsmen, who played an important role in the development of industry, were more easily attracted to the cities. The

---

[1] E. I. Zaozerskaia, Manufaktura pri Petre I (Moskva: Izdatel' stvo Akademii Nauk SSSR), pp. 8-9. According to Zaozerskaia, some 200 factories were established in Russia during Peter's reign.

[2] Ibid., p. 134.

[3] Ibid., pp. 62-65.

[4] Ibid., pp. 128-129.

[5] F. Ia Polianskii, Gorodskoe remeslo i manufaktura v Rossii XVIII v. (Moskva: Izdatel'stvo Moskovskogo Universiteta, 1960), p. 200.

initial advantages for the location of manufacturing enjoyed by the cities, however, were only temporary. Although industrial growth continued to take place in the cities, it was soon over-shadowed by the expansion of industry in the countryside.

Ascendency of the Nobility and the Rise of Estate Industry

The shift in the locational pattern of industrial growth took place within the broader context of the class struggle for political and economic ascendency that intensified following the death of Peter the Great. In this confrontation the state sided with and promoted the interests of the landed gentry at the expense of the urban merchantry. The formation of a coalition of interests between the state and the nobility had a far-reaching impact on the subsequent pattern of Russian economic development. In contrast to the West, where the development of industry was achieved under the initiative and direction of the urban class, in Russia the state never allowed an urban bourgeoisie to fully materialize.[1] The impulse for industrial growth, instead, emanated primarily from the landed feudal aristocracy, the peasantry, and in the final analysis the state itself.

In return for the backing of the state, the gentry were implicitly compelled to assist the state in carrying out its overall policies. One major policy, initiated by Peter the Great and carried on in one fashion or another by his successors, was what may be called the "Westernization" or "modernization" of the Empire. The role of the gentry in this process consisted largely in imitating Western standards. This role, however, among other things involved greatly increased expenditures for the gentry which, in turn, compelled them to seek out new avenues of improving their revenues.[2] To assist the gentry in their quest for larger incomes the state expanded the realm of economic opportunities for them while simultaneously curtailing the range of economic activity for the merchantry.

---

[1]Yves Barel, Le développement économique de la Russie tsariste ("Publications de la Faculté de Droit et des Sciences Economiques de Grenoble: Série Economie du Développement," Vol. 3; Paris: Mouton & Cie, 1968), p. 245.

[2]Arcadius Kahan, "The Costs of 'Westernization' in Russia : The Gentry and the Economy in the Eighteenth Century," Slavic Review, XXV (March, 1966), p. 41.

The most important contribution to the cause of the gentry was in the consolidation and expansion of serfdom. The right to own serfs, aside from the state, had for all practical purposes become the exclusive privilege of the nobility in the 17th century, and, with a brief exception, the general thrust of the state's policy during the 18th century was to strengthen this monopoly. The exception to this policy came during the latter part of the reign of Peter the Great, when the problem of supplying industry, and in particular, the metallurgical industry in the Urals, with an adequate supply of labor became acute. By a decree in 1721 Peter gave the noble as well as the merchant entrepreneur the right to purchase entire villages in order to secure a labor force for their industrial establishments.[1] With this decree, 'the right to own serfs . . . became the key to industrial production," and there subsequently took place a shift from free, hired labor to forced serf labor in the factories of the Empire.[2] The cities, however, derived little direct benefit from the newly bestowed privilege upon the merchantry, since it actually encouraged the merchant entrepreneur to locate his factory in the countryside rather than in the city. The decree did, nevertheless, expand the realm of opportunity for the merchant to participate in industrial development. The merchant's role in this phase of industrial expansion, however, was short-lived, largely because shortly after the death of Peter the Great,the state, under pressure from the gentry, gradually restricted the right of merchants to purchase serfs and in 1762 abolished the right altogether.[3] As a consequence, the prominent position occupied by merchant-owned factories in the structure of Russian industry yielded to the factory of the noble.

While the merchantry was being denied access to serf labor and thus forced to depend on comparatively more expensive hired labor to work their factories, the gentry, seeking to increase their income, turned to the development of manufacturing on their estates. Utilizing the presence of an unpaid, servile labor force on their estates and with the encouragement of the state in the form of guarantying markets for their products or even bestowing upon them industrial monopolies, as in the distillation of spirits, many

[1]Zaozerskaia, p. 135.

[2]Bill, p. 72.

[3]Tugan-Baranovskii, p. 24. In 1798, however, the right was reinstated, but severely restricted. It was abolished again in 1816. Ibid., pp. 67-69.

gentry became directly involved in the establishment of manufacturing on their estates. Gentry-owned enterprises were most prominently represented in the metallurgical, woolen, and distilling industries during the 18th century and sugar beet refining was added to their domain in the 19th century.[1]

Not only did the state facilitate the entry of the gentry into manufacturing, but it also bestowed upon them various privileges to engage in trade, which had traditionally been the exclusive domain of the merchantry. Particularly with the publication of the Customs Statute in 1755, the gentry gained the unlimited right to engage in wholesale and retail trade in the products of their estates and of their peasants.[2] The decree allowed the gentry as well as their peasants to capture a share of the domestic trade, which contributed to the further decline of the merchantry and in the process led to the further deterioration of the economic position of the cities.

Growth of Rural Peasant Industry

In addition to the rise of gentry industry another serious threat to the industrial development of the cities was the growth of the manufacture of commodities in the countryside by peasants for sale on the market, known in Russia as the _kustar_ (handicraft) industry. The impetus to the development of the _kustar_ industry was twofold. On one hand the increasing financial burden placed on the peasantry by the state and the gentry compelled the peasants to seek alternative sources of income other than agriculture. On the other hand, the development of rural peasant industry was promoted by the gentry and the state since both parties benefited through increased tax revenues.

The peasantry, moreover, benefited from a number of economic changes initiated by the government in the latter part of the 18th century in an effort to stimulate industrial expansion. The state, through a series of legal acts, moved to enlarge the sphere of economic freedom by abolishing many of the exclusive privileges, inducements, and regulations which had effectively limited competition and suppressed entrepreneurial initiative. Of particular

---

[1]F. Ia Polianskii, _Ekonomicheskii stroi manufaktury v Rossii XVIII veka_ (Moskva: Izdatel'stvo Akademii Nauk SSSR, 1956), pp. 337-349.

[2]Kahan, pp. 59-60.

importance was a decree promulgated in 1775 which granted the
right, "to one and all . . . , to establish all sorts of mills and
crafts without requiring any permission from higher or lower
authorities."[1]

Although part of the kustar industry evolved from simple
household craft production for personal and estate consumption,
the main route of the development of the kustar industry was the
result of an evolutionary process based upon the development of
large-scale industry.[2]

The initial success of the large factory during the early
part of the 18th century was based on technical know-how rather
than on machinery. Work was done in the factory without the aid
of expensive equipment and tools, but rather by hand. The superiority of the factory thus lay with the possession of particular
skills among the workers. But once the peasants were able to
familiarize themselves with the new technical methods of production, they were able to engage in small-scale manufacturing and
successfully compete with factory production.[3]

The diffusion of the technical skills and know-how into the
countryside followed several paths.[4] The development of the
kustar industry was greatly furthered by the gentry, many of whom
had their serfs trained in various crafts by sending them to work
in urban or rural factories and then assisting them in establishing
various sorts of craft production and small-scale manufacturing on
their estates. In a similar fashion industry was introduced into
the villages by peasants, especially state peasants, returning
from working in the factories. Since the particular skills involved in manufacturing at the time were fairly easily acquired
and the capital requirements to establish a small operation in
the peasant's house or even a small workshop were low, many peasants were able to engage in manufacturing on their own account.
Finally, the kustar industry frequently grew up alongside a factory
established in a rural locality with the workers learning the trade
and entering into production with materials supplied by the factory

---

[1]V. N. Bernadskii, Ocherki iz istorii klassovoi bor'by i
obshchestvenno-politicheskoi mysli Rossii v tret'ei chetverti
XVIII veka ("Leningradskii gosudarstvennyi pedagogicheskii institut
imeni A. I. Gertsena: Uchenyi zapiski," Tom 229; Leningrad, 1962),
p. 87.

[2]Tugan-Baranovskii, pp. 172-174.

[3]Ibid., p. 204.

[4]Ibid., pp. 185-186, 202.

or middlemen. This process was greatly furthered by the growing practice of manufacturers to "farm-out" work at various stages of production to the peasants either for work in their homes or in their workshops. Consequently, a well-developed cottage industry sprang up around many factories in the countryside.

Effects of Peasant Enterprises on the Development of Industry in Cities

The rise of the _kustar_ industry in Russia had serious repercussions on the industrial development of the cities during the 18th century and especially during the first half of the 19th century. The most immediate effect was in the competition for markets. Unlike the gentry-owned industry, which produced primarily for state demands, peasant manufacturing competed directly with the workshops of the urban artisans and the factories of the merchants for the satisfaction of the demands, limited as they were, of the masses for more cheaply produced commodities. Although the peasants were most prominently represented in the textile industries (linen, wool, silk, and especially cotton), they also engaged in metal and wood working, in the production of tallow, soap, candles, leather and fur goods, footwear, and many other commodities. These were essentially the same commodities manufactured in the urban centers, but because the products of the peasants had "the advantage of cheapness which attracts most purchasers,"[1] the _kustar_ industry was not only successful in satisfying the relatively narrow consumption needs of the village market, but was also able to compete with urban manufacturing for the broader and more diverse urban market. Consequently, although the cities remained dependent on the countryside for food supplies, the emergence and rapid growth of the _kustar_ industry hindered the reverse flow of manufactured goods from the cities to the villages from fully developing. By the end of the 18th century the bulk of locally used consumer goods were supplied by rural peasant industries, and their significance in the economy did not decline until after the emancipation.[2]

---

[1] Tugan-Baranovskii, p. 191, quoting a report from the Governor of Kaluga Guberniia to the Minister of Finance in 1835.

[2] Dmitri B. Shimkin, "The Entrepreneur in Tsarist and Soviet Russia," _Explorations in Entrepreneurial History_, II (November, 1949), p. 27.

In addition to industry, the peasants became actively involved in domestic trade. As many of the restrictions on peasant commercial activity were removed or relaxed, the peasants were able to seize a considerable share of domestic trade which was formerly held by the merchants and burghers. The peasants became particularly prominent at the rural markets and fairs, whose role in the commodity circulation of the country was enhanced as the volume of domestic trade increased and as long as the inadequacies of transportation continued to impede the movement of goods over any great distance. The increased significance of rural markets and fairs, in turn, "diminished the commercial importance of the cities."[1] The peasants, moreover, infringed upon the interests of the merchants not only by undermining their position in the countryside, but also by competing directly with them on the urban market. Many of the independent peasant manufacturers frequently undertook the direct marketing of their products in the cities, while other producers sold their products to peasant middlemen-turned-traders and to itinerant peddlars who in turn brought the goods to the cities and fairs for sale.[2]

The increase in the trading activity of the peasantry adversely affected the development of the cities by hindering the process of capital accumulation. The commercial competition of the peasants, by reducing the wealth of the urban merchantry, lessened their potential for investment in industrial enterprise. At the same time the redistribution of wealth brought little benefit to the cities. The merchant wealth that was diminished by the peasant traders, as one observer noted, "cannot be replaced by the latter since most of them belong to the gentry and, since their capital and persons are thus subject to their masters' authority, cannot constitute a real urban population or a stable capitalist group."[3] The capital accumulated by the peasantry was, of course, often skimmed off by their masters who preferred to spend it on the amenities of life rather than saving and investing it in productive undertakings.

Impediments to Industrial Development in the Cities

Aside from the immediate effects on urban economic development, the growth of the kustar industry in the latter part of the 18th

---

[1]Bernadskii, p. 69.

[2]Blum, pp. 290-291.

[3]Sbornik svedenii po vedomstvu ministerstva finansov (No. 3, 1865), quoted in Tugan-Baranovskii, p. 181, footnote 16.

century and during the 19th century provided an infrastructure from which much of the subsequent growth in industry took place. The training and experience acquired in kustar industries provided Russia with a new generation of industrial entrepreneurs and formed a cadre of workers possessing the necessary skills and work habits suitable for the development of modern capitalist factory industry.[1]

Lack of Entrepreneurial Talent

One of the major obstacles in the path of industrial development in the cities was a dearth of entrepreneurial talent. The entrepreneurial role of the merchantry, which was so prominent in the early phases of industrial development during the 18th century, gave way in the 19th century to a new generation of industrial entrepreneurs who emerged primarily from the ranks of the peasantry.[2] The rise of the kustar industry provided the opportunity for many peasants to acquire the skills and business acumen necessary to successfully compete in the emerging capitalist system and the state and the gentry allowed them sufficient freedom within limits to apply their newly acquired talents to the development of industry. The cities, however, were unable to reap the full economic benefits from this development since these new peasant entrepreneurs were for the most part unable to leave the countryside because of serfdom and, at the same time, were denied ready access to participate fully in urban life by the restrictions regulating membership in the urban estate.[3] Consequently, they were forced to exercise their entrepreneurial talents in the countryside.

Although the prevalent form of peasant entrepreneurship, handicraft and small-scale enterprise, increasingly succumbed to the competition from the emergence of modern, large-scale, capitalist factory production, many of these peasant entrepreneurs played an important role in the transition from manual to machine production. In many instances the emergence of mechanized factory production took place in the midst of an old kustar region and was initiated by the larger and more successful peasant manufacturers who introduced and adapted modern technology to their particular industry.[4] Although this development brought a radical change in many of the

---

[1] V. I. Lenin, The Development of Capitalism in Russia, translated from Volume 3 of the Progress Publisher's edition of Lenin's Collected Works, fifth Russian edition (Moscow: Progress Publishers, Third Printing, 1967), p. 434.

[2] Ryndziunskii, "Gorodskoe naselenie," p. 350.

[3] Ibid., p. 351.

[4] Liashchenko, p. 482.

productive, economic, and technical conditions and relationships prevailing in the countryside, it did not entail a shift in the geographic location of production. Thus the rise of modern factory industry in the countryside was in part due to the subsequent evolution of kustar production into factory production, a process initiated and guided by peasant industrial entrepreneurs.

Scarcity of Labor

A far more serious handicap to the development of industry in the cities was the persistent lack of an abundant supply of cheap labor. While the growth of manufacturing, especially in the 19th century, created a great demand for labor, the supply became increasingly scarce in the cities because of the institution of serfdom and the development of rural industry. The growing scarcity of labor naturally drove up its costs, and thereby made it substantially more difficult for urban-located industry to compete with industry located in the countryside and accessible to abundant supplies of cheap labor.[1] Consequently, the geographic disparity in labor costs provided a strong attraction for the establishment of industry in the countryside.

At the beginning of the 18th century most of the factory labor was hired and consisted mainly of "free" urban residents, fugitive serfs, and various categories of persons who had not yet been attached to the serf estate. But as the demand for labor grew the factory owners turned increasingly to the serfs, first by purchasing them for factory labor, and later by hiring them with the permission of their lords.

After 1721 many urban factory owners were able to secure a labor force through the direct purchase of serfs. But to settle compactly a mass of rightless serfs in a city whose total environment was hostile to them turned out to be not only difficult, but also expensive.[2] The experiment with forced serf labor, therefore, did not prove very successful in the cities. The privilege granted to non-gentry factory owners to purchase serfs was abrogated in 1762 but the decline in the use of serf labor in the cities had already set in as many urban factory owners increasingly discovered that the utilization of forced serf labor was comparatively more expensive in the long run than the use of hired labor. Not only

---

[1]Polianskii, Ekonomicheskii stroi manufaktury v Rossii, pp. 151-152, 262-263.

[2]Ryndziunskii, Gorodskoe grazhdanstvo . . . , p. 443.

was serf labor less efficient than hired labor, both in the cities
and in the countryside, but for the urban factory owners there were
also potentially high fixed costs involved in the use of such labor.
Under the conditions for purchasing serfs for factory work, the
serfs could not be separated from the factory nor could they be
used for other work. Thus the owner was responsible for the support of his serfs whether there was work in the factory year round
or not.[1] While in the countryside, the serfs, during periods of
unemployment, could at least draw some of their livelihood from the
land, such possibilities were obviously limited in the cities.
Nevertheless, in spite of the disadvantages of forced serf labor,
many factory owners felt that without access to such labor they
could not effectively compete with rural industry, and although
the use of serf labor declined steadily, it did not entirely dis-
appear from the urban scene. The practice persisted well into the
first half of the 19th century, although it became limited mainly
to the provincial cities and primarily to larger-sized, gentry-
owned manufactories.[2]

The shift to the use of hired labor rather than forced labor
in industry was made possible through the rise of the obrok system.
Particularly in the non-Black Earth regions of the northwestern
and north-central parts of European Russia, where agriculture was
carried out under more marginal conditions and was, on the whole,
less profitable than in the Black Earth regions, many of the gentry
in an effort to increase their revenues increasingly turned to the
practice of commuting the obligated labor services of their serfs
into monetary rents, or obrok.[3] The serfs, in turn, were thus compelled to seek out new avenues of increasing their cash incomes
and one of the available means was to hire themselves out, with
the permission of their masters, as wage laborers in the growing
industrial sector. At the same time the gentry also began to di-
vest themselves from a direct entrepreneurial role as the spread
of the obrok system provided them with larger monetary returns.[4]

---

[1] Tugan-Baranovskii, p. 98.

[2] Ryndziunskii, Gorodskoe grazhdanstvo . . . , p. 431.

[3] Henry Rosovsky, "The Serf Entrepreneur in Russia," Explorations in Entrepreneurial History, VI (May, 1954), pp. 209-210.

[4] Ibid., p. 210.

The cities, however, even with the expansion of the supply of hired labor through the spread of the _obrok_ system, still remained at a disadvantage in relation to the attraction of a permanent labor force for the development of industry.[1] The supply of wage laborers for the cities still remained restricted to the extent to which the gentry and civil officials were willing to give permission to the serfs to leave temporarily the villages. Moreover, the stability of the labor force for industry also depended on the will of the same authorities, who in most instances were not directly interested in manufacturing and who were alien to the industrial-capitalist complex.[2] It was not surprising, therefore, that the gentry were reluctant to permit many of their serfs to venture too far from their estates or remain away from the estate for too long of a period. Consequently, the nearer to the villages industry was situated, the greater were the chances for securing an adequate and stable working force. Moreover, the degree to which the peasants preferred or were compelled to till their holdings during the growing season played an important role in the location of industry. In this regard the _kustar_ industry and seasonal manufacturing enjoyed a distinct advantage over urban industry in that the former more easily fit the rhythm of work patterns in the countryside.[3] As a result of these limitations the cities continued to remain at a disadvantage in securing a permanent labor force that could provide the basis for the growth of industry. Even the emancipation did not alter significantly the relative supply and location of labor for non-agricultural occupations. As pointed out previously, the character of the reform, by assigning to the _obshchina_ and the _mir_ such a strong role in the life of the post-reform village, perpetuated the main obstacles inherent in serfdom to the formation of a permanent labor force in Russia and particularly in the cities. Even the system of granting passports for temporary sojourns outside of the village, because of the precarious stipulations governing their validity, made a peasant's position as an urban laborer tenuous and vulnerable to pressures from the village.[4]

---

[1] Polianskii, _Gorodskoe remeslo i manufaktury_ . . . , p. 73.

[2] Blum, p. 321.

[3] Polianskii, _Ekonomicheskii stroi manufaktury v Rossii_, p.236.

[4] Gerschenkron, "Russia: Agrarian Policies and Industrialization, 1861-1914," pp. 195-196.

Introduction of Advanced Technology and the Development of Factory Industry

With the rapid growth of factory industry during the post-reform period the demand for labor sharply increased, while the institutional barriers which kept the peasants bound to the villages made labor a comparatively scarce and expensive factor of production. At the same time the competition for labor among the kustar industry, rural factory industry, and urban industry steadily drove up its costs. The cost of labor for urban industry was particularly high since in order to overcome the inherent advantages of working in the countryside and the greater expenses of living in the cities, the factory owners were forced to offer higher wages if they were to attract labor. In response to this unfavorable situation factory owners increasingly turned to technological innovations to cut costs.[1]

The recourse to labor-saving, capital-intensive technology, however, did not eliminate the serious deficiency in the process of industrialization represented by the inadequate supply of labor and, all too often its inferior quality, but merely attenuated the handicap. In fact, if industrialization was to proceed at a rapid pace, as it did in Russia during the latter part of the 19th century, increasing amounts of labor were required. Consequently, the attraction of adequate supplies of cheap labor continued to exert a powerful influence on the location of factory industry.

The introduction of advanced technology in the manufacturing process, beginning especially after 1840, was accompanied, however, by a decline in many of the existing industries. Handicraft industries and especially factories that still continued to utilize forced serf labor prior to the emancipation found it increasingly difficult to compete with the newer forms of factory production based on machines. This process, however, affected both the cities and the countryside.

Effect on Existing Urban Manufacturing

The industries of many provincial cities in European Russia were particularly hard hit by the competition from the growth of technically advanced enterprises and recovery for many of these cities was slow if it took place at all. Thus many cities in Kaluga guberniia, which formerly were centers of the linen industry,

---

[1]Tugan-Baranovskii, p. 209.

were severely affected by the emergence of advanced enterprises,
particularly in St. Petersburg, during the latter decades prior to
the reforms.[1] The city of Voronezh, which as an important center
of cloth production had appeared to one observer at the beginning
of the 19th century as, "truly a factory town," with its foothills,
"completely strewn with factory buildings," had only three cloth
factories left by 1856 and none by the end of the following decade.[2]
Cloth production in Voronezh, "which had been based entirely on
forced labor, declined mainly as a result of competition from
Moscow merchant factories operated by free labor."[3] The emancipation of the peasantry, "only dealt the coup de grace to a declining
industry."[4] The same fate overtook two of the oldest and largest
factories in the Empire, located in Kazan' and Yaroslavl'. The
immense possessional cloth factory in Kazan', which dated from the
time of Peter the Great and as late as the middle 1830's employed
about 3,000 serfs, "began to decay rapidly in the 1840's"[5] By the
middle of the 1860's only some 260 persons were still employed in
this cloth factory. Likewise, the Great Yaroslavl' Factory, which
was renowned for its fine linen production and was, "the oldest
establishment of the sort in Russia, having been founded in 1722,"
had by 1850, "lost much of its former importance."[6] Whereas some
2,000 serfs were employed in this factory at the beginning of the
19th century, by 1850 it gave employment to only about 150 weavers,
all free men. The reason for its decline was simply stated: "the
processes of manufacture are antiquated."[7]

---

[1]Ryndziunskii, "Gorodskoe naselenie," p. 329.

[2]Pamiatnaia knizhka Voronezhskoi gubernii na 1865-66 gg.,
p. 50, quoted in Tugan-Baranovskii, p. 249.

[3]Tugan-Baranovskii, p. 250.

[4]Ibid.

[5]Ibid.

[6]Tegoborskii, I, p. 517.

[7]Ibid.

Effect on Urban and Rural Handicraft Production

With the development of large-scale, capitalist factory production, the handicraft industries were also steadily driven out of
the major branches of production. Faced on one hand with declining
prices for manufactured goods brought about by mass production, and
on the other hand with increasing costs of raw materials, labor,
fuel, and other factors of production with growing demand for their
use, the various forms of handicraft production found their competi-
tive position in the market place steadily deteriorating. Although
precise data on the value of production from small industry and
handicrafts are unavailable, it has been estimated that the value
of production from this sector of industry declined from approximately one-half of the value of factory production at around the time
of the reforms, to less than one-fifth on the eve of the First
World War.[1] Nevertheless, handicraft industry tenaciously clung on
to its existence. To counter the forces over which they had little
control, handicraftsmen resorted to various means to perpetuate
their increasingly tenuous position. Immediate responses took the
form of lengthening the working period and reducing the margin of
profit and thereby the standard of living. Longer-term solutions
involved the formation of various types of cooperative organiza-
tions, either for the purchase of materials or the marketing of
final products. These efforts met with greater success among the
rural handicraft producers than the urban. In the cities handicraft production by the beginning of the 20th century became increasingly restricted primarily to the forms of small auxiliary
crafts in fields that had not yet been adapted to large-scale production, or had been turned into a form of "home-work" in the
service of large commercial firms, especially in the garment industry.[2]

Although the relative importance of the value of production
from the handicraft industries sharply declined during the post-
reform period, this form of industry continued to remain very important in terms of employment. According to the estimates of
A. G. Rashin, the number of persons employed in small industry and
handicrafts as late as 1913 amounted to about one million persons in
the cities and approximately two million persons in the countryside.[3]

[1] Goldsmith, p. 468.

[2] Liashchenko, p. 552.

[3] A. G. Rashin, "O chislennosti i territorial'nom razmeshchenii
rabochikh Rossii v period kapitalizma," Istoricheskie Zapiski, XLVI
(1954), pp. 145, 150, 160.

The combined total of employment in this sector was approximately
equal to the number of persons employed in factory industry and
mining together. These totals, of course, are not exactly comparative since workers in handicraft industries frequently were employed
only for a portion of the year. The decline of the handicraft industries, however, did have a positive side effect for the development of factory industry, since as handicraftsmen were forced out
of production they provided a ready supply of labor for the factories.

Attractions of Urban Locations for Factory Industry

The process of the introduction of modern technology and the
simultaneous rise of modern, capitalist factory production in
Russia had varied consequences on the industrial development of
cities. To be sure, many cities, particularly the larger ones,
attracted a significant share of the growth in factory industry.
Urban locations possessed certain distinct advantages for the
attraction of industry. The rapid growth of the urban population
provided industrialists with a greatly enlarged market and supply
of labor. The urban market became a particularly important factor
during the post-reform period since the deteriorating economic
conditions in the countryside and the increased tax burden placed
on the peasantry to help finance the industrialization drive reduced
the purchasing power of the peasantry for manufactured goods.
Consequently, the urban market acquired greater importance than its
proportion of the population. Moreover, the expansion of the railroad network, in which the cities were the connecting nodes, enlarged
the potential market areas for urban manufacturers while at the same
time providing them with reduced assembly and distribution costs.

Certain cities, by virtue of their relative size, location,
and administrative significance, offered industrialists comparatively greater accessibility to financial and credit facilities, technology, and government officials. The development of large-scale
industry required large sums of capital. While individuals, the
state, and foreigners provided investment capital to Russian industry, the role of commercial banks and stock exchanges became increasingly important in Russia. These resources, however, were
largely concentrated in St. Petersburg and Moscow.[2] Likewise, the

---

[1]Rashin, Formirovanie rabochego klassa v Rossii, p. 343.

[2]Liashchenko, p. 702.

major stock exchange was located in St. Petersburg, while secondary ones were found in Moscow, Warsaw, Riga, Khar'kov, and Odessa.[1]

The rapid development of large-scale industry in Russia was made possible with the massive infusion of modern technology. Since virtually all of this technology was imported from abroad, those cities situated on the main channels of international inter-course with the West and at the top of the urban hierarchy enjoyed distinct advantages over others. The rapid development of Russia's "window to the West," St. Petersburg, into one of the leading in-dustrial centers of the Empire was greatly facilitated by the fact that it was the main port of entry for modern technology.

Finally, accessibility to government officials played an impor-tant role in the attraction of industry to some cities, especially the capital cities. Relations between government and private en-terprise were close and continuous in Russia and, consequently, "were of greater significance to the individual enterprise than those in western Europe."[2] Because of the state's intimate role in directing the industrialization of the country, the success or failure of many industrial endeavors frequently "depended on the administrative decisions of key officials."[3] Since such decisions seldom were based on cost or quality considerations, but rather on the pursuit of personal profit, ready accessibility and personal contact with government officials often entered into the locational decision-making process of many entrepreneurs. Such contacts were maximized in the cities and especially in the administrative cen-ters of the Empire.

Advantages of Rural Sites for Factory Industry

Despite the many locational advantages afforded by the cities, the growth of modern factory industry in Russia spread with parti-cular rapidity outside the cities and even penetrated, "deep into remote areas that would seem to be isolated from the world of big capitalist enterprise."[4] New factory construction was noticeable not so much in the large, already populated centers:

---

[1] Ibid., 712.

[2] John P. McKay, Pioneers for Profit: French Entrepreneurship and Russian Industrialization, 1885-1913 (Chicago: The University of Chicago Press, 1970), p. 268.

[3] Ibid., p. 269.

[4] Lenin, p. 528.

> "but in new localities, in the provinces, in the
> hitherto remote villages and hamlets . . . . Nearly to
> half-forgotten small stations, stations, and among
> quiet villages and hamlets, like mushrooms all sorts
> of factories and plants grow, and now and then even
> whole factories with leviathan buildings appear.
> And there, where earlier wagged countryside roads
> over which not even a single peasant cart passed by,
> now multi-storied factory buildings hum and buzz, to
> which lines of carts stretch from all directions." 1

The spread of factory industry into the rural areas was motivated largely by one factor: "While the erection of factories in the countryside," involved, "quite a few inconveniences," it did, however, "guarantee a supply of cheap labor."[2] Since the peasants were prevented from going to the factories because of the system of collective responsibility and other barriers to leaving the villages, the factories went to the peasants. In Kostroma guberniia, for example:

> "The Vychuga factory owners, considering it all
> important to acquire a cheap and permanent labor
> force, already in the 1860's began the separation
> of their factories and transferring them into non-
> factory areas, where it was possible to acquire a
> cheaper labor force . . . ."[3]

There were other characteristics of the labor force situated in the countryside that made it appealing for the location of factory industry. Because of the long tradition of kustar production many rural localities offered a labor force that possessed considerable industrial skill and has become accustomed to the discipline necessary for modern factory work. The growth of the textile industry in the Central Industrial region which, "began to develop rapidly after 1870 in the form of capitalist manufacturing plants," arose, "in those localities where an adequate supply of skilled workers was available among the former kustars and individual household craftsmen"[4] In reference to the silk weaving industry, one

---

[1] E. Diubiuk, "Fabrika v derevne. (Pis'mo iz Vladimira)," Sovremennyi Mir, (Aprel', 1911), p. 277.

[2] Lenin, p. 530.

[3] P. Makar'ev, Fabrichno-zavodskaia promyshlennost' Kostromskoi gubernii nakanune mirovoi voiny (Kostroma, 1924) p. 61, quoted in Rashin, Formirovanie rabochego klassa Rossii, p. 210-211.

[4] Liashchenko, p. 546.

observer noted that: "Factories cannot be erected in any village
and in any number," but rather, "the factory must follow the weaver
into the villages where . . . a contingent of proficient workers has
been formed."[1] Moreover, the labor force in the countryside was
often less demanding than in the cities.[2] Because the standards of
living were abysmally low in the countryside, workers were more apt
to be docile and less prone to disruptive practices as a means to
protest low wages, dismissals, and unhealthy and unsafe working conditions. As the tempo of strikes increased and the efforts at
unionizing gained momentum in the cities this aspect of the rural
labor force undoubtedly acquired greater significance for the location of industry.

Finally, there were a number of secondary factors that often
enhanced the attraction of rural sites for industry and helped to
account for the predominance of manufacturing in the countryside.
Factories located outside of the city often required "less formali-
ty, troubles, and expenditures for their construction and maintenance, "and in many instances, "the (low) purchase and rent values
of land, closeness to water and timber, cheap motive power and
fuels," were decisive factors in the selection of a site in the
countryside for the erection of a factory rather than in the cities.[3]

---

[1]Promysly Vladimirskoi gubernii, IV, p. 22, quoted in Lenin,
p. 435.

[2]Diubiuk, p. 281.

[3]Pogozhev, p. 68.

CHAPTER XI

SUMMARY AND CONCLUSIONS

The 19th century was a period of rapid urban growth in the
Russian Empire. Between 1811 and 1910 the number of cities increased from 570 to 932, with the number of cities containing
50,000 or more inhabitants increasing from 22 to 206. During the
same interval the total population of cities in the Empire grew
from 2,780,337 to 23,553,583, resulting in a net addition to the
urban population of 20,773,246 persons. This represented an increase in the urban population of 7.5 times or an average annual
rate of growth of 2.2 per cent.

The analysis of the patterns of urban growth in this study
was divided into two broad periods, each characterized by different
sets of social and economic forces, separated by a transitional
period coinciding with preparation and implementation of the Great
Reforms.

During the first forty-five years of this study, 1811-1856,
a period characterized by the presence of serfdom, urban growth
was comparatively slow and erratic. The urban population grew at
an average annual rate of 1.6 per cent as slightly less than three
million persons were added to the population of cities. The growth
of cities during the pre-reform period was based largely on the increase in the volume of domestic trade, primarily in the form of
periodic fairs and markets, and on the expansion of settlement,
particularly into the southern and eastern regions of European
Russia. In the absence of any notable improvement in the means of
transportation, however, these two processes tended to promote a
pattern of urban growth that was characterized more by the uniformity of its distribution than by its concentration. In fact, the
percentage of the urban population residing in cities with 50,000
or more inhabitants actually declined slightly during this period
from 25 per cent in 1811 to 24 per cent in 1856. With the exception of St. Petersburg and Moscow, whose political and administrative significance rivaled their economic role, and Odessa,
which became the primary outlet for the export of wheat, cities
in the Russian Empire remained small.

With the abolition of serfdom in 1861 a major barrier to the movement of population and the growth of cities was removed. While the impact of the emancipation on economic development was delayed somewhat, the effects on the growth of cities was most immediate and pronounced. In the period between 1856 and 1870 the urban population of Russia increased by nearly 35 per cent or 2,026,397 persons, especially as a result of the displacement of several million persons from the countryside associated with abolition of serfdom. In addition, the annexations of Tsarist Poland and parts of Central Asia brought 1,126,243 urban inhabitants into the Russian Empire.

The post-reform period, 1870-1910, was characterized by a growth in the urban population of unprecedented proportions. Nearly 15 million persons were added to the population of cities during this period, a figure representing about 72 per cent of the total growth in the urban population of the Russian Empire during the entire period of study. The average annual rate of increase over these forty years was 2.5 per cent. Another major feature of the pattern of urban development in this period was the increasing degree of the concentration of the urban population into a limited number of large cities. By the end of this period, 40 per cent of the urban population of the Russian Empire was concentrated into 30 cities of 100,000 inhabitants or more.

The principal factors behind the growth in the urban population and its concentration into large cities during the post-reform period were a number of forces that became significant with rapid economic development. Of foremost importance was the construction of railroads. Between 1867 and 1910 the railroad network was expanded from 5,038 km. to 66,581 km. While providing the primary catalyst to economic expansion in general, the growth of railroads promoted the concentration of economic activities into a limited number of cities by conferring upon them cost advantages over other cities in the assembly and distribution of goods.

As a consequence of the enlargement of markets and increased regional specialization that accompanied the expansion of the railroad network, the volume of domestic trade grew rapidly. The importance of periodic fairs and markets during the post-reform period gave way to permanent forms of trade as commercial functions and facilities became increasingly centralized in the cities. Another important feature of this period was the nearly fourfold increase in the value of foreign trade. The growth in foreign trade was a particularly important factor in the rapid development of many cities on the Baltic and Black Sea coasts.

Continued expansion of settlements during the post-reform period also contributed significantly to the growth of cities in outlying areas, especially in the North Caucasian Foreland, Western and Eastern Siberia, and the Central Asian Steppe.

The most spectacular feature of economic development in the post-reform period, however, was the rapid growth of industry, particularly the emergence of large-scale factory industry. Throughout the period industrial output rose at an average annual rate of 5 per cent, and in certain periods, especially in the last decade of the century, the rate of industrial expansion was even greater.

As impressive as industrial development was in Tsarist Russia, however, it did not have a great impact on urban growth. Of the 334 cities in the Russian Empire which attained a population of 10,000 or more inhabitants by 1897, only 66 cities had more than 30 per cent of their gainfully occupied population employed in manufacturing of all types, including handicraft production, and only 33 cities had 40 per cent or more. Moreover, of the 54 largest cities in 1897, those with a population of 50,000 persons or more, only 11 had 30 per cent or more of their gainfully occupied populations employed in manufacturing. Consequently, while the development of industry was of primary importance in explaining the growth of a comparatively small number of cities such as Moscow, St. Petersburg, Łódź, Ivanovo, and Tula, it was only of secondary significance in accounting for the over-all increase in the urban population of the Russian Empire.

The absence of a close relationship between urban and industrial development was a reflection of the distinctive pattern urban-industrial growth assumed in Tsarist Russia during the 19th century, a pattern that varied from the western experience in two significant respects.

First of all, while urban and industrial growth occurred simultaneously in Tsarist Russia, they were not spatially coincident. Nearly 52 per cent of the persons gainfully occupied in manufacturing of all types in 1897 and 61 per cent of the total employment in factory industry in 1902 were located outside the cities.

Secondly, the cities in Russia did not play a prominent role in industrialization. Unlike their counterparts in the West, the cities in the Russian Empire did not become the organizational centers of industry.

The failure of cities to draw together industrial production was the result primarily of their inability to attract large and permanent supplies of labor upon which the growth of industry was contingent and to nurture the formation of an independent and dynamic entrepreneurial class capable of initiating and guiding industrial development. Both of these factors were inextricably interwoven with the institutional structures and historical traditions of Russian society.

Serfdom was, of course, the single greatest barrier to the movement of labor, and while its abolition in 1861 improved the mobility of labor, the conditions of the emancipation, particularly the political and social roles assigned to the village mir, effectively prevented for several decades a massive redistribution of the labor force from materializing.

The quality of labor that did become available to the cities, either through the system of obrok, the issuing of passports, or even through illegal departures, was also affected adversely by the institutional arrangements of Russian society. In particular, the formation of a permanent and reliable labor force in the cities was greatly impeded by a web of legal, social, economic, and personal links which more or less effectively tied the urban worker of peasant origins to the countryside.

Conditions in the city itself, moreover, also hindered the formation of a labor force suitable for industry. Unlike in Western Europe, where the principle, "city air makes men free," was firmly established, in Russia the police apparatus stood ready to return peasants who had entered the city illegally or had overstayed their permitted sojourn either to their owners, as was the case under serfdom, or, after the emancipation, to their village communes. The acquisition of a permanent domicile in the city was impossible for many and difficult for most immigrants from the countryside.

State attitudes and policies, which consistently promoted the interests of the landed gentry at the expense of the urban merchantry, were also instrumental in fostering the growth of industry outside the cities. The state encouraged the gentry to establish industries on their estates by providing them with a virtual monopoly on cheap labor, access to markets, subsidies, and other incentives. The development of industry as well as trade among the peasantry was stimulated as the state, under pressure from the gentry, steadily removed virtually all the restrictions which had been placed on the peasants to engage in such activities.

The gentry, moreover, generally encouraged peasant involvement in trade an d industry as it was a means of increasing their revenues and oftentimes played a direct role in the development of peasant industry by providing capital and having their peasants trained in various industrial skills.

The formation of a reservoir of entrepreneurial talent in the cities, moreover, was hindered by the same general policies of the state which promoted the development of industry in the countryside and by institutional barriers to mobility. The urban merchantry, in particular, which played a prominent role in the early stages of industrial development in Russia, found it increasingly difficult to shift their talents and capital from commercial to industrial ventures. The loss of their exclusive privileges to engage in trade and establish industries, the inability to secure access to cheap labor, and the competition from goods produced, often more cheaply, in the countryside dampened the merchants' interest and reduced their financial capability to develop industries in the cities. While few merchants were willing or able to make the transition to industrialists, the cities were at the same time deprived of the talents of the new class of entrepreneurs which emerged from the ranks of the peasantry. Institutional barriers in the countryside, which impeded permanent departures from the villages, and in the cities, which hindered the acquisition of full citizenship, forced most of these new entrepreneurs to exercise their talents in the countryside.

Finally, in contrast to the West, the rapid growth in the urban population of the Russian Empire did not result in any significant structural changes in the relative distribution of the rural and urban population and their economic activities. Despite the addition of more than 20 million persons to the population of cities, the level of urbanization remained low. During the ninety-nine-year period of this study the per cent of the total population residing in cities increased only modestly from 6.3 per cent in 1811 to 14.7 per cent in 1910.

The reason why the urban growth which took place in the Russian Empire during the 19th century had such a slight impact on the level of urbanization was the rapid growth in the rural population and, equally important, the institutional constraints on the mobility of the population which acted to impound the growth in the rural population in the countryside. Like Western Europe, Russia experienced a demographic revolution, but unlike Western Europe the growth in the population was not accompanied by a significant redistribution of the population.

The demographic revolution in the countryside does provide a partial explanation of the growth in the population of the cities in the Russian Empire. Throughout the period under study the increase in the urban population was largely the result of in-migration from the countryside. The increase in the volume of rural to urban migration, however, must be viewed not so much as the consequence of the growth of economic opportunities in the cities as it was simply the absolute increase in the number of persons who possessed the freedom to move, first through the emancipation of the serfs in 1861 and later through the Stolypin reforms of 1905-1906.

APPENDIX   I

POPULATION OF CITIES IN THE RUSSIAN EMPIRE,

1811-1910

The guberniias are arranged in the Russian alphabetical order, as they typically occur in Russian sources, for European guberniias, followed by Poland, Caucasus, Siberia and Central Asia.

The cities in the appendix are arranged according to the guberniia in which they were situated as of 1910. The cities in each guberniia are ordered according to descending size of population in 1910. The names of cities and their spellings, transliterated according to the Library of Congress system, are given as they appeared in: Russia. Tsentral'nyi statisticheskii komitet. Goroda Rossii v 1910 godu (S.-Peterburg, 1914).

Included in the appendix are all settlements, regardless of size, which were designated as goroda, that is, cities, by 1910. Also included are settlements designated as posady or mestechka which had a population of 2,000 or more inhabitants in 1910 and appeared for three or more consecutive dates in the basic statistical sources. Thus to qualify for placement in the appendix such settlements had to appear in the statistical sources for 1885, 1897, and 1910. This latter criterion was adopted because of the rather amorphous denotation and connotation of what constituted a city in Russia during the 19th century. In addition to cities proper, or goroda, such settlements as posady and mestechka were also legally considered as urban settlements. Not all such settlements, however, were included in the statistical sources. Nevertheless a number of such settlements were consistently included in most, if not all, of the statistical publications and, consequently, were considered de facto as cities, if not de jure.

In several instances, where data were lacking for a given year from a long sequence, the population of the city was estimated for the given year by dividing the difference of the population for the previous and subsequent periods and adding the result to the figures for the previous period. Such estimates are denoted by an asterisk.

For Tsarist Poland the columns in the appendix are not added to derive a total urban population for the guberniias in 1810, 1825, 1840, and 1857 since it is not part of this study prior to the reforms and because of the inconsistencies in the pre-reform Polish and post-reform Russian definition and designation of cities and their numbers. Population data for the cities in Tsarist Poland in the pre-reform period are provided, where available, only as a convenience to the reader in order to examine long-term growth trends. Population data for fourteen cities in 1870 became available only after the completion of the study and, therefore, were not included in the final calculations of the urban population. The population data for these cities are enclosed by parentheses.

In Bessarabia data on the population of a number of cities are lacking for 1870 because such cities were temporarily detached from the Russian Empire. Because they were not part of the Empire at this time, no effort was made to estimate their populations nor were their populations included in the total urban population of the guberniia for 1870.

EUROPEAN RUSSIA

	1811	1825	1840	1856	1870	1885	1897	1910
ARKHANGEL'SK								
1. Arkhangel'sk	10,951	21,823	9,589	15,157	19,540	17,761	20,882	34,125
2. Onega	1,078	1,294	1,530	1,516	2,329	2,643	2,541	3,820
3. Mezen'	1,515	1,485	1,647	1,542	1,845	1,595	1,847	2,620
4. Shenkursk	435	458	545	670	1,015	1,293	1,492	1,764
5. Pinega	395	535	670	632	748	1,066	994	1,435
6. Kem'	1,153	1,117	1,864	1,722	2,027	2,102	2,447	1,352
7. Kholmogory	1,145	1,323	905	1,068	1,158	1,072	1,112	719
8. Kola	842	734	770	507	743	765	615	683
9. Aleksandrovsk	–	–	–	–	–	–	–	524
	17,514	28,769	17,520	22,814	29,405	28,297	31,930	47,042
ASTRAKHAN'								
10. Astrakhan'	37,820	37,320	45,938	34,582	48,220	70,554	112,880	142,491
11. Krasnyi-Iar	2,284	2,767	3,577	4,636	8,246	6,071	5,593	12,721
12. Chernyi-Iar	2,248	2,728	1,903	3,778	6,155	4,792	4,226	5,723
13. Tsarev	–	–	2,454	4,378	8,191	6,921	6,977	5,654
14. Enotaevsk	856	853	1,060	2,029	2,510	2,591	2,826	3,653
	43,208	43,668	54,932	49,403	73,322	90,929	132,502	170,242
BESSARABIIA								
15. Kishinev	–	–	42,636	63,469	102,427	120,074	108,483	125,000
16. Bendery	–	–	10,012	14,879	24,625	44,684	31,797	59,758
17. Izmail	–	–	21,908	31,779		33,084	22,295	35,708
18. Bel'tsy	–	–	4,514	6,646	4,959	10,943	18,478	23,625
19. Akkerman	–	–	25,339	19,807	39,201	41,178	28,258	21,287
20. Khotin	–	–	11,068	13,074	18,148	17,890	18,398	21,160
21. Orgeev	–	–	4,092	4,119	5,883	6,326	12,336	18,000
22. Soroki	–	–	2,243	5,054	7,161	11,876	15,351	17,067
23. Kiliia	–	–	5,394	5,563		8,014	11,618	15,088
24. Bolgrad	–	–				8,179	12,300	13,802
25. Reni	–	–	6,304	8,263		6,077	6,941	9,600
26. Kagul	–	–	454	3,808		5,980	7,077	8,530
27. Vilkovo Posad	–	–	1,109	1,610		2,784	4,225	4,921
28. Shabo Posad	–	–				4,043	3,717	4,800
			135,073	178,071	202,404	321,132	301,274	378,346

	1811	1825	1840	1856	1870	1885	1897	1910
VIL'NA								
29. Vil'na	56,314	46,655	54,499	45,881	64,217	102,845	154,532	192,746
30. Smorgon'	–	–	–	–	–	–	8,908	16,228
31. Lida	1,326	1,493	3,517	2,196	3,333	8,123	9,323	14,837
32. Novo-Vileisk	–	–	–	–	–	–	–	10,182
33. Oshmiany	1,830	1,022	1,462	1,725	4,560	4,547	7,214	7,868
34. Disna	1,405	2,801	2,867	3,804	6,111	8,250	6,756	7,303
35. Druia	–	2,447	2,235	2,196	3,877	5,524	4,742	6,580
36. Sventsiany	429	1,013	4,848	4,795	5,854	8,515	6,025	6,025
37. Troki	1,487	818	1,135	5,733	2,191	2,456	3,240	4,402
38. Vileika	543	727	841	2,122	2,953	4,012	3,560	3,903
39. Radoshkovichi	916	381	1,580	1,222	1,351	2,631	2,615	2,414
	64,250	57,357	72,984	69,674	94,447	146,903	206,915	272,488
VITEBSK								
40. Dvinsk	1,843	2,881	11,361	11,106	29,462	69,033	69,675	109,689
41. Vitebsk	16,905	16,867	17,989	20,728	28,088	54,676	65,871	103,411
42. Polotsk	6,320	7,066	10,685	11,967	11,928	19,134	20,294	30,878
43. Rezhitsa	760	205	1,091	1,304	8,951	10,149	10,795	19,600
44. Nevel'	2,925	2,897	5,934	6,695	8,951	7,310	9,349	17,031
45. Velizh	5,670	7,206	7,655	10,279	7,858	16,372	12,193	15,232
46. Sebezh	2,020	2,627	1,734	2,847	3,211	3,821	4,326	7,586
47. Lepel'	555	1,777	2,014	2,344	4,640	6,003	6,284	7,504
48. Gorodok	1,704	1,678	2,239	3,361	2,944	5,618	5,023	6,171
49. Drissa	544	712	1,149	1,298	5,099	3,490	4,238	5,615
50. Liutsin	–	1,372	4,414	4,312	3,759	5,460	5,140	5,607
51. Surazh	1,165	1,202	1,531	1,991	3,094	5,085	2,731	4,429
	40,411	46,490	67,796	78,232	115,066	206,151	215,919	332,753
VLADIMIR								
52. Ivanovo-Voznesensk	–	–	–	1,332	3,289	32,579	54,208	100,000
53. Vladimir	5,694	9,859	12,035	12,606	16,422	18,305	28,479	32,708
54. Shuia	1,612	1,895	3,428	9,314	10,444	15,733	19,583	24,372
55. Kovrov	911	1,150	1,648	2,223	4,893	8,227	14,571	21,230
56. Murom	5,277	5,850	9,882	10,819	10,703	13,987	13,271	15,751

VLADIMIR

	1811	1825	1840	1856	1870	1885	1897	1910
57. Pereslavl'-Zaleskii	5,829	5,769	4,231	5,376	7,210	7,431	10,639	12,000
58. Melenki	2,350	2,171	3,574	4,566	5,597	6,169	8,909	9,222
59. Viazniki	3,114	3,135	4,027	5,306	4,411	5,154	8,862	8,469
60. Aleksandrov	2,504	2,379	2,150	3,407	6,779	6,724	6,810	7,420
61. Iur'ev-Pol'skii	2,419	2,582	2,582	2,920	4,779	5,453	5,759	6,800
62. Suzdal'	5,040	4,578	5,209	6,064	7,047	6,668	6,412	6,029
63. Kirzhacn	1,090	1,138	1,641	2,137	2,851	3,335	4,851	4,651
64. Sudogda	746	1,375	1,159	2,499	2,499	1,987	3,182	4,221
65. Gavrilovskii Posad	1,233	1,309	1,512	1,827	1,957	2,033	3,037*	4,040
66. Pokrov	989	992	1,667	2,721	2,886	2,719	2,785	3,835
67. Gorokhovets	1,532	1,813	2,286	2,255	2,574	2,824	2,297	3,220
	40,340	45,995	57,369	75,821	94,331	139,328	193,655	263,968

VOLOGDA

	1811	1825	1840	1856	1870	1885	1897	1910
68. Vologda	9,564	9,699	13,118	14,159	17,223	17,391	27,705	38,700
69. Velikii-Ustiug	7,447	7,017	8,763	7,959	7,792	8,119	11,137	18,707
70. Ust'-Sysol'sk	2,132	2,258	3,113	3,093	3,570	4,225	4,464	5,285
71. Tot'ma	2,778	2,776	2,573	2,870	3,315	3,412	4,947	4,891
72. Griazovets	1,438	1,683	2,416	2,868	2,174	2,301	3,205	4,497
73. Kadnikov	473	739	1,784	2,166	1,583	1,436	2,406	2,838
74. Nikol'sk	667	902	1,041	1,238	1,748	1,889	2,553	2,497
75. Vel'sk	395	565	1,008	773	1,362	1,441	1,989	2,381
76. Sol'vychegodsk	1,773	1,152	1,222	1,265	1,304	1,313	1,788	1,602
77. Iarensk	805	882	1,108	973	1,169	1,281	993	1,619
78. Lal'sk	910	788	790	856	536	695	1,124	1,307
79. Krasnoborsk	429	546	480	465	655	676	671	812
	28,481	29,007	37,416	38,685	42,431	44,179	62,982	85,136

VOLYNIIA

	1811	1825	1840	1856	1870	1885	1897	1910
80. Zhitomir	8,176	13,403	16,670	29,350	35,739	55,875	65,895	88,365
81. Rovno	2,924	3,903	5,581	4,875	6,300	7,357	24,573	38,103
82. Lutsk	2,349	5,985	7,447	6,524	11,464	17,354	15,804	31,300
83. Kovel'	3,735	2,615	4,184	3,380	4,765	14,552	17,697	28,942
84. Kremenets	4,293	7,089	10,290	8,693	11,039	11,840	17,704	25,045
85. Starokonstantinov	4,713	9,284	11,030	10,529	15,165	19,025	16,377	24,439

	1811	1825	1840	1856	1870	1885	1897	1910
VOLYNIIA								
86. Dubno	5,589	10,579	9,670	8,092	7,212	8,942	14,257	24,263
87. Novogorod-Volynskii	2,254	4,151	6,199	6,469	8,814	14,242	16,904	21,502
88. Ostrog	4,602	8,830	9,729	8,853	7,707	16,637	14,749	19,433
89. Vladimir-Volynskii	2,375	5,985	7,447	6,524	5,109	8,752	9,883	18,293
90. Zaslavl'	4,474	2,937	8,724	8,110	7,360	11,695	12,611	15,838
91. Ovruch	756	2,255	3,894	4,468	5,841	6,671	7,393	12,269
92. Zdolbunovo	–	–	–	–	–	–	4,692	10,448
	46,240	76,048	98,730	103,569	126,515	192,942	238,539	358,240
GRODNA								
127. Sokolka	1,830	2,436	2,604	8,201	3,443	4,125	7,598	5,830
128. Vasil'kov	1,066	970	1,404	1,244	1,497	2,960	3,880	5,314
129. Goniondz	1,249	884	2,426	2,467	1,846	4,345	3,436	4,240
130. Knyshin	1,136	964	2,077	2,259	2,924	6,840	3,864	4,045
131. Kleshcheli	1,146	735	1,366	1,234	1,516	1,998	2,013	3,900
132. Narev	–	1,095	1,772	1,806	1,187	2,826	1,434	3,686
133. Sukhovolia	848	1,439	1,905	1,880	2,168	3,505	3,203	3,411
134. Ianov	645	1,439	1,780	1,435	1,980	2,727	2,296	2,678
135. Mel'nik	782	454	883	842	822	1,198	1,485	2,639
136. Drogichin	898	729	774	1,401	1,110	1,100	1,707	2,300
137. Druskeniki	–	–	–	–	–	–	–	2,151
138. Surazh	948	288	1,054	1,064	851	1,100	1,599	2,105
139. Novyi Dvor	616	550	862	928	1,325	1,707	1,300	1,924
140. Odel'sk	–	622	1,439	1,002	1,473	1,886	1,462	1,742
141. Dombrova	745	944	1,306	1,100	1,186	1,878	1,988	1,584
142. Kuznitsa	547	644	1,187	996	1,271	1,077	1,346	1,170
143. Koritsyn	305	313	826	747	808	603	683	773
	42,684	57,144	86,360	110,754	131,148	224,006	260,742	340,499
EKATERINOSLAV								
144. Ekaterinoslav	8,583	8,412	8,476	13,031	24,167	46,876	112,839	211,905
145. Lugansk	–	–	–	–	10,059	15,505	20,404	63,313
146. Mariupol'	2,674	3,673	3,679	6,858	9,774	17,331	31,116	51,398
147. Aleksandrovsk	994	1,716	5,192	2,829	4,507	6,707	18,849	38,225
148. Pavlograd	3,517	3,949	5,634	6,957	11,391	14,774	15,775	30,645
149. Novomoskovsk	7,034	7,919	10,069	9,588	10,515	18,285	12,883	26,879

EKATERINOSLAV

	1811	1825	1840	1856	1870	1885	1897	1910
150. Bakhmut	3,190	3,190	6,394	8,928	17,999	14,630	19,316	25,147
151. Nikopol'	-	3,336	5,560	6,312	9,706	8,144	17,097	23,806
152. Verkhne-dneprovsk	1,115	1,011	2,809	2,521	4,077	7,570	6,701	12,225
153. Slavianoserbsk	1,013	1,974	2,122	2,431	3,156	5,049	3,122	4,040
	28,120	35,180	49,935	59,455	105,351	154,871	258,102	487,583

ZEMLIA VOISKOGO DONSKA

	1811	1825	1840	1856	1870	1885	1897	1910
154. Rostov-na-Donu	3,995	5,236	9,050	12,587	44,443	61,256	119,476	172,274
155. Tagonrog	7,402	8,389	22,472	18,515	48,186	56,047	51,437	68,369
156. Nakhichevan'-na-Donu	9,060	7,511	10,821	13,959	16,258	17,347	28,427	43,442
157. Novocherkassk	6,239	8,535	17,623	17,910	18,611	32,646	51,963	41,273
158. Azov Posad	-	991	2,295	5,296	16,791	16,581	17,024	29,246
159. Aleksandrovsk-Grushevskii	-	-	-	-	-	13,157	16,479	23,096
	26,696	30,662	62,261	68,537	143,588	197,034	284,806	377,700

KAZAN'

	1811	1825	1840	1856	1870	1885	1897	1910
160. Kazan'	53,907	36,963	41,304	56,257	86,262	139,915	129,959	184,465
161. Chistopol'	6,692	5,246	7,557	9,860	13,035	24,288	20,104	24,671
162. Mariinskii Posad	-	-	-	-	2,876	4,796	3,319	6,167
163. Tetiushi	1,062	1,438	1,752	2,324	3,297	3,934	4,754	5,868
164. Cheboksary	4,395	4,432	4,908	4,672	3,564	5,081	4,738	5,474
165. Koz'modem'iansk	4,984	3,483	4,244	5,008	5,845	9,205	5,284	5,440
166. Mamadysh	4,155	4,046	3,772	3,703	4,123	5,073	4,195	5,180
167. Laishev	1,802	2,180	2,545	3,389	4,654	5,220	3,743	3,203
168. Iadrin	1,494	1,814	1,671	2,412	2,530	2,596	2,454	3,135
169. Sviiazhsk	1,399	1,969	1,510	1,803	2,553	2,883	2,365	3,033
170. Spassk	991	1,325	2,178	1,519	2,820	3,227	2,770	2,902
171. Tsivil'sk	1,089	1,248	937	1,516	1,883	1,829	2,336	2,529
172. Troitskii Posad	-	-	-	1,784	2,024	2,583	2,298*	2,012
173. Tsarevokokshaisk	1,076	891	1,042	1,151	1,124	1,538	1,658	1,854
174. Arsk	947	401	1,207	1,366	1,507	1,100	1,228	1,209
	83,993	65,436	74,627	96,664	138,097	213,268	191,205	257,142

		1910	1897	1885	1870	1856	1840	1825	1811
KALUGA									
175.	Kaluga	53,791	49,513	40,102	38,608	31,027	35,290	26,431	23,137
176.	Zhizdra	12,430	6,004	11,678	11,703	10,947	8,200	7,022	5,469
177.	Borovsk	11,791	8,414	9,584	9,491	9,121	8,102	6,844	6,660
178.	Kozel'sk	9,762	5,619	5,841	7,368	7,929	8,464	4,541	4,652
179.	Sukhinichi	6,954	5,447	6,186	6,038	6,740	5,057	—	—
180.	Medyn	6,161	4,387	8,057	7,781	5,647	2,755	2,886	1,810
181.	Maloiaslovets	5,318	2,497	4,557	5,173	2,848	2,304	1,623	1,413
182.	Meshchovsk	3,964	3,635	5,164	5,431	5,272	4,181	2,955	2,297
183.	Peremyshl'	3,889	1,712	3,095	2,999	2,124	2,703	2,135	1,960
184.	Mosal'sk	3,254	2,655	2,463	3,200	3,472	2,612	2,225	1,761
185.	Serpeisk	2,000	1,034	1,971	1,936	1,786	1,652	1,304	1,231
186.	Tarusa	1,928	1,989	2,599	2,922	2,623	2,233	1,535	1,305
187.	Likhvin	1,767	1,612	2,690	2,224	2,947	2,641	1,971	2,022
188.	Vorotynsk	1,088	777	1,352	1,461	1,595	1,417	1,161	1,176
		124,097	95,295	105,339	106,335	94,078	87,611	62,635	54,893
KIEV									
189.	Kiev	527,287	247,723	165,561	79,773	62,497	47,424	24,369	23,318
190.	Berdichev	75,338	53,351	77,223	52,563	50,281	35,592	21,470*	7,347
191.	Cherkasy	42,759	29,600	20,755	13,914	11,945	8,684	5,809	5,339
192.	Uman'	41,276	31,016	15,976	15,393	11,175	7,877	4,744	4,913
193.	Zvenigorodka	24,694	16,923	11,562	11,375	7,790	7,003	3,749	2,926
194.	Skvira	22,574	17,958	15,550	10,061	8,445	5,891	3,561	3,623
195.	Lipovets	16,606	8,658	18,438	6,710	5,611	5,936	3,087	3,681
196.	Vasil'kov	16,538	13,132	18,020	16,597	10,191	8,971	5,419	5,047
197.	Tarashcha	15,350	11,259	15,801	11,420	7,230	5,110	2,814	2,048
198.	Radomysl'	15,041	10,906	7,086	5,905	7,644	4,505	2,357	3,370
199.	Chigirin	14,856	9,872	16,009	9,677	7,367	5,414	2,736	2,468
200.	Kanev	12,228	8,855	8,652	7,418	6,372	4,465	3,661	2,504
		824,547	459,253	380,633	240,806	196,548	146,872	83,776	66,584
KOVNA									
201.	Kovna	84,315	70,920	50,493	33,050	20,003	8,525	5,122	1,569
202.	Shavli	21,275	16,128	20,619	13,343	5,404	2,870	923	2,670
203.	Vil'komir	13,706	13,532	16,240	11,118	6,230	5,766	4,153	2,651
204.	Ponevezh	13,446	12,968	17,428	7,224	5,610	6,375	2,120	1,878

	1811	1825	1840	1856	1870	1885	1897	1910
KOVNA								
205. Rossieny	2,400	2,169	1,420	8,296	10,700	11,512	7,455	10,482
206. Tel'shi	1,061	2,085	3,585	5,122	6,481	11,028	6,205	7,842
207. Novoaleksandrovsk	-	-	817	3,012	6,115	6,825	6,359	7,002
208. Vidzi	3,076	922	2,618	1,032	2,116	6,052	5,103	5,942
209. Shadov	-	1,280	1,950*	2,620	2,020	4,063	4,474	5,183
	15,305	18,774	33,926	58,329	92,167	144,260	143,144	169,193
KOSTROMA								
210. Kostroma	10,030	16,847	13,490	14,834	27,178	28,171	41,336	67,274
211. Kineshma	2,449	2,411	3,680	2,116	3,857	4,042	7,575	25,500
212. Galich	4,023	5,181	5,070	5,865	5,620	5,742	6,237	6,960
213. Makar'ev	1,882	2,642	2,980	3,597	5,202	5,549	6,046	6,302
214. Vetluga	916	1,102	1,770	2,998	3,939	4,350	5,179	5,569
215. Iur'evets	2,158	1,876	2,320	2,524	2,867	2,901	4,776	4,817
216. Soligalich	2,309	2,193	2,560	2,720	3,223	3,303	3,419	4,034
217. Bui	722	746	980	2,303	1,913	2,155	2,624	3,681
218. Nerekhta	1,771	1,578	2,020	2,296	3,385	3,334	3,092	3,361
219. Puchezh Posad	1,152	1,167	1,070	913	2,410	2,315	2,497	3,203
220. Kologriv	394	493	1,070	1,269	1,835	2,082	2,565	2,860
221. Chukhloma	830	971	1,340	2,016	1,949	1,978	2,202	2,481
222. Ples	1,501	1,467	2,100	2,360	2,418	2,461	2,164	2,190
223. Lukh	1,368	1,339	1,560	1,438	1,985	1,995	1,965	1,813
224. Varnavin	367	575	630	1,023	1,151	1,232	1,444	1,678
225. Unzha	712	868	1,100	1,181	1,506	1,687	1,284	1,604
226. Sudislavl'	540	716	1,030	1,183	1,018	1,053	1,362	1,520
227. Kadyi	553	463	600	819	841	946	1,095	1,235
	33,677	42,635	45,380	51,455	72,297	75,296	96,862	146,082
KURLIAND								
228. Libava	5,696	6,735	10,992	8,333	10,767	29,688	64,489	90,744
229. Mitava	10,818	12,458	20,321	17,403	22,185	30,039	35,131	35,011
230. Griva	-	-	-	-	-	-	8,009	12,240
231. Tukkum	1,359	2,269	2,804	2,701	3,751	6,678	7,555	12,000
232. Vindava	1,032	1,385	1,873	4,263	4,108	6,094	7,127	10,200
233. Gol'dingen	1,572	2,690	4,053	4,818	4,752	9,628	9,720	9,645
234. Fridrikhshtadt	773	678	1,279	2,151	3,915	6,242	5,175	6,005
235. Iakobshtadt	1,428	2,065	3,316	3,080	4,567	5,579	5,829	5,891

	1811	1825	1840	1856	1870	1885	1897	1910
KURLIAND								
236. Bausk	1,152	1,676	2,248	5,722	4,240	6,532	6,544	5,000
237. Tal'sen	—	—	—	—	—	—	4,200	4,357
238. Frauenburg	—	—	—	—	—	—	3,570	4,244
239. Gazenpot	1,394	743	2,312	6,030	3,344	3,631	3,340	3,840
240. Illukst	—	—	—	—	—	—	3,652	3,593
241. Polangen	—	—	—	—	—	—	2,149	2,353
242. Subbat	—	—	—	—	—	—	2,047	2,067
243. Doblen	—	—	—	—	—	—	—	1,973
244. Tsabel'n	—	—	—	—	—	—	—	1,468
245. Kandava	—	—	—	—	—	—	—	1,380
246. Grobin	797	778	1,167	1,167	1,858	1,566	1,490	1,359
247. Pil'ten	429	440	1,075	1,100	1,496	1,507	1,509	1,355
248. Sasmaken	—	—	—	—	—	—	—	1,304
249. Durben	—	—	—	—	—	—	—	596
	26,450	31,917	51,440	56,768	64,983	107,184	171,536	216,625
KURSK								
250. Kursk	23,481	15,800	30,469	40,771	31,754	49,657	75,721	87,963
251. Belgorod	8,231	9,033	8,382	12,796	16,097	22,676	26,564	31,666
252. Oboian	3,662	6,658	5,122	5,386	6,322	8,155	11,832	13,634
253. Ryl'sk	4,956	5,781	6,859	7,210	9,445	11,572	11,549	12,500
254. Korocha	2,523	2,575	4,253	6,002	6,563	9,409	10,235	10,763
255. Putivl'	3,563	4,675	4,520	6,104	7,046	10,565	9,955	9,991
256. Staryi Oskol'	4,115	4,850	5,129	7,535	7,191	10,960	15,617	9,022
257. Shchigry	988	1,541	2,425	3,733	4,946	6,363	6,061	6,940
258. L'gov	1,293	1,251	2,228	2,971	3,882	4,485	4,321	6,699
259. Graivoron	—	—	6,796	3,553	4,626	5,145	6,340	6,689
260. Sudzha	7,092	7,006	4,661	4,519	4,582	4,979	7,433	6,432
261. Dmitriev	997	1,703	2,329	2,756	3,004	4,313	6,073	6,105
262. Fatezh	3,159	2,662	3,417	4,657	5,528	5,183	6,034	5,038
263. Miropol'e	7,552	7,687*	7,822	8,911	10,754	3,289	10,101	4,288
264. Novyi Oskol'	3,379	4,885	1,130	966	2,837	1,660	2,996	3,898
265. Tim	1,474	1,420	1,506	2,830	4,860	4,553	7,377	2,861
266. Khotmyzhsk	2,318	707	342	364	534	915	2,863	2,639
267. Bogatyi	314	687*	1,060	1,257	1,863	338	455	1,119
	79,097	78,921	98,450	122,321	131,834	164,217	221,527	228,247

	1811	1825	1840	1857	1870	1885	1897	1910
LIFLIAND								
268. Riga	31,967	38,794	59,960	70,463	99,892	175,332	282,230	370,000
269. Iur'ev	6,006	8,450	12,203	12,914	20,540	30,643	42,308	43,940
270. Valk	1,025	1,195	870	1,936	2,923	4,318	10,922	20,500
271. Pernov	2,373	4,392	4,530	5,684	9,568	13,221	12,898	14,500
272. Fellin	1,052	1,781	1,736	2,094	2,888	5,336	7,736	7,600
273. Venden	769	1,063	1,732	1,338	3,522	4,333	6,356	6,806
274. Vol'mar	524	544	932	1,125	2,051	2,580	5,050	4,930
275. Arensburg	2,372	1,693	2,993	3,736	3,136	3,456	4,603	4,669
276. Shlok	-	295	525	437	789	1,375	2,114	4,500
277. Verro	561	679	813	1,472	2,010	2,795	4,152	4,211
278. Lemzal'	666	586	877	1,108	1,442	1,839	2,412	3,500
	47,315	59,472	87,171	102,307	148,761	245,228	380,781	485,156
MINSK								
279. Minsk	11,205	15,626	23,602	25,525	35,563	53,399	90,912	105,441
280. Bobruisk	2,137	6,829	5,701	17,103	26,872	57,444	34,336	40,218
281. Pinsk	2,415	4,217	6,816	10,368	17,718	26,251	28,368	36,441
282. Borisov	3,166	2,188	5,839	5,656	5,882	17,373	15,063	19,147
283. Slutsk	3,478	4,707	6,895	7,490	9,882	19,208	14,349	16,146
284. Rechitsa	1,865	2,440	3,312	5,657	4,247	6,956	9,280	12,054
285. Mozyr'	2,801	2,921	3,868	4,601	4,166	10,554	8,076	10,619
286. Nesvizh	-	3,544	4,230	4,975	7,266	9,165	8,459	9,417
287. Novogrudok	2,320	1,865	3,673	5,864	8,553	11,701	7,887	8,422
288. Igumen	804	894	1,713	2,780	2,190	4,095	4,573	5,617
289. Dokshitsy	633	898	1,966	1,545	1,970	4,759	3,642	4,404
290. Osipovichi	-	-	-	-	-	-	-	1,695
	30,824	46,129	67,615	91,544	124,083	220,905	224,945	269,621
MOGILEV								
291. Gomel'	1,409	1,494	2,363	10,113	13,030	26,192	36,775	96,149
292. Mogilev	5,808	11,632	17,868	22,815	40,431	41,899	43,119	52,528
293. Rogachev	744	1,635	2,249	3,379	7,009	5,615	9,038	21,300
294. Orsha	1,951	2,158	2,814	2,869	5,024	4,715	13,061	18,967
295. Mstislavl'	2,974	2,974	6,014	6,599	6,648	7,803	8,514	16,171
296. Groki	-	-	-	-	5,035	5,092	6,735	8,028
297. Staryi Bykhov	2,553	3,410	5,223	6,247	5,172	6,074	6,381	7,863

		1811	1825	1840	1856	1870	1885	1897	1910
MOGILEV									
298.	Chausy	2,409	3,986	4,373	4,772	4,167	5,202	4,960	6,845
299.	Klimovichi	1,210	962	1,829	2,267	2,010	3,355	4,714	6,542
300.	Cherikov	1,797	2,134	3,028	3,295	3,853	3,987	5,249	6,225
301.	Senno	984	1,279	1,028	1,856	2,508	3,110	4,100	5,708
302.	Kopys'	1,874	2,265	2,293	3,117	1,860	3,393	3,384	5,644
303.	Babinovichi	368	488	1,145	1,125	729	1,012	1,157	1,448
		24,081	34,417	50,227	68,454	97,476	117,449	147,187	253,418
MOSCOW									
304.	Moscow	81,053	241,514	349,068	368,765	460,894	753,469	1,038,591	1,481,240
305.	Serpukhov	5,219	5,412	13,585	15,440	16,620	20,983	30,571	36,795
306.	Kolomna	7,416	8,044	14,341	13,830	18,808	28,114	20,277	27,600
307.	Sergievskii Posad	2,148	4,226	4,032	12,077	27,471	29,342	15,155	21,698
308.	Bogorodsk	818	943	1,379	1,219	2,064	2,311	11,102	16,046
309.	Pavlovskii Posad	–	–	–	2,915	4,465	6,898	9,991	15,929
310.	Podol'sk	942	1,089	1,849	3,674	11,033	11,199	3,798	9,060
311.	Dmitrov	4,055	4,850	6,583	6,842	7,529	9,154	4,480	5,608
312.	Volokolamsk	1,429	1,209	1,526	2,109	2,851	889	3,095	5,134
313.	Klin	1,258	1,320	3,085	3,914	6,643	7,635	4,655	4,691
314.	Bronnitsy	1,885	1,658	2,734	4,692	3,424	6,093	3,897	4,324
315.	Mozhaisk	2,383	1,645	2,572	3,216	4,160	4,412	3,194	4,203
316.	Ruza	1,801	1,931	2,345	2,975	3,991	5,436	3,349	3,808
317.	Vereia	4,055	5,091	5,687	5,310	5,502	5,502	3,707	3,629
318.	Zvenigorod	1,070	1,510	1,532	2,377	1,759	2,288	2,381	3,109
319.	Voskresensk	578	601	616	1,291	5,959	1,625	2,289	2,446
		216,110	281,043	410,934	450,646	583,273	895,340	1,159,528	1,645,320
NIZHEGOROD									
320.	Nizhnii Novgorod	14,412	15,965	31,921	35,803	44,190	66,585	90,053	101,114
321.	Arzamas	7,835	7,217	8,931	10,349	10,406	11,770	10,592	13,033
322.	Pochinki	5,422	4,866	6,727	8,243	7,224	7,614	9,851	11,252
323.	Gorbatov	1,770	2,192	2,509	3,222	2,683	3,149	4,604	5,063
324.	Semenov	1,531	1,925	1,917	2,799	2,961	2,900	3,752	4,786
325.	Balakhna	3,975	3,400	3,891	3,638	3,905	5,143	5,120	4,657
326.	Vasil'-Sursk	1,602	1,728	1,811	2,112	2,507	3,092	3,799	4,030

	1811	1825	1840	1856	1870	1885	1897	1910
NIZHGOROD								
327. Ardatov	1,669	1,941	2,738	2,739	3,108	3,170	3,546	3,573
328. Lukoianov	1,848	2,011	2,832	2,892	2,371	1,750	2,117	2,313
329. Kniaginin	1,898	1,277	1,885	6,656	1,708	1,940	2,737	2,167
330. Sergach	2,435	2,399	3,311	3,430	3,629	1,556	4,530	1,725
331. Makar'ev	1,555	1,689	1,808	2,445	1,656	1,596	1,560	1,125
332. Perevoz	524	527	503	2,066	634	738	770	898
	46,476	47,137	70,784	86,394	86,982	111,003	142,731	155,736
NOVGOROD								
333. Novgorod	6,341	5,445	16,781	12,758	17,093	23,980	25,736	26,438
334. Staraia Russa	6,828	6,566	8,168	8,044	14,756	13,537	15,183	19,986
335. Borovichi	5,393	3,932	5,807	8,644	8,338	10,147	9,431	13,857
336. Malaia Vyshera Posad	—	—	—	—	—	4,076	4,851	10,006
337. Cherepovets	1,404	1,258	1,649	2,706	3,540	5,952	6,948	9,419
338. Tikhvin	3,889	3,803	5,688	6,359	5,969	6,554	6,589	8,344
339. Ustiuzhna	2,584	3,167	1,029	5,058	6,900	7,603	5,111	7,456
340. Belozersk	2,807	2,955	4,785	4,144	4,754	4,506	5,015	5,331
341. Kirillov	2,154	2,112	2,450	2,651	3,092	4,345	4,306	5,246
342. Valdai	3,238	3,870	4,319	4,880	3,734	4,307	2,907	4,956
343. Kresttsy	1,844	2,073	1,337	2,576	3,173	2,807	2,596	3,006
344. Demiansk	—	567	640	1,652	1,474	1,338	1,648	2,038
	36,482	35,748	52,653	59,472	72,823	86,152	90,321	116,083
OLONETS								
345. Petrozavodsk	4,729	5,189	5,064	10,144	10,901	12,182	12,522	13,049
346. Vytegra	2,206	2,130	1,982	2,467	2,880	2,610	4,502	5,382
347. Kargopol'	2,516	2,246	1,587	1,955	2,048	2,539	3,057	3,133
348. Olonets	1,080	967	572	1,155	1,341	1,384	1,246	2,175
349. Pudozh	959	1,027	1,086	1,025	1,106	1,356	1,455	1,826
350. Lodeinoe Pole	507	1,306	581	1,127	1,133	1,202	1,432	1,648
351. Povenets	533	499	569	520	518	823	1,294	1,482
	12,530	13,364	11,441	18,393	19,927	22,096	25,508	28,695

		1811	1825	1840	1856	1870	1885	1897	1910
OREL									
352.	Orel	24,617	26,816	32,600	35,281	44,281	78,091	69,735	91,051
353.	Elets	14,678	12,385	25,880	23,188	30,540	39,302	46,956	58,100
354.	Briansk	4,821	6,840	8,518	11,254	14,657	16,475	24,781	30,440-
355.	Livny	2,773	4,016	6,837	10,073	12,975	25,104	20,448	22,240
356.	Bolkhov	9,683	12,833	13,332	17,216	19,224	26,532	21,446	21,329
357.	Karachev	6,549	7,180	5,726	9,896	11,267	15,493	19,381	20,660
358.	Mtsensk	8,077	8,961	8,221	12,288	14,159	15,019	9,823	14,058
359.	Maloarkhangel'sk	3,150	3,854	2,801	4,266	4,891	5,019	7,785	8,578
360.	Sevsk	4,350	6,121	7,098	5,768	8,798	8,486	9,248	8,256
361.	Trubshevsk	2,885	3,277	5,170	4,021	5,451	5,275	7,416	7,845
362.	Dmitrovsk	3,596	4,019	5,752	5,567	5,992	6,707	5,291	7,556
363.	Kromy	1,646	1,935	3,092	2,593	2,992	3,074	5,586	4,945
		86,825	98,237	125,027	141,411	175,227	243,669	244,008	295,058
ORENBURG									
364.	Orenburg	5,449	6,050	14,644	13,662	35,623	56,371	72,425	91,240
365.	Cheliabinsk	2,445	3,054	3,507	4,322	5,811	9,542	19,998	70,472
366.	Troitsk	1,850	2,553	3,715	3,134	8,298	17,254	23,299	35,110
367.	Orsk	—	—	—	—	4,584	20,014	14,016	21,610
368.	Verkhneural'sk	2,280	2,992	3,003	3,360	4,957	9,860	11,095	16,300
369.	Iletskaia Zashchita	—	—	—	—	2,886	7,355	11,768	15,412
370.	Seitovskii Posad	—	—	—	—	—	6,795	8,733	11,097
		12,024	14,649	24,869	24,478	62,159	127,191	161,334	261,241
PENZA									
371.	Penza	14,822	13,128	19,479	23,772	30,462	44,735	59,981	79,552
372.	Kerensk	5,806	6,269	7,362	7,946	5,197	13,587	4,004	16,070
373.	Saransk	9,109	8,215	10,109	5,443	13,438	13,921	14,584	15,281
374.	Mokshan	5,576	6,040	8,192	10,139	14,404	13,367	10,044	11,068
375.	Krasnoslobodsk	6,292	4,539	7,719	6,176	5,253	7,899	7,381	8,435
376.	Troisk	4,683	4,263	4,230	4,988	5,351	5,892	5,822	7,631
377.	Chembar	2,689	2,593	2,741	4,146	4,048	5,753	5,345	6,361
378.	Nizhnii Lomov	5,819	3,002	6,441	8,904	10,171	9,792	9,996	5,710
379.	Insar	3,942	2,975	2,971	7,433	3,604	6,138	4,244	5,400
380.	Gorodishche	3,435	3,162	4,292	4,517	3,617	3,790	3,965	4,586
381.	Shishkeev	2,754	2,687	2,689	4,802	5,297	3,712	3,810	4,229

	1811	1825	1840	1856	1870	1885	1897	1910
PENZA								
382. Narovchat	3,747	3,626	3,967	3,479	4,541	4,673	4,710	2,116
383. Verkhnii Lomov	4,929	5,490	5,666	6,315	8,414	6,518	5,952	718
	73,603	65,989	85,858	98,060	114,797	139,777	139,838	167,157
PERM								
384. Ekaterinburg	4,119	11,889	16,669	16,939	25,133	31,923	43,239	70,000
385. Perm	3,057	7,254	11,972	9,484	22,288	32,909	45,205	61,614
386. Kungur'	5,683	7,175	8,370	9,854	10,804	11,855	14,295	19,638
387. Shadrinsk	—	2,364	589	4,672	7,194	14,740	11,678	14,000
388. Kamyshlov	347	1,304	1,459	1,693	2,164	3,167	8,210	9,908
389. Irbit	—	3,174	3,043	3,230	4,212	5,347	20,062	8,590
390. Osa	—	1,505	1,566	1,276	2,815	2,989	5,067	7,119
391. Krasnoufimsk	3,046	3,233	1,568	2,402	3,682	4,438	6,251	7,100
392. Dediukhin	—	—	2,706	3,724	3,611	4,498	3,318	4,303
393. Solikamsk	2,288	2,369	2,840	2,760	3,733	3,901	4,073	4,003
394. Cherdyn'	—	2,641	2,765	3,283	3,261	3,485	3,658	3,742
395. Verkhotur'e	2,226	2,232	2,358	3,050	3,485	2,834	3,179	3,387
396. Okhansk	—	718	859	985	1,633	3,516	1,894	2,387
397. Dalmatov	—	2,470	2,819	4,570	4,337	1,648	564	1,889
398. Alapaevsk	—	2,770	2,833	5,084	5,422	6,951	8,646	1,662
	20,766	51,098	62,416	73,006	103,774	134,201	179,339	219,258
PODOLIIA								
399. Kamenets-Podol'sk	3,632	6,849	14,700	18,262	22,611	35,989	35,934	49,611
400. Vinnitsa	3,482	4,995	9,212	8,988	18,780	18,733	30,563	47,841
401. Proskurov	2,270	3,060	5,763	5,952	11,451	17,929	22,855	40,611
402. Mogilev-na-Dnestre	6,978	8,198	9,304	8,930	18,029	16,274	22,315	32,604
403. Zhmerinka	—	—	—	—	—	—	12,908	28,670
404. Balta	3,628	5,106	8,931	12,306	18,842	32,983	23,363	27,925
405. Bar	2,447	4,030	6,791	4,694	7,789	13,434	9,982	22,660
406. Khmel'nik	3,759	4,787	4,540	8,540	7,787	12,228	11,657	18,381
407. Gaisin	2,096	2,477	4,855	6,071	9,417	9,791	9,374	14,102
408. Litin	2,038	3,422	3,633	5,863	7,081	9,071	9,420	12,882
409. Bratslav	1,470	2,149	3,588	4,222	5,525	6,836	7,863	11,428

	1910	1897	1885	1870	1856	1840	1825	1811
PODOLIIA								
410. Ol'gopol'	11,341	8,134	6,198	6,922	4,396	2,478	1,421	1,970
411. Letichev	10,549	7,248	7,342	4,772	4,745	2,978	2,147	1,668
412. Novaia Ushitsa	8,035	6,371	4,993	4,502	3,497	—	—	—
413. Iampol'	7,481	6,605	5,463	4,305	3,446	2,827	2,294	1,812
414. Staraia Ushita	7,251	4,176	4,346	3,708	1,941	2,540	1,173	1,085
415. Sal'nitsa	4,469	3,699	2,451	3,265	1,920	1,532*	1,143	1,183
416. Verbovets	3,559	2,311	2,036	2,121	721	931*	1,141	665
	359,400	234,778	206,097	156,907	104,494	84,603	54,392	40,183
POLTAVA								
417. Kremenchug	88,425	63,007	41,625	30,472	20,030	17,533	7,748	8,350
418. Poltava	59,880	53,703	42,210	33,979	20,516	15,966	10,557	10,083
419. Romny	30,754	22,510	12,784	5,952	5,446	4,951	3,559	4,156
420. Priluki	29,109	18,532	15,231	12,878	9,500	8,185	5,830	5,973
421. Pereiaslavl'	18,156	14,614	13,794	9,287	7,540	8,373	5,422	4,327
422. Mirgorod	16,992	10,037	8,682	7,445	8,699	7,523	7,375	6,502
423. Lubny	16,961	10,097	10,317	5,205	2,802	2,516	1,972	2,208
424. Piriatin	16,702	8,022	5,977	4,887	3,697	3,324	2,343	2,667
425. Kobeliaki	14,365	8,487	14,197	12,989	7,260	8,422	6,628	7,612
426. Zolotonosha	13,835	8,739	8,417	7,896	6,286	5,319	4,344	4,159
427. Konstantinograd	12,935	6,455	6,890	4,679	3,139	2,400	2,767	1,124
428. Zen'kov	12,767	10,443	13,775	10,589	8,577	8,954	7,019	6,553
429. Khorol'	11,603	7,997	5,842	5,501	3,720	3,869	2,717	3,188
430. Lokhvitsa	10,742	8,911	9,978	7,903	3,122	5,571	4,947	3,875
431. Gradizhsk	10,500	9,486	10,586	7,107	7,340	3,174	5,139	4,313
432. Gadiach	10,285	7,721	9,754	8,425	6,007	5,928	3,529	3,335
433. Glinsk	7,613	3,533	4,575	2,857	2,704	2,996	2,375	2,471
	381,624	274,294	234,634	178,051	130,385	115,004	84,271	80,596
PSKOV								
434. Pskov	36,069	30,478	21,684	18,331	16,329	10,269	8,685	9,290
435. Velikie Luki	10,188	8,466	6,809	5,714	5,637	4,900	3,735	3,493
436. Toropets	8,443	7,368	5,943	4,989	6,000	6,084	4,967	5,055
437. Opochka	8,041	5,735	4,943	2,617	4,275	2,472	2,103	3,052
438. Ostrov	7,061	6,268	4,284	3,625	2,581	2,275	1,416	1,445
439. Kholm	6,541	5,894	5,718	4,718	5,056	3,858	2,789	2,277
440. Porkhov	6,452	5,551	3,996	3,399	5,929	4,900	3,275	2,708

	1811	1825	1840	1856	1870	1885	1897	1910
PSKOV								
441. Sol'tsa Posad	2,480	2,799	5,847	4,855	5,042	5,903	3,981	6,051
442. Aleksandrovskii Posad	-	1,237	1,801	1,043	2,734	2,944	3,082	3,718
443. Novorzhev	695	615	1,425	1,346	1,658	1,925	2,838	3,667
444. Pechora	910	925	1,299	1,186	1,305	1,360	1,690*	2,019
	31,945	32,546	45,130	54,237	54,432	64,915	81,351	98,250
RIAZAN'								
445. Riazan'	7,751	18,326	18,951	21,499	19,990	30,327	46,122	41,433
446. Egor'evsk	1,246	1,341	2,058	5,629	5,101	6,179	19,239	29,183
447. Kasimov	5,763	6,409	7,305	9,602	14,102	15,478	13,547	17,081
448. Skopin	7,426	7,613	11,294	11,217	9,447	10,421	13,247	16,844
449. Zaraisk	4,462	5,490	6,373	6,332	5,037	5,918	8,054	8,830
450. Sapozhok	2,248	2,536	3,473	4,356	2,817	2,945	8,550	6,216
451. Ranenburg	2,025	2,840	4,578	6,351	4,594	4,298	15,331	5,823
452. Spask	2,796	3,080	4,894	4,743	3,652	4,383	4,759	5,753
453. Riazhsk	1,216	2,648	3,026	2,882	2,931	4,563	14,835	5,474
454. Dankov	1,439	1,558	2,448	3,291	2,153	2,491	9,121	4,618
455. Mikhailov	2,355	2,153	3,489	4,526	3,309	3,000	9,162	4,556
456. Pronsk	1,193	1,247	1,293	2,017	1,641	1,764	7,907	3,958
	39,920	54,941	69,181	82,545	74,804	91,767	169,874	149,769
SAMARA								
457. Samara	4,370	5,199	13,732	24,405	51,947	75,478	89,999	145,568
458. Buguruslan	2,084	2,713	3,824	5,431	7,938	20,062	12,109	21,459
459. Buzuluk	1,652	2,200	2,311	5,626	14,876	19,562	14,362	18,757
460. Novouzensk	-	-	4,719	5,509	7,543	12,034	13,261	18,075
461. Melekes Posad	-	-	-	-	-	6,834	8,463	15,252
462. Nikolaevsk	-	-	2,902	5,687	9,794	10,433	12,504	15,000
463. Bugul'ma	2,283	2,719	4,339	3,598	5,279	13,819	7,581	9,569
464. Stavropol'	2,084	2,165	3,381	4,166	4,265	4,883	5,969	6,510
465. Sergievsk	-	1,115	1,966*	2,817	3,978	2,710	3,057	4,536
	12,473	16,111	37,174	57,239	105,620	165,815	164,305	254,726

SAINT PETERSBURG

		1811	1825	1840	1856	1870	1885	1897	1910
466.	Saint Petersburg	335,616	438,112	470,202	490,808	667,207	861,303	1,264,920	1,566,000
467.	Kronshtadt	-	26,193	54,717	39,905	47,166	42,603	59,525	68,673
468.	Tsarskoe Selo	1,920	6,044	12,859	10,833	14,465	16,838	22,480	30,340
469.	Narva	3,057	6,388	4,589	6,131	6,482	12,188	16,599	21,542
470.	Gatchina	-	2,554	6,250	5,248	8,890	11,557	14,824	18,183
471.	Kolpino Posad	-	-	-	-	-	8,076	12,241	15,845
472.	Petergof	-	-	2,209	6,951	7,875	9,516	11,316	15,485
473.	Luga	511	2,210	808	1,398	1,541	1,834	5,617	10,000
474.	Oranienbaum	1,330	1,305	2,048	3,392	4,043	3,523	5,458	8,987
475.	Shissel'burg	2,259	2,693	2,855	3,134	7,892	5,542	5,284	7,802
476.	Pavlovsk	-	2,175	3,219	2,382	2,993	3,702	5,113	6,252
477.	Iamburg	482	802	2,126	2,057	2,490	3,343	4,584	4,150
478.	Novaia Ladoga	2,188	3,255	3,337	3,435	4,179	3,566	3,927	3,783
479.	Gdov	1,117	839	1,634	2,287	1,393	2,827	2,106	2,665
		348,480	492,570	566,853	577,961	776,616	986,418	1,433,994	1,769,707

SARATOV

		1811	1825	1840	1856	1870	1885	1897	1910
480.	Saratov	26,744	38,280	42,237	61,610	85,220	122,829	137,147	217,418
481.	Tsaritsyn	3,834	4,055	4,426	7,193	11,826	35,997	55,186	100,811
482.	Vol'sk	8,510	10,849	14,009	21,499	31,269	36,315	27,058	36,134
483.	Kuznetsk	6,891	7,190	9,560	11,774	14,185	18,350	20,473	27,388
484.	Kamyshin	3,202	3,266	8,100	10,438	15,698	15,257	16,264	22,200
485.	Balashov	2,173	2,711	4,008	6,630	6,910	10,135	10,300	21,927
486.	Petrovsk	6,921	5,439	6,544	9,367	10,771	15,316	13,304	19,346
487.	Khvalynsk	3,549	3,964	7,707	12,948	15,628	21,980	15,127	18,261
488.	Dubovskii Posad	4,417	3,397	6,753	11,611	12,737	14,543	16,255	17,700
489.	Atkarsk	2,794	1,364	4,450	6,390	15,199	7,816	7,300	12,779
490.	Serdobsk	5,317	2,417	3,258	9,985	12,202	10,738	7,381	12,452
		74,352	82,932	111,052	169,445	231,645	309,276	325,804	506,416

SIMBIRSK

		1811	1825	1840	1856	1870	1885	1897	1910
491.	Simbirsk	13,319	14,994	17,739	26,521	26,822	39,047	41,684	52,378
492.	Syzran'	7,089	9,025	12,932	17,837	19,443	28,624	32,383	45,256
493.	Alatyr'	3,396	3,565	4,960	7,713	8,451	14,077	12,209	19,411
494.	Sengilei	2,487	2,484	3,190	4,085	3,501	5,172	5,734	8,811
495.	Ardatov	2,311	2,721	4,192	4,291	4,735	5,624	4,855	6,355
496.	Buinsk	2,631	3,040	3,071	3,443	4,127	5,091	4,213	5,271

	1811	1825	1840	1856	1870	1885	1897	1910
SIMBIRSK								
497. Korsun'	3,027	3,711	4,308	4,100	3,736	4,078	3,805	4,541
498. Kurmysh	1,206	1,060	962	1,914	1,925	2,412	3,166	2,660
	35,466	40,600	51,354	69,904	72,740	104,125	108,049	144,683
SMOLENSK								
499. Smolensk	12,405	10,767	11,010	9,187	24,332	34,348	46,699	59,000
500. Viaz'ma	7,955	7,841	10,488	10,213	11,637	13,148	15,645	28,900
501. Roslavl'	3,934	3,886	5,598	6,287	6,638	9,725	17,776	27,473
502. Belyi	3,131	3,614	4,493	6,200	6,631	8,923	6,952	11,200
503. Dorogobuzh	4,694	4,146	5,558	6,133	9,099	8,727	6,486	10,300
504. Gzhatsk	2,709	3,243	3,784	3,817	8,242	6,995	6,324	9,493
505. Porech'e	2,887	3,058	3,806	3,757	4,998	5,998	5,688	7,604
506. Sychevka	1,846	2,425	3,432	3,465	4,059	4,984	4,773	6,287
507. Dukhovshchitsa	1,340	1,726	2,325	2,713	3,550	3,636	3,109	5,430
508. Krasnyi	1,494	1,220	1,434	2,135	3,493	3,383	2,753	4,019
509. Iukhnov	887	1,145	1,414	1,803	3,072	3,503	2,249	2,310
510. El'nia	1,340	1,638	2,785	3,743	3,861	5,907	2,441	2,000
	44,655	44,709	56,127	59,453	89,612	109,277	120,895	174,016
TAVRIDA								
511. Sevastopol'	—	21,920	41,145	6,213	13,259	33,803	53,595	77,378
512. Simferopol'	2,460	3,672	12,891	26,481	17,129	36,503	49,078	66,452
513. Kerch-Enikol'	1,454	2,185	8,228	12,660	22,449	29,084	34,785	54,144
514. Feodosiia	—	5,545	4,709	8,530	8,482	12,406	24,096	35,916
515. Berdiansk	—	—	3,435	9,702	12,223	20,861	26,496	34,214
516. Evpatoriia	5,278	11,145	9,820	5,437	8,294	15,970	17,913	30,432
517. Aleshki	—	2,177	4,060	4,206	8,187	4,302	8,999	22,901
518. Ialta	—	—	371	255	1,369	—	13,155	21,874
519. Melitopol'	—	—	—	3,687	4,852	12,774	15,489	18,025
520. Karasubazar	6,886	11,237	12,104	15,240	11,669	12,800	12,968	17,122
521. Bakhchisarai	8,872	9,165	12,391	12,161	10,528	14,193	12,959	15,689
522. Genichensk	—	—	—	—	—	—	8,061	12,955
523. Orekhov	—	4,305	5,557	4,263	5,600	4,611	5,996	7,352
524. Nogaisk	—	—	961	2,104	3,022	3,896	3,963	6,129
525. Staryi Krym	—	2,164	1,176	1,714	1,143	3,264	3,330	5,752
526. Perekop	2,717	4,254	4,045	7,405	4,331	6,692	5,279	5,406
527. Alushta	—	—	—	—	—	—	2,182	4,105

	1811	1825	1840	1856	1870	1885	1897	1910
TAVRIDA								
528. Balaklava	—	—	371	255	695	2,347	1,215	2,240
	27,667	77,769	121,354	121,218	133,232	222,577	299,559	438,086
TAMBOV								
529. Tambov	16,830	18,354	16,789	21,950	26,403	36,688	48,015	60,729
530. Kozlov	12,390	13,528	20,682	20,554	25,522	27,892	40,297	60,215
531. Morshansk	4,914	6,674	9,993	12,278	19,504	21,190	26,458	30,490
532. Borisoglebsk	4,323	2,202	5,379	8,052	12,610	13,007	22,309	29,137
533. Lipetsk	4,892	5,926	8,033	11,300	14,213	15,860	20,524	23,541
534. Kirsanov	1,560	2,828	3,517	6,047	7,203	7,672	9,331	10,676
535. Spassk	5,008	5,281	7,906	4,453	5,018	5,484	6,439	10,014
536. Elat'ma	5,499	4,841	6,053	6,590	7,107	7,562	4,578	9,331
537. Kadom	—	3,988	5,329*	6,670	7,107	7,492	6,314	8,865
538. Temnikov	4,350	4,990	5,962	6,842	6,592	7,107	5,399	8,083
539. Lebedian'	3,746	2,541	3,845	4,989	6,010	6,248	12,774	7,500
540. Usman'	4,268	5,525	7,540	5,467	7,488	7,665	9,986	7,469
541. Shatsk	6,752	4,729	5,483	6,207	7,261	7,663	13,840	5,310
	74,532	81,407	106,511	121,369	152,038	171,530	226,264	271,360
TVER'								
542. Tver'	17,528	33,119	17,085	12,867	38,248	39,280	53,544	62,652
543. Rzhev	9,016	9,120	15,228	13,621	18,732	35,810	21,265	23,606
544. Vyshnii Volochek	6,239	7,176	8,782	8,340	17,408	15,838	16,612	17,521
545. Torzhok	10,115	10,493	13,571	10,160	12,910	14,574	12,698	13,723
546. Ostashkov	7,164	7,852	10,502	9,163	10,806	11,592	10,445	10,736
547. Bezhetsk	2,560	2,683	2,586	3,588	6,845	6,668	9,450	9,893
548. Kashin	3,779	4,490	6,417	5,161	7,516	6,873	7,544	7,867
549. Staritsa	2,343	2,593	3,082	3,444	5,600	4,709	6,368	6,914
550. Kaliazin	4,518	3,066	6,389	6,324	7,167	7,988	5,496	5,670
551. Ves'egonsk	2,009	2,070	2,256	2,947	3,586	2,629	3,457	3,528
552. Zubtsov	1,588	1,776	3,036	2,976	3,301	4,191	2,992	3,202
553. Krasnyi Kholm	1,542	1,557	1,666	1,827	1,932	1,791	2,514	2,680
554. Pogoreloe Gorodishche	1,210	1,215	1,588*	1,961	2,188	2,129	2,337*	2,545
555. Korcheva Posad	999	1,171	1,480	1,859	1,850	3,417	2,384	2,500
	70,610	88,381	93,668	84,238	138,089	157,489	157,106	173,037

TULA

No.	City	1811	1825	1840	1856	1870	1885	1897	1910
556.	Tula	52,084	38,391	51,735	50,641	57,374	63,928	114,733	125,147
557.	Belev	6,900	6,562	8,818	7,745	8,640	9,484	9,562	14,348
558.	Efremov	3,494	3,899	7,366	9,801	7,402	9,801	9,038	8,997
559.	Odoev	2,610	2,027	2,932	3,934	4,681	5,172	4,317	7,375
560.	Kashira	1,807	2,044	3,967	3,221	3,873	4,725	4,038	7,304
561.	Bogoroditsk	4,286	3,903	5,362	4,664	7,982	7,980	4,768	6,224
562.	Venev	3,139	2,712	3,925	4,301	4,459	3,474	5,167	5,366
563.	Epifan	1,160	2,641	2,914	2,982	4,697	3,882	4,174	5,065
564.	Novosil'	1,581	1,685	2,264	2,521	3,027	4,623	2,912	3,682
565.	Aleksin	2,090	1,790	2,318	2,170	3,891	5,426	3,465	2,600
566.	Krapivna	1,384	1,927	2,693	2,923	2,446	1,732	6,146	2,529
567.	Chern'	1,147	1,540	1,538	3,386	3,978	2,666	3,660	2,507
		81,682	69,121	95,832	98,289	112,450	122,893	171,980	191,144

UFA

No.	City	1811	1825	1840	1856	1870	1885	1897	1910
568.	Ufa	9,181	7,589	16,501	12,894	20,917	26,251	49,275	99,614
569.	Zlatoust	—	—	—	5,501	16,629	19,014	20,502	32,101
570.	Sterlitamak	2,143	2,437	3,613	2,908	6,037	9,097	15,550	18,738
571.	Birsk	2,548	2,077	1,963	4,713	4,001	8,428	8,589	14,796
572.	Menzelinsk	2,825	3,690	4,269	2,252	4,995	6,108	7,552	8,573
573.	Belebei	688	993	1,187	—	2,565	4,224	5,835	7,814
		17,385	16,786	27,533	28,268	55,104	73,122	107,303	181,636

KHAR'KOV

No.	City	1811	1825	1840	1856	1870	1885	1897	1910
574.	Khar'kov	10,431	17,424	29,395	30,600	81,028	171,416	173,989	244,526
575.	Sumy	9,053	9,700	11,712	12,120	14,126	15,831	27,564	48,241
576.	Akhtyrka	11,599	13,556	14,640	13,583	17,820	24,086	23,399	29,936
577.	Slaviansk	—	4,081	6,205	7,822	11,689	16,183	15,792	21,000
578.	Belopol'e	9,762	1,906	10,479	10,568	12,256	12,803	15,215	18,214
579.	Lebedin	4,059	10,878	10,439	10,102	11,897	15,311	14,301	16,793
580.	Izium	3,445	5,739	7,628	7,685	12,962	18,134	13,108	16,644
581.	Volchansk	9,722	4,941	5,970	7,845	9,365	14,259	11,020	14,544
582.	Valki	7,224	7,011	7,309	7,998	7,630	5,507	7,938	13,751
583.	Bogodukhov	6,534	9,338	8,619	9,172	9,801	12,443	11,752	13,668
584.	Kupiansk	—	4,698	3,460	3,643	4,247	3,197	6,893	13,525
585.	Zolochev	—	5,984	5,709	6,423	5,995	6,584	6,573	10,600
586.	Chuguev	—	—	—	8,130	10,061	10,147	12,592	6,900
587.	Krasnokutsk	—	4,448	5,838	5,409	5,678	6,087	6,860	6,771
588.	Starobelsk	—	968	1,923	6,023	12,960	8,270	9,801	5,939
589.	Nedrigailov	—	4,213	3,976	4,740	5,061	6,694	5,873	5,706
590.	Zmiev	1,967	2,399	2,905	3,400	4,050	4,604	4,673	4,257

		1811	1825	1840	1856	1870	1885	1897	1910
KHERSON									
591.	Odessa	10,988	40,562	60,055	101,320	139,462	240,000	403,815	620,143-
592.	Nikolaev	4,190	15,762	28,664	44,280	73,681	67,249	92,012	103,391
593.	Kherson	8,972	8,073	22,589	33,813	46,320	67,349	59,076	91,858
594.	Elisavetgrad	4,822	9,326	11,410*	13,494	35,179	58,496	61,488	75,800
595.	Tiraspol'	4,000	4,479	6,639	7,015	16,692	23,541	31,616	35,242
596.	Anan'ev	—	—	—	6,506	15,983	14,259	16,684	22,193
597.	Aleksandriia	785	1,566	4,834	5,527	10,521	17,441	14,007	20,505
598.	Vosnesensk	—	—	—	5,235	9,458	11,629	15,748	19,300
599.	Bobrinets	—	—	5,708	8,061	7,137	10,680	14,281	18,470
600.	Novogeorgievsk	2,628	4,170	5,227*	6,183	10,225	8,694	11,594	13,441
601.	Berislav	1,735	2,900	4,763	6,301	8,078	11,093	12,149	12,081
602.	Dubossary	2,651	4,817	4,212	5,316	6,402	9,697	12,089	11,391
603.	Berezovka	—	—	—	—	—	—	6,154	10,620
604.	Ochakov	1,335	1,665	4,831	4,789	5,227	8,032	10,786	10,620
605.	Bogoiavlensk Posad	—	—	—	—	—	6,970	7,385	10,546
606.	Ol'viopol'	1,956	1,158	1,061*	964	5,397	5,368	6,884	9,639
607.	Grigoriopol'	2,809	2,318	3,658	5,402	6,791	8,656	7,605	8,993
608.	Berezniagovatyi Posad	—	—	—	—	—	4,297	6,578	8,640
609.	Visunsk Posad	—	—	—	—	—	5,057	6,599	8,579
610.	Ovidiopol'	964	1,123	2,921	3,254	4,687	5,776	5,187	5,544
611.	Kalinovka Posad	—	—	—	—	—	3,277	4,076	5,419
612.	Novaia Praga Posad	—	—	—	—	—	10,421	12,622	4,993
613.	Maiaki	—	—	—	—	—	3,740	4,575	4,850
614.	Novomirgorod	—	—	—	6,582	7,785	3,280	9,364	4,750
615.	Voskresensk Posad	—	—	—	—	5,893	3,024	3,093	4,244
616.	Pokrovsk Posad	—	—	—	—	—	996	2,196	4,121
		47,834	97,919	166,572	264,042	414,918	609,022	837,663	1,145,373
CHERNIGOV									
617.	Nezhin	12,587	11,687	16,819	16,342	21,590	43,023	32,113	51,905
618.	Chernigov	4,534	6,976	11,100	4,279	16,174	26,703	27,716	31,784
619.	Konotop	4,417	5,576	7,610	8,612	9,946	16,418	18,770	27,400
620.	Starodub	5,547	5,673	8,867	7,733	12,333	24,388	12,381	20,957
621.	Glukhov	5,393	4,483	8,806	8,856	13,398	16,440	14,828	20,670
622.	Novozybkov	4,935	3,711	5,688	7,167	7,612	11,924	15,362	20,541
623.	Krolevets	4,403	6,543	6,188	6,205	8,145	9,190	10,384	16,672
624.	Borzna	5,711	6,086	7,679	6,746	7,574	13,798	12,526	14,750
625.	Klintsy Posad	—	—	—	—	—	11,635	12,166	13,696

CHERNIGOV

		1811	1825	1840	1856	1870	1885	1897	1910
626.	Novgorod Sever-skii	3,860	6,181	5,599	5,065	6,405	8,021	9,182	12,512
627.	Dobrianka Posad	—	—	—	—	—	9,368	6,038	10,500
628.	Berezna	5,711	5,278	6,701	7,839	9,790	11,086	9,922	10,286
629.	Osyer	2,392	3,350	3,298	3,537	2,831	3,548	5,370	8,564
630.	Mglin	4,646	4,751	6,767	7,106	6,165	10,982	7,640	8,542
631.	Sosnitsa	4,417	4,362	5,074	5,276	5,657	6,774	7,087	8,230
632.	Klimov Posad	—	—	—	—	—	6,605	5,023	8,000
633.	Korop	4,861	3,395	4,180	5,150	5,381	5,463	6,262	7,387
634.	Gorodnia	927	2,140	2,468	2,451	2,473	4,238	4,310	7,026
635.	Surazh	2,517	677	1,409	3,120	3,770	5,175	4,006	6,525
636.	Luzhki Posad	—	—	—	—	—	5,701	2,744	6,159
637.	Pogar	4,262	3,901	3,812	10,184	4,487	3,944	4,965	6,110
638.	Voronok Posad	—	—	—	—	—	5,771	3,707	4,950
639.	Kozelets	2,302	2,884	3,785	2,014	5,078	4,430	5,141	4,933
640.	Sviatskaia Posad	—	—	—	—	—	2,991	2,389	4,145
641.	Churovichi Posad	—	—	—	—	—	4,092	3,611	3,611
642.	Mit'kovka Posad	—	—	—	—	—	2,380	2,214	2,214
643.	Novoe Mesto	—	—	—	—	990	1,422	1,488	2,025
		84,064	88,482	117,290	121,739	149,799	275,410	247,345	340,094

ESTLIAND

		1811	1825	1840	1856	1870	1885	1897	1910
644.	Revel'	17,592	21,219	24,041	20,284	31,400	51,277	64,572	98,995
645.	Vezenberg	492	1,014	1,192	1,380	2,455	3,612	5,890	5,890
646.	Gapsal'	636	1,088	1,003	1,230	2,200	2,875	3,212	3,228
647.	Veisenshtein	929	926	3,011	1,015	1,786	2,033	2,507	3,082
648.	Baltiiskii Port	203	381	310	368	664	960	900	1,216
		19,852	24,628	29,557	24,277	38,505	60,757	77,081	112,419

IAROSLAVL'

		1811	1825	1840	1856	1870	1885	1897	1910
649.	Iaroslavl'	23,760	20,271	34,913	26,915	26,429	34,799	71,616	111,876
650.	Rybinsk	3,064	3,501	5,745	8,643	15,047	19,571	25,290	31,485
651.	Rostov	5,813	5,508	7,858	9,598	9,683	11,898	13,715	18,250
652.	Romanovo-Borisoglebsk	4,340	5,118	4,805	5,121	5,571	5,999	6,682	12,321
653.	Uglich	7,192	7,778	7,483	9,999	13,069	11,183	9,698	9,698

IAROSLAVL'

		1811	1825	1840	1856	1870	1885	1897	1910
654.	Danilov	1,579	1,849	3,024	2,911	4,365	6,099	4,286	4,770
655.	Mologa	3,348	3,055	4,345	4,681	4,440	6,439	4,253	4,280
656.	Poshekhon'e	3,020	3,359	4,551	2,907	3,951	6,034	4,033	4,027
657.	Liubim	1,543	2,017	2,237	2,207	2,398	3,275	3,000	3,329
658.	Petrovsk	1,033	1,080	1,502	1,142	1,574	1,644	1,505	2,291
659.	Myshkin	1,019	1,107	1,948	2,064	3,014	2,525	2,232	2,257
	Total	55,711	54,643	78,411	76,188	89,541	109,466	146,310	214,584
	European Russia	2,669,805	3,264,772	4,559,069	5,277,906	7,033,996	9,903,210	12,278,280	16,641,707

WARSZAWA

		1811	1825	1840	1856	1870	1885	1897	1910
660.	Warsaw	77,727	123,433	140,471	156,072	297,090	454,298	683,692	781,179
661.	Włocławek	2,002	3,644	5,244	6,253	12,445	12,163	22,907	37,403
662.	Pułtusk	2,520	3,755	4,222	4,321	7,689	12,946	15,968	18,636
663.	Kutno	2,712	4,001	4,038	5,868	8,228	9,209	11,250	15,186
664.	Łowicz	2,635	6,693	5,313	5,465	7,605	7,922	12,368	14,487
665.	Kałuszyn	1,641	1,826	—	4,234	(6,115)	7,318	8,737	13,626
666.	Płońsk	2,388	3,658	—	3,959	5,812	6,775	7,900	11,680
667.	Skierniewice	1,649	1,713	—	2,656	5,038	5,717	10,745	11,532
668.	Nasielsk	2,197	3,050	—	3,118	(4,478)	5,191	4,693	8,112
669.	Gostynin	561	1,523	—		5,907	4,551	6,747	7,776
670.	Nowy Dwór	841	—	—	899	5,217	5,331	7,302	7,720
671.	Gąbin	1,368	2,395	3,451	3,926	5,249	5,113	5,137	7,320
672.	Radzymin	917	1,054	1,862	2,250	3,866	3,989	4,172	7,196
673.	Mszczonów	1,537	1,704	—	3,537	4,871	5,982	5,124	7,120
67–.	Mińsk	529	646	773	1,203	2,548	3,281	9,286	7,053
675.	Zakroczym	588	1,189	—	2,917	4,709	5,465	4,518	6,835
676.	Sochaczew	2,055	2,600	3,378	3,848	5,297	6,503	6,038	6,808
677.	Grójec	1,037	1,601	—	2,510	4,491	4,410	6,028	6,106
678.	Warka	1,087	2,018	—	2,600	4,289	5,151	4,272	6,034
679.	Nieszawa	817	1,397	—	1,846	2,639	2,984	2,639	4,955
680.	Błonie	786	938	967	1,140	1,740	1,862	2,974	4,826
681.	Brześć Kujawski	912	1,230	1,400	1,696	2,008	1,857	2,744	3,530
						396,738	578,018	845,241	995,120
						(407,331)			

		1810	1825	1840	1857	1870	1885	1897	1910
KALISZ									
682.	Kalisz	7,256	11,400	12,043	12,066	18,058	20,216	24,418	52,903
683.	Zduńska Wola	—	2,000	—	6,347	8,640	9,376	15,910	23,452
684.	Ozorków	—	3,250	—	6,577	9,058	10,276	11,533	18,327
685.	Koło	1,942	2,904	—	4,610	6,499	8,098	9,359	11,655
686.	Łęczyca	2,573	3,291	4,597	5,159	6,488	8,298	8,863	11,196
687.	Konin	1,840	3,608	4,695	5,147	8,008	7,027	8,522	10,073
688.	Turek	744	1,594	3,563	4,773	7,007	7,320	8,118	9,243
689.	Sieradz	1,678	2,652	4,014	5,256	6,398	6,414	7,005	8,551
690.	Wieluń	1,710	2,989	—	3,816	5,763	5,268	7,850	7,287
691.	Słupca	1,454	1,620	—	1,745	2,266	3,043	3,852	6,183
692.	Błaszki	643	1,360	—	2,806	3,770	4,055	3,995	6,063
693.	Warta	1,779	2,625	2,976	3,224	4,490	4,893	3,418	5,644
694.	Dąbie	998	1,722	—	2,980	3,213	3,803	3,149	4,511
						89,658	98,091	115,992	174,747
KIELCE									
695.	Kielce	1,971	3,611	4,377	3,841	7,838	10,633	23,178	32,381
696.	Pińczów	2,559	4,176	—	4,213	5,290	6,607	9,075	10,862
697.	Chęciny	1,368	2,558	—	3,876	5,194	6,219	6,178	10,095
698.	Chmielnik	986	1,514	—	3,098	5,181	6,935	6,888	10,037
699.	Włoszczowa Posad	724	1,353	—	2,175	(2,585)	4,510	3,724	7,842
700.	Andrzejewo Posad	661	728	—	835	(1,057)	3,639	4,717	6,773
701.	Działoszyce	884	1,749	—	3,006	4,167	5,585	4,606	6,764
702.	Olkusz	720	1,157	1,486	1,650	2,276	7,205	3,441	6,255
703.	Miechów	1,212	1,171	1,206	1,427	1,595	2,184	4,175	3,810
						31,541	53,517	65,982	94,819
						(35,183)			
ŁOMŻA									
704.	Łomża	1,866	3,302	3,937	5,881	13,335	14,450	26,093	25,806
705.	Ostrołęka	1,195	1,484	1,927	3,371	5,865	5,120	12,949	15,985
706.	Ostrów	1,376	1,792	—	3,972	6,142	7,800	10,471	15,209
707.	Maków	2,214	4,160	—	5,217	6,527	6,293	7,206	9,003
708.	Tykocin	2,978	3,305	4,931	4,947	(5,309)	5,960	4,212	7,080
709.	Kolno	1,196	1,965	—	3,350	4,672	5,786	4,891	6,995
710.	Szczuczyn	1,915	3,084	2,890	2,996	4,457	5,090	5,756	6,198
						40,898	50,499	71,578	86,276
						(46,207)			

		1810	1825	1840	1857	1870	1885	1897	1910
LUBLIN									
711.	Lublin	7,105	13,159	14,322	15,629	24,456	39,908	50,385	65,870
712.	Chełm	1,792	2,216	3,291	3,662	4,891	10,611	18,452	22,685
713.	Zamość	4,065	4,709	4,721	4,035	8,733	8,147	14,705	14,033
714.	Hrubieszów	2,535	3,992	5,430	5,859	7,654	8,922	10,639	13,478
715.	Biłgoraj	2,642	2,945	4,745	5,037	6,705	6,884	5,846	11,434
716.	Tomaszów	1,928	2,824	3,761	3,686	4,802	5,784	6,233	9,548
717.	Kraśnik	1,385	3,333	3,723	3,249	(3,937)	5,353	8,257	9,178
718.	Novo Aleksandriia	-	-	-	-	-	3,130	8,617	9,178
719.	Krasnystaw	801	2,952	3,622	3,614	5,588	6,200	9,846	8,383
720.	Lubartów	2,207	3,193	3,224	3,264	3,791	5,024	5,237	8,333
721.	Janów	2,004	3,199	3,811	3,229	6,415	5,868	7,919	8,127
722.	Dubienka	2,567	1,808	-	3,013	(3,981)	4,686	4,799	8,085
723.	Szczebrzeszyn	2,575	3,233	4,584	4,204	(4,217)	5,771	6,122	7,574
724.	Łęczna	1,442	2,488	-	2,613	(3,055)	3,871	3,767	4,999
						73,035	120,159	160,824	200,905
						(88,225)			
PIOTRKÓW									
725.	Łódź	514	939	19,999	24,655	39,078	113,413	314,020	415,604
726.	Sosnowiec	-	-	-	-	-	-	9,048	98,748
727.	Częstochowa	2,233	5,060	7,303	8,637	14,830	21,167	45,045	72,652
728.	Będzin	1,310	2,254	-	4,060	6,236	8,584	23,757	49,623
729.	Piotrków	2,667	2,343	3,324	3,697	14,289	24,866	31,182	41,181
730.	Pabianice	893	963	-	4,365	6,399	11,895	26,765	38,932
731.	Tomaszów	-	-	3,761	5,136	7,015	16,533	21,005	27,493
732.	Zgierz	673	3,162	7,316	8,337	11,468	14,533	19,108	23,208
733.	Radomsko	1,198	1,709	2,727	2,956	4,670	8,641	12,392	19,725
734.	Brzeziny	1,756	3,186	4,113	4,933	6,185	7,213	7,648	15,608
735.	Rawa	2,204	3,189	4,231	4,567	5,597	6,560	6,412	10,029
736.	Łask	1,716	1,809	-	3,693	4,408	5,514	4,229	6,374
						120,175	238,735	520,611	819,177
PŁOCK									
737.	Płock	5,421	7,646	11,556	12,430	19,189	20,660	26,966	30,771
738.	Mława	1,705	2,216	3,164	3,290	6,134	7,062	13,440	18,652
739.	Przasnysz	2,059	3,376	3,876	3,766	6,948	8,025	9,128	10,390
740.	Sierpc	1,972	2,583	-	4,905	6,629	7,103	8,634	9,040

	1810	1825	1840	1857	1870	1885	1897	1910
PŁOCK								
741. Ciechanów	1,735	2,384	—	3,338	5,249	6,274	10,656	8,929
742. Rypin	1,126	1,619	—	2,272	3,417	3,542	5,961	7,552
743. Lipno	1,590	3,008	3,485	3,884	5,463	6,349	6,807	7,258
744. Wyszogród	2,876	3,305	—	3,820	4,423	4,443	4,160	4,689
745. Dobrzhń	1,460	1,890	—	1,861	2,218	3,011	2,485	3,019
					59,670	66,469	88,237	100,300
RADOM								
746. Radom	1,742	3,628	5,845	7,962	11,339	12,402	29,896	49,194
747. Ostrowiec	1,608	1,768	—	3,411	4,080	5,290	9,768	13,507
748. Staszów	2,355	3,107	4,877	5,069	6,078	7,748	8,724	10,830
749. Szydłowiec	1,565	2,830	3,602	3,796	4,797	6,262	7,435	10,272
750. Końskie	1,829	3,208	4,069	3,587	4,343	5,242	8,130	9,959
751. Kozienice	1,962	2,094	2,874	2,902	3,059	4,874	6,882	9,261
752. Przedbórz	951	2,535	—	4,268	5,151	6,235	5,927	8,731
753. Opatów	2,112	2,406	3,116	3,491	4,918	5,586	6,603	8,102
754. Opoczno	1,844	3,363	2,787	3,334	4,441	5,326	6,079	7,654
755. Sandomierz	1,421	3,086	3,279	3,191	4,767	5,905	6,556	7,325
756. Iłża Posad	1,119	1,790	—	1,978	(2,843)	3,862	4,230	6,028
					52,973	68,552	100,230	140,863
					(55,816)			
SIEDLCE								
757. Siedlce	2,738	4,414	6,471	7,521	10,013	13,606	26,234	34,072
758. Biała	2,477	3,586	3,588	3,881	5,662	8,375	13,090	22,042
759. Miedzyrzec	2,686	4,340	—	8,062	(9,000)	10,449	13,760	16,620
760. Węgrów	3,314	3,013	3,902	3,859	4,892	7,915	8,268	12,463
761. Włodawa	2,238	3,162	4,436	5,500	6,102	6,910	6,673	11,734
762. Sokołów	2,043	3,005	—	3,677	4,815	7,083	7,265	11,037
763. Łuków	1,297	3,206	2,941	3,122	4,148	6,210	9,363	10,231
764. Żelechów	1,864	2,246	2,899	3,412	(4,300)	6,058	7,140	8,393
765. Parczew	1,580	2,725	—	3,368	(4,000)	5,488	6,660	7,822
766. Radzyń	1,371	1,954	1,958	2,472	4,351	4,109	5,937	7,312
767. Terespol	868	1,366	—	2,585	(2,750)	3,649	4,107	5,514
768. Garwolin	808	912	1,431	1,719	2,344	3,988	5,341	5,168
					42,327	83,840	113,838	152,408
					(62,377)			

SUWAŁKI

	1810	1825	1840	1857	1870	1885	1897	1910
769. Suwałki	1,444	2,116	7,321	10,584	16,585	19,113	22,648	32,962
770. Augustów	—	3,086	6,972	3,115	9,453	10,326	12,743	15,258
771. Kalwaria	—	—	7,628	—	9,418	10,641	9,378	15,022
772. Volkovyshki	—	—	—	—	6,706	10,080	5,788	6,699
773. Mariampol'	1,619	2,668	2,992	3,283	5,611	6,400	6,737	6,074
774. Sejny	—	—	3,528	—	4,035	4,969	3,778	5,383
775. Vladislavov	—	—	—	—	9,306	6,176	4,595	3,984
776. Verzhbolev	—	—	—	—	3,554	3,866	3,293	3,483
777. Preny	—	—	—	—	3,090	3,812	2,477	3,162
778. Shaki	—	—	—	—	3,549	3,969	2,211	3,042
Total					71,307	79,352	73,648	95,069
Tsarist Poland					978,322	1,437,232	2,156,181	2,859,684
					(1,035,949)			

CAUCASUS

	1811	1825	1840	1856	1870	1885	1897	1910
BAKU								
779. Baku	—	—	6,834	8,374	15,480	15,480	45,679	232,200
780. Kuba	—	—	3,295	9,618	12,836	12,836	13,730	24,361
781. Shemakha	—	—	16,273	20,433	23,869	28,545	20,007	22,206
782. Sal'iany	—	—	—	—	—	—	11,787	20,904
783. Lenkoran	—	—	1,286	3,966	4,848	5,618	8,733	5,938
784. Geokchai	—	—	—	—	—	—	2,201	3,780
			26,788	42,391	57,033	93,572	169,995	309,389
DAGESTAN								
785. Derbent	—	—	10,713	13,870	15,739	14,185	14,649	10,072
786. Petrovsk	—	—	—	—	4,323	3,749	9,753	4,209
787. Temir-Khan-Shura	—	—	—	—	5,090	3,356	9,214	2,689
			10,713	13,870	25,152	21,290	33,616	16,970
ELISAVETPOL'								
788. Elisavetpol'	—	9,843	7,790	10,938	16,167	20,294	33,625	60,361
789. Shusha	—	—	8,421	15,194	19,945	26,806	25,881	39,379
790. Nukha	—	—	13,566	17,945	24,994	25,757	24,734	36,695
791. Geriusy	—	—	—	—	—	—	2,349	2,381
		9,843	29,777	44,077	61,106	72,857	86,589	138,816

	1811	1825	1840	1857	1870	1885	1897	1910
KARS								
792. Kars	—	—	—	—	—	3,137	20,805	24,550
793. Kagyzman'	—	—	—	—	—	3,298	10,518	10,789
						6,435	31,323	35,339
KUBAN								
794. Ekaterinodar		4,312	6,616*	8,919	19,244	39,610	65,606	92,254
795. Eisk		—	—	17,539	26,785	27,915	35,414	46,308
796. Maikop		—	—	—	—	27,945	34,327	44,102
797. Temriuk		3,906	2,764*	1,441	6,519	13,656	14,734	17,731
798. Anapa		—	—	—	5,037	7,604	6,944	11,429
		8,218	9,290	27,890	57,585	116,730	157,025	211,824
KUTAIS-BATUM-SUKHUM								
799. Kutais		3,367	2,575	3,856	10,525	20,227	32,476	55,965
800. Batum		—	—	—	—	11,878	28,508	40,000
801. Sukhum		—	—	—	1,612	1,279	7,998	25,819
802. Poti		—	—	—	3,112	4,785	7,346	16,610
803. Ozurgety		—	138	306	1,485	3,098*	4,710	6,250
804. Redut-Kale		—	—	—	—	—	780	782
		3,367	2,713	4,162	16,734	41,317	81,818	145,426
STAVROPOL'								
805. Stavropol'	1,899	3,603	9,286	17,309	23,612	36,561	41,590	58,863
806. Sviatyi Krest'	—	—	—	—	—	3,597	6,583	14,691
	1,899	3,603	9,286	17,309	23,612	40,158	48,173	73,554
TEREK								
807. Vladikavkaz	—	—	2,132	6,858	5,774*	33,981	43,740	71,105
808. Piatigorsk	823	1,059	—	—	9,594	13,133	18,440	31,242
809. Groznyi	—	—	—	—	2,631	6,214	15,564	25,953
810. Georgievsk	1,092	2,347	2,609	5,595	2,343	8,290	12,115	21,322
811. Mozdok	5,544	6,424	5,778	9,953	11,472*	12,989	9,330	17,068
812. Kislovodsk	—	—	—	—	—	—	—	13,533
813. Kizliar	7,447	8,106	10,282	10,075	9,267	6,429	7,282	10,553
	14,906	17,936	20,801	32,481	41,081	81,036	106,471	190,776
TIFLIS								
814. Tiflis	—	29,859	23,045	38,375	70,591	89,551	159,590	303,150
815. Akhaltsikh	—	—	9,595	13,298	13,775	13,265	15,357	21,463
816. Gori	—	2,144	2,418	3,378	5,183	5,386	10,269	20,729

	1811	1825	1840	1857	1870	1885	1897	1910
TIFLIS								
817. Signakh	—	3,332	3,311	5,278	10,320	10,069	8,994	15,805
818. Telav	—	2,085	3,332	4,800	6,209	8,014	13,929	15,231
819. Akhalkalaki	—	—	—	1,200	2,752*	4,303	5,440	4,816
820. Dushet	—	1,181	1,346	1,925	1,983*	2,041	2,566	2,603
821. Zakataly	—	—	—	—	—	1,231	3,009	1,100
		38,601	43,047	68,254	110,813	133,860	219,154	384,897
CHERNOMORSK								
822. Novorossiisk	—	—	—	—	1,881	8,304	16,897	47,040
823. Tuapse	—	—	—	—	—	—	1,392	10,381
824. Sochi	—	—	—	—	—	—	1,352	9,554
825. Khosta	—	—	—	—	—	—	—	1,214
826. Romanovsk	—	—	—	—	—	—	—	432
					1,881	8,304	19,641	68,621
827. Aleksandropol'	—	—	9,310	11,600	20,600	22,670	30,616	48,446
828. Erivan	—	—	12,310	13,179	15,040	14,555	29,006	33,700
829. Novobaiazet	—	—	—	3,593	4,870	7,120	8,486	10,960
830. Nakhichevan'	—	—	1,983	4,894	8,772	6,911	8,790	8,340
831. Ordubat	—	—	3,237	4,839	4,321	4,112	4,611	5,387
			26,840	38,105	53,603	55,368	81,509	106,833
Total Caucasus	16,805	81,568	179,255	288,539	448,600	670,927	1,035,314	1,682,445
SIBERIA								
AMUR								
832. Blagoveshchensk	—	—	—	—	3,107	9,340	32,834	52,000
833. Zeia-Pristan'	—	—	—	—	—	—	—	5,354
					3,107	9,340	32,834	57,354
ENISEI								
834. Krasnoiarsk	2,946	3,111	6,928	6,409	12,974	19,840	26,699	71,849
835. Kansk	—	859	1,588	1,991	2,582	3,958	7,537	17,512
836. Minusinsk	—	846	1,626	2,178	4,221	10,433	10,231	15,230
837. Eniseisk	5,746	5,673	6,481	5,119	4,141	7,250	11,506	10,855
838. Achinsk	1,176	1,489	2,172	2,287	3,726	7,452	6,699	10,155
839. Turukhansk	578	410	394	330	297	139	212	135
	10,446	12,388	19,189	18,314	27,941	49,072	62,884	125,740

	1811	1825	1840	1857	1870	1885	1897	1910
ZABAIKAL								
840. Chita	–	–	–	854	2,598	5,728	11,511	68,211
841. Verkhneudinsk	2,168	2,024	3,231	3,391	3,520	5,193	8,086	15,158
842. Troitskosavsk	1,028	2,490	5,185	5,359	4,675	6,117	8,788	12,951
843. Nerchinsk	1,736	2,310	3,535	4,721	3,747	4,535	6,639	9,142
844. Mysovsk	–	–	–	–	–	–	–	2,442
845. Barguzin	143	288	275	489	709	1,659	1,378	2,325
846. Aksha	–	–	–	–	–	520	1,627	1,865
847. Selenginsk	655	1,832	945	1,256	1,019	856	1,086	1,015
	5,730	8,944	13,171	16,070	16,268	24,608	39,115	113,109
IRKUTSK								
848. Irkutsk	12,553	14,411	16,773	24,103	32,789	39,226	51,473	93,400
849. Nizhneudinsk	433	432	707	2,430	2,722	3,507	5,752	5,750
850. Kirensk	–	681	832	938	809	999	2,280	2,014
851. Balagansk	314	360*	406	500	917	1,026	1,314	1,920
852. Verkholensk	–	–	–	–	856	955	1,354	1,079
853. Ilimsk	131	325	419*	512	531	596	662	933
	13,431	16,209	19,137	28,483	38,624	46,309	62,835	105,096
PRIMORSK								
854. Vladivostok	–	–	–	–	–	13,050	28,933	90,582
855. Nikol'sk-Ussuriiskii	–	–	–	–	–	–	10,868	47,411
856. Kharbarovsk	–	–	–	–	–	2,500	14,971	42,432
857. Nikolaevsk	–	–	–	–	5,090	2,043	5,684	16,440
	–	–	–	–	5,090	17,593	60,456	196,865
TOBOL'SK								
858. Tiumen'	8,782	10,771	10,803	11,215	15,512	13,948	29,544	33,791
859. Kurgan	744	1,948	1,781	2,925	6,120	8,943	10,301	24,566
860. Tobol'sk	16,934	16,994	14,246	16,120	18,481	20,175	20,425	21,405
861. Ishim	1,321	1,422	2,067	2,483	5,842	7,137	7,153	13,175
862. Tara	3,509	4,298	5,086	5,192	6,469	8,654	7,223	11,785
863. Tiukalinsk	–	842	958	1,457	1,503	3,907	4,018	5,511
864. Ialutorovsk	–	1,962	2,805	3,345	3,936	4,481	3,310	4,399
865. Turinsk	3,002	3,079	3,104	3,735	3,646	4,658	3,167	3,173
866. Berezov	812	990	1,179	1,159	1,669	2,173	1,070	1,329
867. Surgut	–	–	–	–	1,130	1,492	1,120	1,309
	35,104	42,306	42,029	47,631	64,631	75,568	87,351	120,443

	1811	1825	1840	1857	1870	1885	1897	1910
TOMSK								
868. Tomsk	8,631	10,867	12,032	20,202	25,605	36,742	52,210	107,711
869. Novo-Nikolaevsk	–	–	–	–	–	–	8,473	55,695
870. Barnaul	–	–	9,456	10,922	13,529	17,118	21,073	46,771
871. Biisk	2,183	1,716	2,728	3,140	6,329	17,560	17,213	28,091
872. Mariinsk	–	–	–	–	6,531	13,072	8,216	18,662
873. Kolyvan'	868	1,206	1,321	2,469	3,418	13,158	11,711	11,063
874. Kainsk	2,438	1,724	1,997	2,676	5,212	8,160	5,884	6,486
875. Kuznetsk	1,079	877	2,712	1,670	3,253	5,712	3,117	3,808
876. Narym	–	–	882	1,008	1,921	1,641	1,129	841
	15,199	16,390	31,128	42,087	65,798	113,163	129,026	279,128
IAKUTSK								
877. Iakutsk	1,604	2,438	1,761	2,823	4,562	5,698	6,535	8,209
878. Olekminsk	–	–	91	209	299	757	1,144	970
879. Viliuisk	–	–	242	359	333	463	611	713
880. Sredne-Kolymsk	–	–	126	283	499	495	538	605
881. Verkhoiansk	–	–	93	113	145	278	354	377
	1,604	2,438	2,313	3,787	5,838	7,691	9,182	10,874
Total Siberia	81,514	98,675	126,967	156,372	226,974	343,344	483,683	1,008,609

CENTRAL ASIA

	1811	1825	1840	1857	1870	1885	1897	1910
AKMOLINSK								
882. Omsk	4,577	8,496	11,705	16,416	30,559	33,759	37,376	127,865
883. Petropavlovsk	5,056	3,495	4,127	7,313	11,406	13,985	19,686	38,123
884. Akmolinsk	–	–	–	–	5,529	4,743	9,688	13,654
885. Kokchetav	–	–	–	–	–	5,755	4,962	4,173
886. Atbasar	–	–	–	–	–	1,557	3,038	2,859
	9,633	11,991	15,832	23,729	47,494	59,799	74,750	186,737
ZAKASPIISK								
887. Askhabad	–	–	–	–	–	10,945	19,426	51,036
888. Merv	–	–	–	–	–	11,070	8,533	19,969
889. Krasnovodsk	–	–	–	–	–	665	6,322	7,775
890. Kizil'-Arvat	–	–	–	–	–	1,755	4,098	5,406
891. Aleksandrovskii Fort	–	–	–	–	–	644	895	926
						25,079	39,274	85,112

	1811	1825	1840	1856	1870	1885	1897	1910
SAMARKAND								
892. Samarkand	–	–	–	–	17,900	33,117	55,128	87,243
893. Khodzhent	–	–	–	–		34,800	30,109	39,977
894. Uratiube	–	–	–	–	9,885	14,600	20,621	22,191
895. Dzhizak	–	–	–	–	3,866	21,800	15,710	12,011
896. Katta-Kurgan	–	–	–	–		16,000	10,087	10,621
897. Pendzhekent	–	–	–	–		5,896	3,658	4,112
					31,651	126,213	135,313	176,155
SEMIPALATINSK								
898. Semipalatinsk	2,580	5,849	5,221	6,489	10,140	16,830	26,246	29,387
899. Ust' Kamenogrosk	–	1,304	2,181	2,202	3,489	6,673	8,721	12,462
900. Pavlodar	–	–	–	–	1,320	2,817	7,738	7,744
901. Zaisan	–	–	–	–		2,349	4,402	5,147
902. Karkaraly	–	–	–			2,075	4,451	2,635
903. Kokpekty	–	–	–	2,142	1,274	3,503	2,930	1,506
	2,580	7,153	7,402	10,833	16,223	34,247	54,488	58,881
SEMIRECH'E								
904. Vernyi	–	–	–	–	11,583	21,521	22,740	36,382
905. Dzharkent	–	–	–	–		6,778	16,094	25,231
906. Przheval'sk	–	–	–	–	447	3,828	8,108	15,180
907. Pishpek	–	–	–	–		2,227	6,615	13,777
908. Lepsinsk	–	–	–	–		1,392	3,230	9,681
909. Kopal	–	–	–	–	4,161	2,356	6,183	4,656
					16,191	38,102	62,970	104,907
SYR-DAR'IA								
910. Tashkent	–	–	–	–	86,233	121,410	155,673	200,191
911. Aulie-ata	–	–	–	–		5,700	11,722	19,202
912. Turkestan	–	–	–	–	5,490	3,700	11,253	16,279
913. Chimkent	–	–	–	–	5,422	9,080	11,194	15,542
914. Kazalinsk	–	–	–	–	2,934	5,772	7,585	12,337
915. Perovsk	–	–	–	–		5,280	5,058	8,328
916. Petro-Aleksandrovsk	–	–	–	–		820	3,111	2,788
					100,079	151,762	205,596	274,667
TURGAI								
917. Kustanai	–	–	–	–		7,325	14,275	23,124
918. Aktiubinsk	–	–	–	–		862	2,817	10,836
919. Irgiz	–	–	–	–		679	1,542	1,405
920. Turgai	–	–	–	–		381	896	872
						9,247	19,530	36,237

	1811	1825	1840	1857	1870	1885	1897	1910
URAL'SK								
921. Ural'sk	—	10,780	12,597	10,822	17,590	26,054	36,466	27,681
922. Iletsk	—	—	—	—	—	6,049	7,154	12,180
923. Gur'ev	—	—	—	—	2,838	5,954	9,322	7,947
924. Kalmykov	—	—	—	—	883	1,381	1,924	3,048
925. Temir	—	—	—	—	—	—	616	2,527
		10,780	12,597	10,822	21,311	39,438	55,482	53,383
FERGANA								
926. Kokand	—	—	—	—	—	54,043	81,354	113,700
927. Andizhan	—	—	—	—	—	30,620	47,627	76,367
928. Namagan	—	—	—	—	—	31,074	62,017	72,493
929. Staryi Margelan	—	—	—	—	—	25,354	36,490	46,782
930. Osh	—	—	—	—	—	13,527	34,157	45,351
931. Skobelev	—	—	—	—	—	2,565	8,928	15,554
932. Chust	—	—	—	—	—	8,027	13,785	14,810
						165,210	284,358	385,057
Total Central Asia	12,213	29,924	35,831	45,384	232,949	649,097	931,761	1,361,138
Total Russian Empire	2,780,337	3,474,939	4,901,122	5,768,201	8,920,841	13,003,810	16,885,219	23,553,583

Sources for Appendix I

1811   K. German, Statisticheskiia issledovaniia otnositel'no Rossiiskoi Imperii. Chast' I. O narodonaselenii (S.-Peterburg, 1819).

Konstantin Arsen'ev, Nachertanie statistiki Rossiiskogo Gosudarstva, sostavlennoe glavnogo pedagogicheskogo instituta. Chast' pervaia. O sostoianii naroda (Sanktpeterburg, 1818).

1825   Russia. Departament politsii ispolnitel'noi. Statisticheskoe izobrazhenie gorodov i posadov Rossiiskoi Imperii po 1825 god (Sanktpeterburg, 1829).

1840 ____. Ministerstvo vnutrennikh del. Statisticheskoe otdelenie. Statisticheskii tablitsy o sostoianii gorodov Rossiiskoi Imperii, Velikogo Kniazhestva Finliandskogo i Tsarstva Pol'skogo (Sanktpeterburg, 1842).

1856 ____. Tsentral'nyi statisticheskii komitet. Statisticheskiia tablitsy Rossiiskoi Imperii za 1856-i god. Vypusk pervyi (S.-Peterburg, 1858).

1870 ____. Statisticheskii vremennik Rossiiskoi Imperii. II. Vypusk desiatyi. Ekono-micheskoe sostoianie gorodov (Sanktpeterburg, 1875).

1885 gg. ____. Statistika Rossiiskoi Imperii. Tom I. Sbornik svedenii po Rossii za 1884-1885 gg. Gorodskiia poseleniia Imperii (Sanktpeterburg, 1887).

1897 ____. Pervaia vseobshchaia perepis' naseleniia Rossiiskoi Imperii 1897 g. Vypusk 5. Okonchatel'no ustanovlennoe pri razrabotke perepisi. Nalichnoe naselenie gorodov (S.-Peterburg, 1905).

____. _____. Goroda i poseleniia v uezdakh imeiushchie 2,000 i bolee zhitelei (S.-Peterburg, 1905).

1905. ____. _____. Goroda Rossii v 1910 godu (S.-Peterburg, 1914).

1910 ____. Statisticheskii ezhegodnik Rossii 1914 g. (S.-Peterburg, 1915). (Data for 1/1/1914 taken for cities of Novorossiisk, Baku, Irkutsk, and Erivan because of the absence of data for 1910).

Obzor Odesskogo Gradonachal'stva za 1911 god (Odessa: Tipografiia "Ved. Odes. Gradon.," (no date). (Data for the city of Odessa is taken for 1911 because of the absence of data for 1910).

Statesman's Yearbook for 1916. (Data for the city of Briansk, Orel Guberniia, is taken for 1911 because of the absence of data for 1910).

A. Jelonek, "Ludność miast i osiedli typu miejskiego na ziemiach Polski od 1810 do 1960 r.," Dokumentacja Geograficzna, 3-4 (1967), pp. 1-62. (Data for Polish cities in 1810, 1825, 1857, and for later dates if not given in the above Russian sources).

APPENDIX   II

OCCUPATIONAL CATEGORIES OF THE
GAINFULLY EMPLOYED POPULATION
IN THE RUSSIAN EMPIRE,
1897

The data on the occupational characteristics of the gainfully employed population of the Russian Empire collected in the general census of 1897 were organized into 65 occupational headings. For the purposes of this study the 65 occupational headings were grouped into the 14 categories presented below. The arabic numbers before each occupational heading correspond to the numbers used in the official statistical publications of the government.

I. Administration

    1. Administration, courts, and police
    2. Public and social services

II. Armed Forces

    4. Armed forces

III. Religious

    5. Divine service in the Orthodox faith
    6. Divine service in other Christian faiths
    7. Divine service in non-Christian faiths
    8. Persons employed by churches, cemetaries, and other servants

IV. Liberal Professions

    3. Private judicial activity
    9. Teaching and educational activity
   10. Science, literature, and art
   11. Medical and sanitary activity

V. Activity and Service as Private Domestics, Day Laborers, etc.

   13. Domestics, porters, caretakers, day laborers, etc.

VI. Income from Fixed Property, Capital, Inheritance, etc.

   14. Income from fixed property, capital, inheritance, kinship, etc.

VII. Income from State, Private, and Social Institutions

   15. Income and support obtained from state, private, and social institutions

VIII. Agriculture and Related Activities

   17. Agriculture
   18. Apiculture and sericulture
   19. Stock raising
   20. Sylviculture
   21. Fishing and hunting

IX. Mining and Smelting

   22. Mining and the extraction of ores
   23. Smelting of metals

X. Manufacturing

24. Processing of fibrous materials
25. Processing of animal products
26. Processing of wood
27. Processing of metals
28. Processing of mineral matter (ceramics)
29. Production of chemicals and materials related to them
30. Distillation, brewing, and honey fermenting
31. Other beverages and fermented matter
32. Processing of vegetable and animal food products
33. Tobacco and products relating to it
34. Printing
35. Instruments (physical, optical, surgical), watches, toys
36. Jewelry, paintings, articles of culture, luxury, etc.
37. Garment making
39. Manufacture of carriages and construction of wooden vessels
40. Not included in above or undetermined

XI. Construction

38. Construction, repair, and maintenance of residences and other construction work

XII. Transport and Communication

41. Water communications
42. Railroads
43. Carrier's trade
44. Other overland communications and means of transport
45. Mail, telegraph, and telephone

XIII. Trade and Commerce

46. Credit and public commercial institutions
47. Commercial mediation
48. Trade in general without specific determination
49. Trade in live animals
50. Trade in grain products
51. Trade in other products of agriculture
52. Trade in construction materials and fuels
53. Trade in household articles
54. Trade in metal goods, machines, and weapons
55. Trade in fabrics and articles of cloth
56. Trade in leather, skins, etc.
57. Trade in articles of luxury, science, art, culture, etc.
58. Trade in other articles
59. Street hawking
60. Inns, hotels, rooming houses, and clubs
61. Pubs and Taverns
62. Facilities of cleanliness and hygiene

XIV. Others

12. Service in charitable institutions
16. Deprived of freedom and serving sentence
64. Prostitution
65. Persons whose occupations were not indicated

Sources: Tsentral'nyi statisticheskii komitet. *Pervaia vseobshchaia perepis' naseleniia Rossiiskoi Imperii 1897 g.* Volumes 1-89 (S.-Peterburg, 1899-1904), and ___ . ___ . Obshchii svod po Imperii rezul'tatov razrabotki dannykh Pervoi vseobshchei perepisi naseleniia, proizvedennoi 28 ianvaria 1897 goda. II. (S.-Peterburg, 1905), pp. 256-295.

APPENDIX III

SOURCES OF THE FIGURES

SOURCES OF THE FIGURES

Figure 3: Tsentral'nyi statisticheskii komitet. Statisticheskii ezhegodnik Rossii za 1916 (Petrograd, 1918), pp. 50, 51, 85. Finland, Bukhara, and Khiva are not included in data.

Figure 4: Sources are arranged according to year.
For 1811: A. G. Rashin, Naselenie Rossii za 100 let, 1811-1913 (Moskva: Gosudarstvennoe Statisticheskoe Izdatel'stvo, 1956), pp. 27-29. Population of Bessarabia is not included for Russian Empire or European Russia.
For 1840: Population of European Russia was estimated at 49,511,000. This estimate was arrived at by taking the population of European Russia in 1838, 48,825,400 inhabitants, as given in Rashin, op. cit., pp. 28-29, with an adjustment made for annual growth calculated at the average annual rate of growth in the population of European Russia for the period 1811-1863 of .7 per cent as determined by Rashin, op. cit., p. 41.
For 1856: Tsentral'nyi statisticheskii komitet. Statisticheskiia tablitsy Rossiiskoi Imperii za 1856-i god. Vypusk pervyi. Narodonaselenie (S.-Peterburg, 1858).
For 1870: Tsentral'nyi statisticheskii komitet. Statisticheskii vremennik Rossiiskoi Imperii. Vypusk desiatyi. Naselenie Imperii v 1870 g. (Sanktpeterburg, 1875).
For 1885: Tsentral'nyi statisticheskii komitet. Statistika Rossiiskoi Imperii. Sbornik svedenii po Rossii za 1884-1885 gg. Naselenie Imperii v 1885 g. (S.-Peterburg, 1887).
For 1897: Tsentral'nyi statisticheskii komitet. Pervaia vseobshchaia perepis' naseleniia Rossiiskoi Imperii 1897 g. Obshchii svod po Imperii rezul'tatov razrabotke dannykh pervoi vseobshchei perepisi naseleniia proizvedennoi 28 ianvaria 1897 goda (S.-Peterburg, 1905).
For 1910: Tsentral'nyi statisticheskii komitet. Ezhegodnik Rossii v 1910 godu (S.-Peterburg, 1914).

Figure 5: Rashin, Naselenie Rossii za 100 let, pp. 28-29.

Figure 6: Rashin, Naselenie Rossii za 100 let, pp. 44-45.

Figure 7: Rashin, Naselenie Rossii za 100 let, pp. 217-218.

Figure 8: J. William Leasure and Robert A. Lewis, "Internal Migration in Russia in the Late Nineteenth Century," Slavic Review, XXVII (September, 1968), p. 379.

Figure 9: Same as for Figure 8.

Figure 10: Adam Krzyżanowski and Kazimierz Władysław Kumaniecki, Statystyka Polski (Wydana staraniem i nakladem Polskiego Tow. Statystycznego. Krakόw: G. Gebethner, 1915), pp. 5-6.

Figure 11: Donald W. Treadgold, The Great Siberian Migration. Government and Peasant in Resettlement from Emancipation to the First World War (Princeton, N.J.: Princeton University Press, 1957), pp. 33-34.

Figure 12: Based on data in Appendix I.

Figure 13: Based on data in Appendix I.

Figure 14: Based on data in Appendix I.

Figure 15: Based on data in Appendix I.

Figure 16: Based on data presented in: P.A. Khromov, Ekonomicheskoe razvitie Rossii v XIX-XX vekakh, 1800-1917 (Moskva: Gosudarstvennoe Izdatel'stvo Politicheskoi Literatury, 1950), p. 462.

Figure 17: A. G. Rashin, Formirovanie rabochego klassa v Rossii. Istoriko-ekonomicheskie ocherki (Moskva: Izdatel'stvo Sotsial'no-ekonomicheskoi Literatury, 1958), p. 117.

Figure 19: Based on data in Appendix I.

Figure 20: Based on data in Appendix I.

Figure 21: Urban population based on data in Appendix I. Total population from: Tsentral'nyi statisticheskii komitet. Statisticheskii vremennik Rossiiskoi Imperii. Vypusk desiatyi. Naselenie
Imperii v 1870 g. (Sanktpeterburg, 1875) and ___. Ezhegodnik Rossii
1910 godu (S.-Peterburg, 1914).

Figure 22: Urban population based on data in Appendix I. Total population from: Tsentral'nyi statisticheskii komitet. Ezhegodnik Rossii 1910 godu (S.-Peterburg, 1914).

SELECTED   BIBLIOGRAPHY

SELECTED BIBLIOGRAPHY

Basic Statistical Sources

A. Publications of the Tsarist Government

Departament politsii ispolnitel'noi. Statisticheskoe izobrazhenie gorodov i posadov Rossiiskoi Imperii po 1825 god. Sankt-peterburg, 1829.

Ministerstvo vnutrennikh del. Gorodskiia poseleniia v Rossiiskoi Imperii. 7 vols. S.-Peterburg, 1860-1865.

_____. Obozrenie sostoianiia gorodov Rossiiskoi Imperii v 1833 godu. Sanktpeterburg, 1834.

_____. Statisticheskoe obozrenie Sibiri sostavlennoe na osnovanii svedenii, pocherpnutykh iz aktov pravitel'stva i drugikh dostovernykh istochnikov. Sanktpeterburg, 1810.

_____. Khoziaistvennyi departament. Ekonomicheskoe sostoianie gorodskikh poselenii Sibiri. S.-Peterburg, 1882.

_____. Materialy dlia sostavleniia predpolozhenii ob uluchshenii obshchestvennogo upravleniia v gorodakh. Ekonomicheskoe sostoianie gorodskikh poselenii Evropeiskoi Rossii v 1861-62 g. Chast' pervaia. Sanktpeterburg, 1863.

_____. Statisticheskoe otdelenie. Statisticheskiia tablitsy o sostoianii gorodov Rossiiskoi Imperii. Sanktpeterburg, 1840.

_____. _____. Statisticheskiia tablitsy o sostoianii gorodov Rossiiskoi Imperii. S.-Peterburg, 1852.

_____. _____. Statisticheskiia tablitsy o sostoianii gorodov Rossiiskoi Imperii, Velikogo Kniazhestva Finliandskogo i Tsarstva Pol'skogo. Sanktpeterburg, 1842.

Ministerstvo torgovli i promyshlennosti. Otdel torgovli. Remeslenniki i remeslennoe upravlenie v Rossii. Petrograd, 1916.

Tsentral'nyi statisticheskii komitet. Ezhegodnik Rossii 1910 g. God sed'moi. Naselenie Rossiiskoi Imperii k 1-mu ianvaria 1910 goda. S.-Peterburg, 1911.

_____. Goroda i poseleniia v uezdakh imeiushchie 2,000 i bolee zhitelei. S.-Peterburg, 1905. (1897 census)

_____. Goroda Rossii v 1904 godu. S.-Peterburg, 1906.

_____. Goroda Rossii v 1910 godu. S.-Peterburg, 1914.

Tsentral'nyi statisticheskii komitet. Pervaia vseobshchaia perepis'
naseleniia Rossiiskoi Imperii 1897 g. 89 vols. S.-Peter-
burg, 1899-1904.

_____. Pervaia vseobshchaia perepis' naseleniia Rossiiskoi Im-
perii 1897 g. Obshchii svod po Imperii rezul'tatov razrabotki dannykh pervoi vseobshchei perepisi naseleniia proizvedennoi 28 ianvaria 1897 goda. S.-Peterburg, 1905.

_____. Pervaia vseobshchaia perepis' naseleniia Rossiiskoi Im-
perii 1897 g. Vypusk 4. Okonchatel'no ustanovlennoe pri
razrabotke perepisi. Nalichnoe naselenie Imperii po uezdam.
S.-Peterburg, 1905.

_____. Pervaia vseobshchaia perepis' naseleniia Rossiiskoi Im-
perii 1897 g. Vypusk 5. Okonchatel'no ustanovlennoe pri
razrabotke perepisi. Nalichnoe naselenie gorodov. S.-Pe-
terburg, 1905.

_____. Spiski naselennykh mest' Rossiiskoi Imperii po svedeniiam
. . . goda. 62 vols. (21 volumes never issued). Sanktpeterburg, 1861-1885.

_____. Statisticheskii ezhegodnik Rossii 1914 g. S.-Peterburg,
1915.

_____. Statisticheskii ezhegodnik Rossii za 1916. Petrograd,
1918.

_____. Statisticheskiia tablitsy Rossiiskoi Imperii. Vypusk
vtoroi. Nalichnoe naselenie Imperii za 1858 god. A. Bushen.
Sanktpeterburg, 1863.

_____. Statisticheskiia tablitsy Rossiiskoi Imperii za 1856-i
god. Vypusk pervyi. S.-Peterburg, 1858.

_____. Statisticheskii vremennik Rossiiskoi Imperii. I. Otdel
pervyi. Gorodskiia naseleniia. Sanktpeterburg, 1866.

_____. Statisticheskii vremennik Rossiiskoi Imperii. II. Vypusk
pervyi. Ekonomicheskoe sostoianie gorodov. Sanktpeterburg,
1871.

_____. Statisticheskii vremennik Rossiiskoi Imperii. II. Vypusk
desiatyi. Ekonomicheskoe sostoianie gorodov. Sanktpeterburg,
1875.

_____. Statistika Rossiiskoi Imperii. Tom I. Sbornik svedenii
po Rossii za 1884-1885 gg. Gorodskiia poseleniia Imperii.
S.-Peterburg, 1887.

B.   Other Statistical Sources.

Arsen'ev, Konstantin. Nachertanie statistiki Rossiiskogo Gosudarstva,
sostavlennoe glavnogo pedagogicheskogo instituta. Chast'
pervaia. O sostoianii naroda. Sanktpeterburg, 1818.

German, K. Statisticheskiia issledovaniia otnositel'no Rossiiskoi
Imperii. Chast' I. O narodonaselenii. S.-Peterburg, 1819.

Geografichesko-statisticheskii slovar' Rossiiskoi Imperii. Ed. P.
Semenov. 5 vols. Sanktpeterburg. Imperatorskoe Russkoe

geograficheskoe obshchestvo, 1863–1885.

Harris, Chauncy D. "Population of Cities of the Soviet Union, 1897, 1926, 1939, 1959, and 1967. Tables, Maps, and Gazeteer," Soviet Geography: Review and Translation, Vol. 11, No. 5 (May, 1970), pp. 307–444, also separately numbered as special issue, pp. 1–138.

Jelonek, A. "Ludność miast i osiedli typu miejskiego na ziemiach Polski od 1810 do 1960 r.," Dokumentacja Geograficzna, 3–4 (1967), pp. 1–62.

Kabuzan, V. M. Narodonaselenie Rossii v XVIII- pervoi polovine XIX v. Po materialam revezii. Moskva: Izdatel'stvo Akademii Nauk SSSR, 1963.

Krzyżanowski, Adam and Kumaniecki, Kazimierz Władysław . Statystyka Polski. Kraków, 1915.

Leasure, J. William and Lewis, Robert A. Population Changes in Russia and the USSR: A Set of Comparable Territorial Units. "Social Science Monograph Series, Vol. 1, No. 2." San Diego, California: San Diego College Press, 1966.

de Livron, Vikto P. Statisticheskoe obozrenie Rossiiskoi Imperii. Sanktpeterburg, 1874.

Obzor Odesskogo gradonachal'stva za 1911 god. Odessa: Tipografiia "Ved. odes. Gradon." (no date).

Rashin, A. G. Naselenie Rossii za 100 let. (1811–1913 gg.): Statisticheskie ocherki. Moskva: Gosudarstvennoe Statisticheskoe Izdatel'stvo, 1956.

Statesman's Yearbook for 1916.

Volkov, E. Z. Dinamika narodonaseleniia SSSR za vosem'desiat let. Moskva: Gosudarstvennoe Izdatel'stvo, 1930.

General Sources

Ames, Edward. "A Century of Russian Railroad Construction, 1837–1936," The American Slavic and East European Review, VI (No. 18–19, 1947), pp. 57–74.

Barel, Yves. Le développement économique de la Russie tsariste. "Publications De La Faculté de Droit Et Des Sciences Economiques De Grenoble: Série Economie Du Développement, Volume No. 3." Paris: Mouton & Cie., 1968.

Baykov, Alexander. "The Economic Development of Russia," The Economic History Review, 2nd Series, VII (1954), pp. 137–149.

Beckinsale, R. P. and Houston, J. M., eds. Urbanization and Its Problems: Essays in Honor of E. W. Gilbert. Oxford: Basil Blackwell, 1968.

Bendix, Reinhard. Work and Authority in Industry. Ideologies of Management in the Course of Industrialization. New York: John Wiley and Sons, Inc., 1956.

Bernadskii, V. N. Ocherki iz istorii klassovoi bor'by i obshchest-Venno-politcheskoi mysli Rossii v tret'ei chetverti XVIII veka. "Gosudarstvennyi pedagogicheskii institut imeni A. I. Gertsena: Uchenye Zapiski, Tom 229." Leningrad, 1962.

Berry, Brian J. L. and Horton, Frank E., eds. Geographic Perspectives on Urban Systems. Englewood Cliffs, N. J.: Prentice-Hall, Inc., 1970.

Beskrovnyi, L. G., Zaozerskaia, E. I. and Preobrazhenskii, A. A., eds. K voprosu o pervonachal'nom nakoplenii v Rossii XVII-XVIII vy. Sbornik statei. Moskva: Izdatel'stvo Akademii Nauk SSSR, 1958.

Bill, Valentine T. The Forgotten Class: The Russian Bourgeoisie from the Earliest Beginnings to 1900. New York: Frederick A. Praeger, Publishers, 1959.

Black, Cyril E., ed. The Transformation of Russian Society. Aspects of Social Change Since 1861. Cambridge, Mass.: Harvard University Press, 1970.

Blackwell, William L. The Beginnings of Russian Industrialization, 1800-1860. Princeton, N. J.: Princeton University Press, 1968.

Blum, Jerome. Lord and Peasant in Russia from the Ninth to the Nineteenth Century. Princeton, N. J.: Princeton University Press, 1971.

Bobovich, I. M. and Pazhitnova, T. K. Lektsii po istorii narodnogo khoziaistva SSSR. Epokha kapitalizma. Leningrad: Izdatel'stvo Leningradskogo Universiteta, 1961.

Callow, Alexander B., Jr., ed. American Urban History   An Interpretative Reader with Commentaries. New York: Oxford University Press, 1969.

Davis, Kingsley. "The Urbanization of the Human Population," Scientific American, CCXIII (September, 1965), pp. 41-53.

Dickinson, Robert E. The West European City: A Geographical Interpretation. London: Routledge and Kegan Paul, Ltd., 1951.

Ditiatin, I. Ustroistvo i upravlenie gorodov Rossii. Tom I. Goroda Rossii v XVIII stoletii. S.-Peterburg, 1875.

_____. Ustroistvo i upravlenie gorodov Rossii. Tom II. Gorodskoe samoupravlenie v nastoiashchem stoletii. Iaroslavl', 1877.

Diubiuk, E. "Fabrika v derevne. (Pis'mo iz Vladimira)," Sovremennyi Mir, (Aprel', 1911), pp. 274-281.

Dubnow, S. M. History of the Jews in Russia and Poland from the Earliest Times until the Present Day. 3 volumes. Translated from the Russian by I. Friedlaender. Philadelphia: The Jewish Publication Society of America, 1916-1920.

Dyos, H. J., ed. The Study of Urban History. New York: St. Martin's Press, 1968.

Dzhaoshvili, V. Sh. Naselenie Gruzii. Ekonomiko-geograficheskoe issledovanie. Tbilisi: Izdatel'stvo "Metsniereba," 1968.

Ellison, Herbert J. "Economic Modernization of Imperial Russia: Purposes and Achievements." Journal of Economic History, XXV (December, 1965), pp. 523-540.

Entsiklopedicheskii slovar'. 41 volumes issued in 82 parts. I. E. Andreevskii, ed. S.-Peterburg: Izdateli: F. A. Brokgauz and I. A. Efron, 1890-1904.

Foust, C. M. "Russian Expansion to the East through the Eighteenth Century," Journal of Economic History, XXIX (1961), pp. 469-482.

Gerschenkron, Alexander. Continuity in History and Other Essays. Cambridge, Mass.: The Belknap Press of Harvard University Press, 1968.

_____. Economic Backwardness in Historical Perspective. A Book of Essays. Cambridge, Mass.: The Belknap Press of Harvard University Press, 1966.

_____. "The Rate of Industrial Growth in Russia since 1885," Journal of Economic History, VII (Supplement, 1947), pp. 144-174.

Gille, Bertrand. Histoire économique et sociale de la Russie du moyen age au XIX⁰ siècle. Paris: Payot, 1949.

Goldsmith, Raymond W. "The Economic Growth of Tsarist Russia, 1860-1913," Economic Development and Cultural Change, IX (April, 1961), pp. 441-475.

Gregory, Paul. "Economic Growth and Structural Change in Tsarist Russia: A Case of Modern Economic Growth?" Soviet Studies, XXIII (January, 1972), pp. 418-434.

Handlin, Oscar and Burchard, John, eds. The Historian and the City. Cambridge, Mass.: The M.I.T. Press, Second Paperback Edition, 1967.

Harris, Chauncy D. Cities of the Soviet Union. Studies in Their Functions, Size, Density and Growth. "Association of American Geographers: Monograph Series, Volume 5." Chicago: Rand McNally and Company, 1970.

_____, and Ullman, Edward L. "The Nature of Cities," Annals of the American Academy of Political and Social Sciences, CCXLII (1945), pp. 7-17.

Hauser, Philip M. and Schnore, Leo F., eds. The Study of Urbanization. New York: John Wiley and Sons, Inc., 1965.

Henderson, W. O. The Industrial Revolution on the Continent. Germany, France, Russia: 1800-1914. London, Frank Cass and Co., Ltd., 1967.

Iatsunskii, V. K. "Izmeneniia v razmeshchenii naseleniia Evropeiskoi Rossii v 1724-1916 gg.," Istoriia SSSR, I (Mart'-Aprel', 1957), pp. 192-224.

Iatsunskii, V. K. "Promyshlennyi perevorot v Rossii (K probleme vzai-
    medeistviie proizvoditel'nykh sil i proizvodstvennykh otno-
    shenii)," Voprosy Istorii, XII (Dekabr',1952), pp. 48-70.

_____. "Rol' Peterburga v promyshlennom razvitii dorevoliutsionnoi
    Rossii," Voprosy Istorii, XIV (1954), pp. 95-108.

_____. Transport SSSR. Istoriia ego razvitiia i sovremennoe
    sostoianie v sviazi s kratkimi svedeniiami po ekonomike
    transporta. Moskva: NKPS: Transpechat', 1926.

_____. "Znachenie ekonomicheskikh sviazei s Rossii dlia khozia-
    istvennogo razvitiia gorodov pribaltiki v epokhu kapital-
    izma," Istoricheskie Zapiski, XLV (1954), pp. 105-147.

Iofa, L. E. Goroda Urala. Chast' pervaia. Feodal'nyi period.
    Moskva: Gosudarstvennoe Izdatel'stvo Geograficheskoi Lit-
    eratury, 1951.

Kabo, R. M. Goroda Zapadnoi Sibiri. Ocherki istoriko-ekonomiches-
    koi geografii, XVII- pervaia polovina XIX vv. Moskva:
    Gosudarstvennoe Izdatel'stvo Geograficheskoi Literatury,
    1949.

Kabuzan, V. M. Izmeneniia v razmeshchenii naseleniia Rossii v
    XVIII- pervoi polovine XIX v. Po materialam revizii.
    Moskva: "Nauka," 1971.

_____. "Materialy revizii kak istochnik po istorii naseleniia
    Rossii XVIII- pervoi poloviny XIX v. (1718-1858)," Istor-
    iia SSSR, V (Sentiabr'-Oktiabr', 1959), pp. 128-140.

_____. Narodonaselenie Rossii v XVIII- pervoi polovine XIX v.
    Moskva: Izdatel'stvo Akademii Nauk SSSR, 1963.

Kafengauz, B. B., ed. Absoliutizm v Rossii (XVII-XVIII vv.).
    Sbornik statei. Moskva: Izdatel'stvo "Nauka," 1964.

Kahan, Arcadius. "The Costs of 'Westernization' in Russia: The
    Gentry and the Economy in the Eighteenth Century," Slavic
    Review, XXV (March, 1966), pp. 40-66.

_____. "Entrepreneurship in the Early Development of Iron Manu-
    facturing in Russia," Economic Development and Cultural
    Change, X (July, 1962), pp. 395-422.

_____. "Government Policies and the Industrialization of Russia,"
    Journal of Economic History, XXVII (December, 1967), pp.
    460-477.

Khromov, P. A. Ekonomicheskoe razvitie Rossii. Ocherki ekonomiki
    Rossii s drevneishikh vremen do Velikoi Oktiabr'skoi Revo-
    liutsii. Moskva: Izdatel'stvo "Nauka," 1967.

_____. Ekonomicheskoe razvitie Rossii v XIX-XX vekakh, 1800-
    1917. Moskva: Gosudarstvennoe Izdatel'stvo Politicheskoi
    Literatury, 1950.

Kizevetter, A. A. Posadskaia obshchina v Rossii XVIII st. Moskva,
    1903.

Klimov, V. I. "103 vazhneishikh tsentra fabrichno-zavodskoi promyshlennosti Evropeiskoi Rossii v 1900-1914 gg. Opyt prodol-
zheniia tablitsy, sostavlennoi V. I. Leninym," Voprosy Geografii, L (1960), pp. 195-210.

Klokman, Iu. R. Sotsial'no-ekonomicheskaia istoriia Russkogo goroda. Vtoraia polovina XVIII veka. Moskva: Izdatel'stvo
"Nauka," 1967.

Kolb, William L. "The Social Structure and the Function of Cities,"
Economic Development and Cultural Change, III (October,
1954), pp. 30-46.

Kopanev, A. I. Naselenie Peterburga v pervoi polovine XIX veka.
Moskva: Izdatel'stvo Akademii Nauk SSSR, 1957.

Koren, John, ed. The History of Statistics, Their Development, and
Progress in Many Countries. New York: The MacMillan Company,
1918.

Kupriianova, L. V. "Formirovanie gorodskikh proletarskikh tsentrov
Severnogo Kavkaza, 1861-1900 gg.," Istoriia SSSR, III (Mai-
Iiun', 1965), pp. 156-167.

Kurman, M. V. and Lebedinskii, I. V. Naselenie bol'shogo sotsial-
isticheskogo goroda. Moskva: "Statistika," 1968.

Kuznets, Simon. Economic Growth and Structure. Selected Essays.
New York: W. W. Norton and Co., 1965.

Lampard, Eric E. "The History of Cities in the Economically Advanced Areas," Economic Development and Cultural Change,
III (January, 1955), pp. 81-136.

von Laue, Theodore H. Sergei Witte and the Industrialization of
Russia. New York: Columbia University Press, 1969.

Leasure, J. William and Lewis, Robert A. "Internal Migration in
Russia in the Late Nineteenth Century," Slavic Review,
XXVII (September, 1968), pp. 375-394.

_____. "Internal Migration in the USSR: 1897-1926," Demography,
IV (No. 2, 1967), pp. 479-496.

_____. "Regional Population Changes in Russia and the USSR since
1851," Slavic Review, XXV (December, 1966), pp. 663-668.

Lenin, V. I. The Development of Capitalism in Russia. Translation
taken from Volume 3 of the Progress Publishers' edition of
Lenin's Collected Works in 40 volumes. Third Printing.
Moscow: Progress Publishers, 1967.

Lewis, Robert A. and Rowland, Richard H. "Urbanization in Russia
and the USSR: 1897-1966," Annals of the Association of
American Geographers, LIX (December, 1969), pp. 776-796.

Liashchenko, Peter I. History of the National Economy of Russia to
the 1917 Revolution. Translated by L. M. Herman and introduction by Calvin V. Hoover. New York: The MacMillan Company,
1949.

Liubomirov, P. G. Ocherki po istorii Russkoi promyshlennosti v
XVIII i nachale XIX vv. Leningrad: Priboi, 1930.

_____. Ocherki po istorii Russkoi promyshlennosti XVII, XVIII,
i nachalo XIX veka. Moskva: Gosudarstvennoe Izdatel'stvo
Politicheskoi Literatury, 1947.

Livshits, R. S. Razmeshchenie promyshlennosti v dorevoliutsionnoi
Rossii. Moskva: Izdatel'stvo Akademii Nauk SSSR, 1955.

Mavor, James. An Economic History of Russia. Volume I. The Rise
and Fall of Bondage. Volume II (no title). London: J. M.
Dent and Sons, Limited, 1914.

Mavrodin, V. V., ed. Voprosy genezisa kapitalizma v Rossii. Sbornik statei. Leningrad: Izdatel'stvo Leningradskogo Universiteta, 1960.

McKay, John P. Pioneers for Profit. Foreign Entrepreneurship and
Russian Industrialization 1885-1913. Chicago: The University of Chicago Press, 1970.

Mel'nik, I. S., ed. Sibir' eia sovremennoe sostoianie i eia nuzhdy.
Sbornik statei. S. Peterburg, 1908.

Miliukov, P. Ocherki po istorii Russkoi kul'tury. Chast' pervaia.
Naselenie, ekonomicheskii, gosudarstvennyi, i soslovnyi
stroi. S.-Peterburg, 1904.

Miliutin, N. A. "Chislo gorodskikh i zemledel'cheskikh poselenii
v Rossii," "Imperatorskoe Russkoe Geograficheskoe Obshchestvo. Statisticheskii otdel: Trudy. Sbornik statisticheskikh
svedenii o Rossii, Knizhka I." S.-Peterburg, 1851, pp. 229-
239.

Miller, Margaret. The Economic Development of Russia, 1905-1914
with Special Reference to Trade, Industry, and Finance.
London: Frank Cass and Co., Ltd., 1926.

Mullov, P. Istoricheskoe obozrenie pravitel'stvennykh mer po ustroistvu gorodskogo obshchestvennogo upravleniia. "Ministerstvo vnutrennikh del: Materialy dlia sostavleniia
predpolozhenii ob uluchshenii obshchestvennogo upravleniia
v gorodakh." Sanktpeterburg, 1864.

Mumford, Lewis. The City in History: Its Origins, Its Transforma-
tions, and Its Prospects. New York: Harcourt, Brace and
World, Inc., 1961.

Nevolin, K. A. "Izsledovaniia o gorodakh Russkikh," Ministerstvo
vnutrennikh del, Zhurnal, Chast' VIII (1844), pp. 183-198.

Nifontov, A. S. "Formirovanie klassov burzhuaznogo obshchestva v
Russkom gorode vtoroi poloviny XIX v. Po Materialam pere-
pisei naseleniia g. Moskvy v 70-90 kh godakh XIX v.," Istoricheskie Zapiski, LIV (1955), pp. 237-250.

Nowakowski, Stefan, ed. Socjologiczne problemy miasta Polskiego.
Warszawa: Państwowe Wydawnictwo Naukowe, 1964.

Ordinaire, Jean. L'évolution industrielle russe depuis la fin du
XIX siècle. Paris: Marcel Giard, 1927.

Pankratova, A. M. "Proletarizatsiia krest'ianstva i ee rol' v formirovanii promyshlennogo proletariata Rossii, 60-90-e gody XIX v.," Istoricheskie Zapiski, LIV (1955), pp. 194-220.

Parker, W. H. An Historical Geography of Russia. Chicago: Aldine Publishing Company, 1969.

Pazhitnov, K. A. "K voprosu o roli krepostnogo truda v doreformennoi promyshlennosti," Istoricheskie Zapiski, VII (1940), pp. 236-245.

Perloff, Harvey S. and Wingo, Lowdon Jr., eds. Issues in Urban Economics. Baltimore: The Johns Hopkins Press, 1968.

Picheta, V. I. Istoriia narodnogo khoziaistva v Rossii XIX-XX vv. Nachalo industrializatsii i razlozhenie krepostnogo khoziaistva. Moskva: Izdatel'stvo "Russkii Knizhnik," 1922.

Pintner, Walter McKenzie. Russian Economic Policy under Nicholas I. Ithaca, N. Y.: Cornell University Press, 1967.

Pogozhev, A. V. Uchet chislennosti i sostava rabochikh v Rossii. Materialy po statistike truda. S.-Peterburg, 1906.

Pokshishevskii, V. V. "Territorial'noe formirovanie promyshlennogo kompleksa Peterburga v XVIII-XIX vekakh," Voprosy Geografii, XX (1950), pp. 122-162.

_____. Zaselenie Sibiri. Istoriko-geograficheskie ocherki. Irkutsk: Oblastnoe Gosudarstvennoe Izdatel'stvo, 1951.

Polianskii, F. Ia. Ekonomicheskii stroi manufaktury v Rossii XVIII veka. Maskva: Izdatel'stvo Akademii Nauk SSSR, 1956.

_____. Gorodskoe remeslo i manufaktura v Rossii XVIII v. Moskva: Izdatel'stvo Moskovskogo Universiteta, 1960.

_____, Orlov, B. P., and Shemiakin, I. I., eds. Istoriia narodnogo khoziaistva SSSR. Kurs lektsii. Moskva: Izdatel'stvo Sotsial'no-ekonomicheskoi Literatury, 1960.

Postan, M. and Habakkuk, H. J., eds. The Cambridge Economic History. Volume VI. The Industrial Revolutions and After: Incomes, Population and Technological Change (II). Cambridge, England: Cambridge University Press, 1966.

Pred, Allan R. The Spatial Dynamics of U. S. Urban-Industrial Growth; 1800-1914: Interpretive and Theoretical Essays. Cambridge, Mass.: The M.I.T. Press, 1966.

Rashin, A. G. "Dinamika chislennosti i protsessy formirovaniia gorodskogo naseleniia Rossii v XIX- nachale XX vv.," Istoricheskie Zapiski, XXXIV (1950), pp. 32-85.

_____. Formirovanie promyshlennogo proletariata v Rossii. Statistiko-ekonomicheskie ocherki. Moskva: Gosudarstvennoe Sotsial'no-ekonomicheskoe Izdatel'stvo, 1940.

_____. Formirovanie rabochego klassa Rossii. Istoriko-ekonomicheskie ocherki. Moskva: Izdatel'stvo Sotsial'no-ekonomicheskoi Literatury, 1958.

Rashin, A. G. "K voprosu o formirovanii rabochego klassa v Rossii v 30-50-kh godakh XIX v.," Istoricheskie Zapiski, LIII (1955) pp. 144-193.

_____. "O chislennosti i territorial'nom razmeshchenii rabochikh Rossii v period kapitalizma," Istoricheskie Zapiski, XLVI (1954), pp. 126-181.

_____. "Sdvigi v territorial'nom razmeshchenii naseleniia Rossii v XIX i v nachale XX v.," Voprosy Geografii, XX pp. 99-121.

Razgon, A. M. "Promyshlennye i torgovye slobody i sela Vladimirskoi gubernii vo vtoroi polovine XVIII v.," Istoricheskie Zapiski, XXXII (1950), pp. 135-172.

Reissman, Leonard. The Urban Process: Cities in Industrial Societies. New York: The Free Press, 1970.

Rimlinger, Gaston V. "The Expansion of the Labor Market in Capitalist Russia, 1861--917," Journal of Economic History, XXI (1961), pp. 208-215.

Robinson, Geroid Tanquary. Rural Russia under the Old Regime. A History of the Landlord-Peasant World and a Prologue to the Peasant Revolution of 1917. New York: The MacMillan Company, 1932. Berkeley, California: University of California Press, Second Printing, 1969.

Rosovsky, Henry. "The Serf Entrepreneur in Russia," Explorations in Entrepreneurial History, VI (May, 1954), pp. 207-233.

Rozhkov, N. A. Gorod i derevnia v Russkoi istorii. Kratkii ocherk ekonomicheskoi istorii Rossii. Izdanie tret'e, dopolnennoe. S.-Peterburg, 1913.

Rozhkova, M. K. "K voprosu o znachenii iarmarok vo vnutrennei torgovle doreformennoi Rossii. Pervaia polovina XIX v.," Istoricheskie Zapiski, LIV (1955), pp. 298-314.

_____, ed. Ocherki ekonomicheskoi istorii Rossii pervoi poloviny XIX veka. Sbornik statei. Moskva: Izdatel'stvo Sotsial'no-ekonomicheskoi Literatury, 1959.

_____. "Promyshlennost' Moskvy v pervoi chetverti XIX veka," Voprosy Istorii, XI-XII (1946), pp. 88-103.

Rubinshtein, N. L. "Nekotorye voprosy formirovaniia rynka rabochei sily v Rossii XVIII veka," Voprosy Istorii, XXII pp. 74-101.

Rybnikov, A. A. and Orlov, A. S. Kustarnaia promyshlennost' i sbyt kustarnykh izdelii. Moskva, 1913.

Ryndziunskii, P. G. "Gil'deiskaia reforma Kankrina 1824 goda," Istoricheskie Zapiski, XL (1952), pp. 110-139.

_____. Gorodskoe grazhdanstvo doreformennoi Rossii. Moskva: Izdatel'stvo Akademii Nauk SSSR, 1958.

_____. "Krest'iane i gorod v doreformennoi Rossii," Voprosy Istorii, (Sentiabr', 1955), pp. 26-40.

Semenov-Tian-Shanskii, Veniamin. Gorod i derevnia v Evropeiskoi Rossii. Ocherk po ekonomicheskoi geografii s 16 kartami i kartogrammami. "Imperatorskoe Russkoe Geograficheskoe Obshchestvo: Zapiski, Tom X, Vypusk 2." S.-Peterburg, 1910.

Shimkin, Dmitri B. "The Entrepreneur in Tsarist and Soviet Russia," Explorations in Entrepreneurial History, II (November, 1949), pp. 24-34.

Shuster, U. A. "Ekonomicheskaia bor'ba Moskvy s Lozd'iu. Iz istorii Russko-Pol'skikh ekonomicheskikh otnoshenii v 80-kh godakh proshlogo veka," Istoricheskie Zapiski, V (1939), pp. 189-234.

Strumilin, S. G. Ocherki ekonomicheskoi istorii Rossii. Moskva: Izdatel'stvo Sotsial'no-ekonomicheskoi Literatury, 1960.

_____. Ocherki ekonomicheskoi istorii Rossii i SSSR. Moskva: Izdatel'stvo "Nauka," 1966.

de Tegoborski, M. L. Commentaries on the Productive Forces of Russia. 2 volumes. London: Longman, Brown, Green, and Longmans, 1855-1856.

Thiede, Roger L. "Urbanization and Industrialization in Pre-Revolutionary Russia," The Professional Geographer, XXV (February, 1973), pp. 16-21.

Tikhomirov, M. The Towns of Ancient Rus. Translated from the Second Russian Edition by Y. Sdobnikov, edited by D. Skvirskii. Moscow: Foreign Languages Publishing House, 1959.

_____. "Spisok Russkikh gorodov dal'nikh i blizhnikh," Istoricheskie Zapiski, XL (1952), pp. 214-259.

Tisdale, Hope. "The Process of Urbanization," Social Forces, XX (March, 1942), pp. 311-316.

Tokmakoff, George. "Stolypin's Agrarian Reform: An Appraisal," The Russian Review, 30 (April, 1971), pp. 124-138.

Treadgold, Donald W. The Great Siberian Migration. Government and Peasant in Resettlement from Emancipation to the First World War. Princeton, N. J.: Princeton University Press, 1957.

Tugan-Baranovskii, Mikhail I. The Russian Factory in the 19th Century. Translated from the 3rd Russian edition by Arthur Levin and Claora S. Levin under the supervision of Gregory Grossman. Homewood, Illinois: Richard D. Irwin, Inc., 1970.

Ustiugov, N. V., ed. Goroda feodal'noi Rossii. Sbornik statei. Moskva: Izdatel'stvo "Nauka," 1966.

Vodarskii, Ia. E. "Formirovanie promyshlennykh selenii tsentral'no-promyshlennogo raiona Evropeiskoi Rossii," Istoriia SSSR, III (Mai-Iun', 1966), pp. 144-160.

Weber, Adna Ferrin. The Growth of Cities in the Nineteenth Century: A Study in Statistics. "Columbia University: Studies in History, Economics, and Public Law," Volume XI. New York: The MacMillan Company, 1899. Reprinted. Ithaca, N. Y.: Cornell University Press, 1967.

Zaozerskaia, E. I. Manufaktura pri Petre I. Moskva: Izdatel'stvo
     Akademii Nauk SSSR, 1947.

Zhukov, V. I. Goroda Bessarabii 1812-1861 godov. Ocherki sotsial'-
     no-ekonomicheskogo razvitiia. Kishinev: Gosudarstvennoe
     Izdatel'stvo "Kartia Moldoveniaske," 1964.

РЕЗЮМЕ

XIX-ое столетие это период быстрого роста городов Русской Империи. Между 1811 и 1910 годами число городов увеличилось от 570 до 932, а число городов свыше 50,000 жителей возросло с 22 до 206. В тот же период городское население Империи увеличилось от 2,780,337 до 23,553,583 - нетто прирост городского населения составлял 20,773,246 душ. Это было увеличение городского населения в 7.5 раза, или средний прирост 2.2% в год.

Наш анализ характера городского прироста в предлагаемой работе состоит из двух больших периодов, характеризованных различными социальными и экономическими силами, периоды, которые разделялись годами подготовки и проведения в жизнь Великих Реформ.

В течении первых сорока пяти лет (1811-1856) которые изучаются в этой работе - период характеризованный существованием крепостной системы - рост городов был сравнительно медленный и неравномерный. Городское население возрастало в среднем на 1.6% в год, в результате чего городское население увеличилось почти на 3 миллиона душ. Рост городов в этот дореформенный период был следствием развития внутренней торговли, особенно в виде базаров и ярмарок. Второй повод этого роста городов было заселение южных и восточных районов Европейской России.

За отсутствием улучшеной сети транспорта, эти два процесса способствовали росту городов, который характеризовался более своим распределением чем своей сосредоточенностью. Фактически процент городского населения, проживающего в городах свыше 50,000 жителей даже понизился за этот период (1810-1856) с 25 на 24 процента. За исключением Петербурга и Москвы, важных как в административном так и в экономическом смысле, и также Одессы, которая превратилась в самый важный центр экспорта пшеницы, города Русской Империи не показывали роста.

С отменой крепостного права в 1861 году было отстранено самое

важное препятствие для передвижения населения и роста городов.
Влияние отмены крепостничества на экономическое развитие несколько
замедлилось, но влияние на рост городов оказалось большое и немед-
ленное. В период от 1856 до 1870 года городское население России
возрасло почти на 35% или на 2,026,397 душ, главным образом в результате перемещения нескольких миллионов людей из деревни в связи
с раскрепощением. Аннексия Царской Польши и некоторых частей Средней
Азии увеличила дополнительно городское население Империи на 1,126,243
душ.

В пореформеный период (1870-1910) городское население России
возрастало небывалыми темпами. В этом периоде прибавилось в городах
почти 15 миллионов душ. Это составляло около 72% всего роста городского населения в Русской Империи за весь период. Средний годовой
прирост в течении этих сорока лет составлял 2.5%. Другая особенность
характера развития городов в этот период была возрастающая сосредо-
точенность городского населения в ограниченом количестве крупных
городов. В конце этого периода 40% городского населения Русской Империи было сосредоточено в 30-ти городах численностью в 100,000 душ
или больше.

Главные причины этого роста городского населения и его концентрации в крупных городах в этом пореформеном периоде были факторы,
которые явились более мощными с дальнейшим ускоренным экономическим
развитием. Самым важным фактором было построение железных дорог. В
период от 1867 до 1910 года железнодорожная сеть была расширена с
5,030 до 66,581 километров. Развитие железных дорог вызвало сильное
влияние на общую экономическую экспансию. Это развитие транспорта
также способствовало концентрации экономической жизни в ограниченом
количестве городов которые, благодаря этому пользовались выгодными
производственными и торговыми условиями по сравнению с другими го-
родами.

В результате расширения торговли и увеличения районной специализации имевших место наряду с развитием железных дорог, возрос размер внутренней торговли. В пореформеном периоде значительность и роль периодических базаров уменшилась. Постоянные формы торговли и другие комерческие трансакции были сосредоточены в торговых учреждениях крупных городов. Следующим важным фактором этого периода было увеличение внешней торговли в четыре раза. Рост внешней торговли оказался самым важным фактором в резком развитии городов на побережьях Черного и Балтийского морей.

Непрерывное расширение новых поселений в пореформном периоде способствовало в большой мере росту городов в отдаленных районах, особенно в Северо-Кавказской приморской полосе, Западной и Восточной Сибири, и в степях Средней Азии.

Но найболее выдающейся чертой экономического развития пореформенного периода была бурная индустриализация, в особенности развитие большой фабрично-заводской промышленности. В течении этого периода выпуск продукции возрастал в среднем на 5% ежегодно, а в определенных периодах, как например в последнем десятилетии столетия, это возрастание было даже больше.

Это большое индустриальное развитие Царской России не имело большого влияния на рост городов. Из 334 городов Русской Империи которые до 1897 года достигли 10,000 населения или больше, только в 66 городах свыше 30% всех лиц имеющих самостоятельные занятия работало на разных типов фабриках включая кустарную промышленность, и только в 33 городах количество индустриальных рабочих превышало 40%. Кроме того, в 1897 году из 54 крупных городов имеющих 50,000 душ или больше, только 11 имело 30% рабочих занятых в индустрии. Следовательно, в то время когда развитие индустрии создало значительный рост нескольких больших городов, как например Москва, Петербург, Лодзь, Иваново или Тула, оно сыграло второстепенную роль в росте других городов Русской Империи.

Отсутствие близкого соотношения между ростом городов и индустриальным развитием было отличительным признаком характера городского индустриального роста в Царской России в XIX-ом столетии, и это отличалось в двух важных особенностях от западного опыта.

Во первых, в то время как урбанизация и индустриальное развитие имели место в России одновременно, они не совпадали в пространстве. В 1897 году почти 52% рабочих занятых на заводах всех типов, а в 1902 году 61% всех рабочих занятых в индустрии проживало вне городов.

Во вторых, города России не играли большой роли в индустриализации. Противоположно городам Запада, города Российской Империи не являлись организационными центрами индустрии.

Неумение городов притянуть к себе индустриальные предприятия явилось результатом несостоятельности привлекать большие и постоянные кадры рабочих, от которых зависел рост индустрии. Города также не сумели создать условий для образования независимого, динамического класса предпринимателей, способных организовать и управлять индустрией. Оба эти факторы были тесно связаны со структурой государственного устройства и историческими традициями русского общества.

Крепостничество очевидно было самым большим припятствием для свободного передвижения рабочей силы. В то время как отмена крепостного права в 1861 году увеличила возможность передвижения рабочих, условия отмены, особенно политическая и социальная роль сельского мира, не позволили на десятилетия массовому перераспределению рабочей силы.

Качество рабочей силы прибывающей в города - на базе системы оброка, на основании выданых паспортов, или нелегальным выездом из деревень - было также жертвой институций русского общества. Особенно образование постоянной и надежной рабочей силы в городах в большой мере было задержано разными легальными, социальными, экономическими и персональными связями, которые привязывали рабочего крестьянского происхождения к деревне.

Условия в самом городе, тем более, также не позволяли образованию рабочей силы соответствующей требованиям индустрии. В противоположность Западной Европе, где принцип личной свободы был прочно установлен, в России полицейские власти могли делать с выходцами из села что угодно. Крестьяне, которые приезжали в города нелегально или оставались там дольше позволеного времени, отправлялись полицией обратно к их помещикам, или после 1861 года к мирам. Приобретение постоянного жилища в городе для большинства выходцев из села было очень трудно, часто невозможно.

Отношение и политика государства, которые были очень благоприятные для помещиков за счет городского купечества, обусловили рост промышленности вне городов. Государство поощряло помещиков создавать индустриальные предприятия в их имениях представляя им почти полную монополию над рабочей силой, свободный доступ к рынкам, субсидии и прочие выгоды. Развитие промышленности и торговли среди крестьян поощрялось государством, под нажимом помещиков, отменой почти всех ограничений наложенных на крестьян заниматься подобной деятельностью. Помещики в общем поощряли крестьян заниматься торговлей и индустрией как выгодный способ обогащения, и часто играли непосредственную роль в развитии крестьянского кустарного производства предоставляя им капитал и способствуя их обучению разным индустриальным специальностям.

Образование кадров талантливых предпринимателей в городах было дальше задержано той же самой политикой государства, которая способствовала развитию индустрии в сельских местностях, ограничением свободного передвижения рабочих. Городское купечество, которое сыграло большую роль в период раннего индустриального развития в России, больше всего испытывало трудности в перемещении их умения и капиталов из комерческих в индустриальные предприятия. Потеря купцами их исключительных привилегий в торговле и промышленности, невозможность доставать дешевую рабочую силу, и конкуренция товаров произведенных дешевле в деревне, уменшило их заинтересованность и снизило их финансовую возможность развивать промышленность в городах. Тогда как только очень немногие купцы имели способность и желание переключиться на индустриалистов, в то же самое время города не приобрели талантливого нового класса предпринимателей вышедших из крестьян. Легальные припятствия в деревне, которые задерживали выезд навсегда из села, и делали трудным постоянное пребывание в городе, принуждали большинство из этих новых предпринимателей проявить свои способности на селе.

Вконце, в противоположность Западу, стремительный рост городского населения Русской Империи не создал значительных структуральных изменений в относительном размещении сельского и городского населения, в их экономической жизни. Несмотря на увеличение городского населения на свыше 20 миллионов, уровень урбанизации остался низким. В течении 99 лет, периода разсматриваемого в настоящей работе, процент всего населения городов возрос незначительно от 6.3% в 1811 до 14.7% в 1910 году.

Причиной незначительного влияния роста городов Русской Империи в XIX-ом столетии на уровень урбанизации был большой прирост сельского населения. Не менее важным были легальные ограничения в передвижении населения, что являлось причиной задержания лишней рабочей силы на селе. Подобно Западной Европе, в России произошла демографическая революция, но в противоположность Западной Европе увеличение населения не сопровождалось значительным перераспределением.

Демографическая революция на селе частично поясняет рост населения в городах Русской Империи. В течении рассматриваемого периода увеличение городского населения было в основном результатом переселения из сельских местностей. Увеличение миграции из деревни в город должно рассматриваться не как следствие улучшения экономических возможностей в городах, а как результат прироста людей, которые получили возможность передвигаться, сначала благодаря раскрепощению в 1861 году а потом на основании Столыпинских реформ 1905-1906 годов.

THE UNIVERSITY OF CHICAGO
DEPARTMENT OF GEOGRAPHY
RESEARCH PAPERS (Lithographed, 6×9 Inches)

(Available from Department of Geography, The University of Chicago, 5828 S. University Ave., Chicago, Illinois 60637. Price: $6.00 each; by series subscription, $5.00 each.)

106. SAARINEN, THOMAS F. *Perception of the Drought Hazard on the Great Plains* 1966. 183 pp.

107. SOLZMAN, DAVID M. *Waterway Industrial Sites: A Chicago Case Study* 1967. 138 pp.

108. KASPERSON, ROGER E. *The Dodecanese: Diversity and Unity in Island Politics* 1967. 184 pp.

109. LOWENTHAL, DAVID, et al. *Environmental Perception and Behavior.* 1967. 88 pp.

110. REED, WALLACE E. *Areal Interaction in India: Commodity Flows of the Bengal-Bihar Industrial Area* 1967. 210 pp.

112. BOURNE, LARRY S. *Private Redevelopment of the Central City: Spatial Processes of Structural Change in the City of Toronto* 1967. 199 pp.

113. BRUSH, JOHN E., and GAUTHIER, HOWARD L., JR. *Service Centers and Consumer Trips: Studies on the Philadelphia Metropolitan Fringe* 1968. 182 pp.

114. CLARKSON, JAMES D. *The Cultural Ecology of a Chinese Village: Cameron Highlands, Malaysia* 1968. 174 pp.

115. BURTON, IAN; KATES, ROBERT W.; and SNEAD, RODMAN E. *The Human Ecology of Coastal Flood Hazard in Megalopolis* 1968. 196 pp.

117. WONG, SHUE TUCK. *Perception of Choice and Factors Affecting Industrial Water Supply Decisions in Northeastern Illinois* 1968. 96 pp.

118. JOHNSON, DOUGLAS L. *The Nature of Nomadism* 1969. 200 pp.

119. DIENES, LESLIE. *Locational Factors and Locational Developments in the Soviet Chemical Industry* 1969. 285 pp.

120. MIHELIC, DUSAN. *The Political Element in the Port Geography of Trieste* 1969. 104 pp.

121. BAUMANN, DUANE. *The Recreational Use of Domestic Water Supply Reservoirs: Perception and Choice* 1969. 125 pp.

122. LIND, AULIS O. *Coastal Landforms of Cat Island, Bahamas: A Study of Holocene Accretionary Topography and Sea-Level Change* 1969. 156 pp.

123. WHITNEY, JOSEPH. *China: Area, Administration and Nation Building* 1970. 198 pp.

124. EARICKSON, ROBERT. *The Spatial Behavior of Hospital Patients: A Behavioral Approach to Spatial Interaction in Metropolitan Chicago* 1970. 198 pp.

125. DAY, JOHN C. *Managing the Lower Rio Grande: An Experience in International River Development* 1970. 277 pp.

126. MAC IVER, IAN. *Urban Water Supply Alternatives: Perception and Choice in the Grand Basin, Ontario* 1970. 178 pp.

127. GOHEEN, PETER G. *Victorian Toronto, 1850 to 1900: Pattern and Process of Growth* 1970. 278 pp.

128. GOOD, CHARLES M. *Rural Markets and Trade in East Africa* 1970. 252 pp.

129. MEYER, DAVID R. *Spatial Variation of Black Urban Households* 1970. 127 pp.

130. GLADFELTER, BRUCE. *Meseta and Campiña Landforms in Central Spain: A Geomorphology of the Alto Henares Basin* 1971. 204 pp.

131. NEILS, ELAINE M. *Reservation to City: Indian Urbanization and Federal Relocation* 1971. 200 pp.

132. MOLINE, NORMAN T. *Mobility and the Small Town, 1900–1930* 1971. 169 pp.

133. SCHWIND, PAUL J. *Migration and Regional Development in the United States, 1950–1960* 1971. 170 pp.

134. PYLE, GERALD F. *Heart Disease, Cancer and Stroke in Chicago: A Geographical Analysis with Facilities Plans for 1980* 1971. 292 pp.

135. JOHNSON, JAMES F. *Renovated Waste Water: An Alternative Source of Municipal Water Supply in the U.S.* 1971. 155 pp.

136. BUTZER, KARL W. *Recent History of an Ethiopian Delta: The Omo River and the Level of Lake Rudolf* 1971. 184 pp.

137. HARRIS, CHAUNCY D. *Annotated World List of Selected Current Geographical Serials in English, French, and German* 3rd edition 1971. 77 pp.

138. HARRIS, CHAUNCY D., and FELLMANN, JEROME D. *International List of Geographical Serials* 2nd edition 1971. 267 pp.

139. MC MANIS, DOUGLAS R. *European Impressions of the New England Coast, 1497–1620* 1972. 147 pp.

140. COHEN, YEHOSHUA S. *Diffusion of an Innovation in an Urban System: The Spread of Planned Regional Shopping Centers in the United States, 1949–1968* 1972. 136 pp.

141. MITCHELL, NORA. *The Indian Hill-Station: Kodaikanal* 1972. 199 pp.

142. PLATT, RUTHERFORD H. *The Open Space Decision Process: Spatial Allocation of Costs and Benefits* 1972. 189 pp.

143. GOLANT, STEPHEN M. *The Residential Location and Spatial Behavior of the Elderly: A Canadian Example* 1972. 226 pp.

144. PANNELL, CLIFTON W. *T'ai-chung, T'ai-wan: Structure and Function* 1973. 200 pp.

145. LANKFORD, PHILIP M. *Regional Incomes in the United States, 1929–1967: Level, Distribution, Stability, and Growth* 1972. 137 pp.

146. FREEMAN, DONALD B. *International Trade, Migration, and Capital Flows: A Quantitative Analysis of Spatial Economic Interaction* 1973. 202 pp.

147. MYERS, SARAH K. *Language Shift Among Migrants to Lima, Peru* 1973. 204 pp.

148. JOHNSON, DOUGLAS L. *Jabal al-Akhdar, Cyrenaica: An Historical Geography of Settlement and Livelihood* 1973. 240 pp.

149. YEUNG, YUE-MAN. *National Development Policy and Urban Transformation in Singapore: A Study of Public Housing and the Marketing System* 1973. 204 pp.

150. HALL, FRED L. *Location Criteria for High Schools: Student Transportation and Racial Integration* 1973. 156 pp.

151. ROSENBERG, TERRY J. *Residence, Employment, and Mobility of Puerto Ricans in New York City* 1974. 230 pp.

152. MIKESELL, MARVIN W., editor. *Geographers Abroad: Essays on the Problems and Prospects of Research in Foreign Areas* 1973. 296 pp.

153. OSBORN, JAMES. *Area, Development Policy, and the Middle City in Malaysia* 1974. 273 pp.

154. WACHT, WALTER F. *The Domestic Air Transportation Network of the United States* 1974. 98 pp.

155. BERRY, BRIAN J. L., et al. *Land Use, Urban Form and Environmental Quality* 1974. 464 pp.

156. MITCHELL, JAMES K. *Community Response to Coastal Erosion: Individual and Collective Adjustments to Hazard on the Atlantic Shore* 1974. 209 pp.

157. COOK, GILLIAN P. *Spatial Dynamics of Business Growth in the Witwatersrand* 1975. 143 pp.

158. STARR, JOHN T., JR. *The Evolution of Unit Train Operations in the United States: 1960–1969—A Decade of Experience* 1975.

159. PYLE, GERALD F. *The Spatial Dynamics of Crime* 1974. 220 pp.

160. MEYER, JUDITH W. *Diffusion of an American Montessori Education* 1975. 109 pp.

161. SCHMID, JAMES A. *Urban Vegetation: A Review and Chicago Case Study* 1975. 280 pp.

162. LAMB, RICHARD. *Metropolitan Impacts on Rural America* 1975. 210 pp.

163. FEDOR, THOMAS. *Patterns of Urban Growth in the Russian Empire during the Nineteenth Century* 1975. 275 pp.

164. HARRIS, CHAUNCY D. *Guide to Geographical Bibliographies and Reference Works in Russian or on the Soviet Union* 1975. 496 pp.

165. JONES, DONALD W. *Migration and Urban Unemployment in Dualistic Economic Development* 1975. 186 pp.

166. BEDNARZ, ROBERT S. *The Effect of Air Pollution on Property Value* 1975. 118 pp.

167. HANNEMANN, MANFRED. *The Diffusion of the Reformation in Southwestern Germany, 1518-1534* 1975.

168. SUBLETT, MICHAEL D. *Farmers on the Road. Interfarm Migration and the Farming of Noncontiguous Lands in Three Midwestern Townships, 1939-1969* 1975. 228 pp.

169. STETZER, DONALD FOSTER. *Special Districts in Cook County: Toward a Geography of Local Government* 1975. 189 pp.

170. EARLE, CARVILLE V. *The Evolution of a Tidewater Settlement System: All Hallow's Parish, Maryland, 1650–1783* 1975. 249 pp.

171. SPODEK, HOWARD. *Urban-Rural Integration in Regional Development: A Case Study of Saurashtra, India—1800–1960* 1975.

172. COHEN, YEHOSHUA S. and BERRY, BRIAN J. L. *Spatial Components of Manufacturing Change* 1975.

173. HAYES, CHARLES R. *The Dispersed City: The Case of Piedmont, North Carolina* 1975.

174. CARGO, DOUGLAS B. *Solid Wastes: Factors Influencing Generation Rates* 1975.

175. GILLARD, QUENTIN. *Incomes and Accessibility. Metropolitan Labor Force Participation, Commuting, and Income Differentials in the United States, 1960–1970* 1975.

176. MORGAN, DAVID J. *Patterns of Population Distribution: A Residential Preference Model and Its Dynamic* 1975.

177. STOKES, HOUSTON H.; JONES, DONALD W. and NEUBURGER, HUGH M. *Unemployment and Adjustment in the Labor Market: A Comparison between the Regional and National Responses* 1975. 135 pp.